DID I EVER TELL YOU THIS?

SAM NEILL

DID I EVER TELL YOU THIS?

A MEMOIR

TEXT PUBLISHING MELBOURNE AUSTRALIA

The Text Publishing Company acknowledges the Traditional
Owners of the country on which we work, the Wurundjeri
people of the Kulin Nation, and pays respect to their Elders
past and present.

textpublishing.com.au
The Text Publishing Company
Wurundjeri Country, Level 6, Royal Bank Chambers,
287 Collins Street, Melbourne Victoria 3000 Australia

Published by The Text Publishing Company, 2023
Book design by W. H. Chong
Front-cover photograph © Thomas Laisné/Contour, Getty Images

Typeset by J&M Typesetting
Printed and bound in Australia by Griffin Press, an accredited ISO
AS/NZS 14001:2004 Environmental Management System printer

ISBN: 9781922790309 (hardback)
ISBN: 9781922791382 (ebook)
A catalogue record for this book is available from the National
Library of Australia.

Contents

To my children.

I love you and would love to write about you.
But that would be a totally different book...

Thanks

To Dr Orly Lavee and all my friends at St Vincent's.
I wouldn't have started the book without you.
And I would certainly never have finished it.

To Michael Heyward and everyone at Text Publishing for
their unflagging enthusiasm, and all the punctuation.

To everyone who gets a mention—I hope you don't mind.
To everyone who doesn't get a mention—I love you anyway,
and Volume II is all about you.

To all my friends who brought me a candle in those dark,
dark days.

Chapter the First:
What Does Your Daddy Do?

WHEN my youngest daughter, Elena, was small and at a new school of some kind (I didn't like any of them much), the teacher asked the circle of little children around her, 'What does your mummy or your daddy do for a job?'

The little hands went up in the air and the answers flew thick and fast. My mummy's a lawyer. My daddy's a countant. My mummy builds houses. And so on.

When it came to Elena, the answer about me was both perceptive and entirely accurate.

'My daddy sits in caravans.'

Yes, it's true. That's what I've done much of my life: sit in caravans, or trailers as they say in the USA. Sitting, waiting for someone to tell me what to do, somewhere near a film set. I used to sit and read the paper, or sometimes even the script. Nowadays I stare at my iPhone looking for enlightenment—it's never there. Once in a while, there's a knock on the door and the assistant to someone's assistant who is an assistant to someone else might kindly ask you if you'd like a cup of tea. Of course I would. If you're really lucky they might even bring you lunch, but that would be the assistant to the first assistant who brought you tea. When Elena would visit me at work, that is what I would be doing. Sitting in a trailer, in a car park somewhere, having a cuppa, waiting: her daddy at work.

It doesn't sound like a life well lived, does it? At least it's quiet.

But, once in a while, someone does say, 'We need you on set, Mr Neill.' And that's when you emerge, blinking, into the daylight. You walk a few metres and spend a few minutes doing what it is you do. Act. Once in a while, with luck, you might even act well.

And, just possibly, you might even go further, walk a few more metres, and actually live some life. That life, as well as that acting, is what this book is about. There's nothing terribly exceptional about it, but it is mine. I did a *little* more than sit in trailers. Much of it I found amusing and rewarding. It was all a surprise, this I know. I'm far luckier, in hindsight, than I deserved.

But just now I paused for a minute to ponder who exactly I'm writing this for. Is this for my children, or their children? Is it for you, perhaps, this reader who might have a passing interest in a common-or-garden screen actor? As a performer, it's best if you know your audience. What do they want? What should I give them?

But I don't know who you are. It's hard to get the tone right. How intimate should this be? How jolly, how entertaining, am I required to be? It's a bit baffling.

Then the answer came to me, and it was obvious. I am writing for myself. This may be yet another selfish impulse, and I've had, I'm told, many of those over the years.

The thing is, I'm crook. Possibly dying. I may have to speed this up. Suddenly, for the first time in my life, I have time to burn, and time to think. And writing, jotting thoughts and memories down, is a salve. It gets my mind off things.

This book is therefore somewhat flung together. I write in haste. You can drop it any time you like if you're bored, but you are welcome to dip in again whenever you want.

In the meantime, I'm enjoying it, and I hope you might too. Whoever you are...

Ireland

PERHAPS I should start at the beginning. Let's take a stroll down this windy path and I will point things out as we drift past.

I was born in Omagh, County Tyrone, Northern Ireland, in 1947. My parents named me Nigel. We were renting a modest Georgian house, Mullaghmore House, just out of Omagh, surrounded by fields, trees, stone walls and donkeys. My father, Dermot, a New Zealander, was in the British Army, and was stationed at the army depot there after the war, and after his time with the occupying forces in Trieste.

Mum and my brother, Michael, had joined Dad in Italy, and they had a very happy year out there. Dad had word from a brother officer that an Austrian cavalry regiment was being disbanded

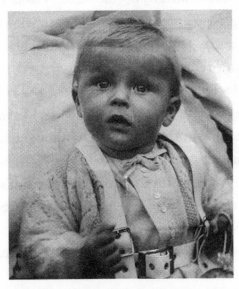

My mother said that as a baby I developed a fear of strange women, who would coo and pinch my cheeks.

in Vienna. He confiscated an enormous old ambulance, drove over a couple of mountain passes and nicked two outstanding horses, which he ferried back over the alps. Dad's job in Trieste was to keep apart the remnants of fascist and communist forces in a region of Italy that has always been in dispute. But mostly he and Mum charged around on horseback, having a great time and conceiving me. Dad claimed the deed was done at the Hotel Danieli, 'one wet afternoon in Venice'. The Danieli was the best hotel in the city, but my parents had no money to speak of, and so I can only imagine that they had some special rate reserved for the occupying forces. Obviously, I was destined for a lifetime of upgrades in five-star hotels.

I'm not entirely sure Dad was home in Omagh when I was born, because it was about this time that he went to Greece for a year. The Greek Civil War was at its height, and Dad served as adviser to a Greek general in the struggle against the communist insurgents there. Like all of Dad's active service, it was never mentioned, though he did tell the story about being stuck up in the mountains surrounded by hostile forces. He and his men were dug in, waiting for reinforcements. To their astonishment they spotted a courier of some kind, hightailing it up the mountain and dodging sniper fire. The messenger arrived safely, and put an important-looking document directly into Dad's hands. He opened it and found it was from Lloyds Bank, informing him that he was overdrawn to the tune of two shillings and sixpence, and if the situation was not immediately rectified they would have no choice but to close his account. For the rest of his life Dad would invariably curse whenever passing a branch of said bank.

And then there was the heartbreak he endured on return. He'd commissioned a rug from these women in a mountain village where the fighting was most intense. It took the best part of a year. He brought it back with him on the ship, and in fact he saw it swing down by crane to the dock at Southampton. It was never seen again; the wharfies pinched it.

But I was born in the kitchen at Mullaghmore. On the kitchen table. Poor Mum; I never did find out why on a table.

'Your father,' my aunt once said in pointed reference to me. 'Now *he* was a handsome man.'

Proceedings were apparently briefly interrupted when the midwife had to shoo out a couple of pigs that managed to break in somehow. This may explain my affection for pigs. One of my best friends is an ageing Kunekune boar, inappropriately named Angelica, whom I rescued some fifteen years ago. He and I are becoming, as pets and owners often do, more and more alike. We are both grumpy, ugly, white-whiskered, and enjoy a good back scratch.

Nineteen forty-seven was also the Chinese Year of the Pig. We were meant for each other.

My mother, Priscilla, was very English, very pretty and very brisk. No nonsense, and I imagine my birth on the kitchen table was little fuss either. She had a new and very fast Connemara pony, and wrote in her memoir, 'Almost as soon as Nigel had been born, I took off hunting on Danny. He was marvellous.' She makes no mention of my being born bright yellow with jaundice.

The kitchen table at Mullaghmore, the scene of my birth.

She was a calm presence who took life with equanimity, and was sociable, funny and generous. Her life was other people, dogs and horses. She was much loved, and she loved us. I will explain Nigel to you in a little while.

I'm afraid I remember nothing clearly of Omagh. But I have

My mother, uncharacteristically wearing lipstick.

gone back a couple of times, and visited Mullaghmore House. It's a small hotel now, and the owner is a charming man, Louis Kelly, who is always wonderfully welcoming when I turn up. We stand around and stare at the kitchen table, the scene of the crime.

He tells great stories. I loved the one about his grandfather, who fell in love with a girl from the other side, whether Catholic or Protestant I can't remember. There was no way that was going to be allowed back then. The young couple went out in a field and lay down on top of a haystack, announcing they were going to stay the night there; both families turned out en masse in a state of outrage. His future grandfather stood up, waved a pistol and said, 'This is a gun. And in the gun are six rounds of ammunition. We will stay the night here. And any man who says otherwise, I will shoot him.' The families backed wisely away, had a talk and returned the next morning. Saying, 'All right, you can come down now, and sure you can get married if you must.'

So romantic and so bloody Irish. I hope I've told it right.

That last time I was leaving Omagh, I walked around and made my peace with the place, pleased to see the rebuild after the hideous bombing in 1998. It's a pretty town that gently slopes towards a lazy river, with splendid views over the soft green hills of County Tyrone. I thought, It's time to go, there is no real connection for me here, even though it's the place of my birth. No one knows me, and that's fine. But I needed to pee, and I needed a cup of tea. I stopped at a roadhouse just out of town, and ordered. And then something happened that floored me. The woman who brought me my tea leant over and said, so quietly, 'We're very proud of you here.' I could have cried.

My earliest memory is being very ill with whooping cough and feeling terribly alone in an enormous white room and it was very cold and scary dark outside.

And, yes, it's true, I was critically ill. Whooping cough could kill you, and Mum said I almost died. I think I must have been perhaps three. I stuttered very badly as a child, and Mum always blamed the whoop for this. I've been back to that very room and it is in fact tiny. I was just small by comparison. And of course I wasn't alone. I had the best mother a little boy could ask for.

By then we were living in a plain whitewashed eighteenth-century house right on the rocks on Tyrella Beach in County Down. Austere and charming, all on its own. You breathed fresh salt air all day, surrounded by the Irish Sea; everything smelt of sweet seaweed. It was called the Watch House, because it had been built for the coastguard back in the day. The sitting room had once housed the boat they would launch to go out and catch smugglers; this, in the 1700s. Smugglers! When I was a child we

The Watch House at low tide. At high tide the sea came right up to the house. Note the windmill.

always seemed to be reading about smugglers or pirates.

Some of my best, albeit hazy, childhood memories are on that windy strand: behind us our white house, the tallest thing on the horizon. Michael, my little sister Juliet and I and our friends would play all kinds of games on the beach, and catch crabs and lobsters around the rocks with fencing wire at low tide.

My father was an officer in the Royal Irish Fusiliers; at that time his battalion was based a few miles down the road. The Irish Fusiliers we thought of as the family regiment. I later met two family members who'd also served with the regiment—an uncle of Dad's, Redmond Neill, and a cousin, Charlie Rattray. They had ramrod-stiff backs, and moustaches just like Dad's.

The Watch House was very isolated, but had electric lighting at least, with power wind-generated by a propeller on a pole and stored in car batteries indoors. There was no shortage of wind. Dad was not a practical man, and once had to replace the propeller, the good one having blown off onto the rocks. Coming back from Belfast, he forgot about the prop beam sticking forwards out of the car roof, drove into the garage and ripped the tiny Standard Ten almost in two in the process. Not a happy day. That was it for electricity. It was candles from then on.

Sometimes Dad would launch his notoriously unreliable clinker-built dinghy, with a Seagull outboard on the back, and we'd all go fishing out into the Irish Sea. That was the first of Dad's awful boats that I knew. Going out with him on the water often meant more of an adventure than you'd like, but we all survived over the years; nobody drowned. That was probably divine intervention rather than good seamanship on Dad's part. I loved adventures with Dad over all those years of my childhood, except when it came to reversing a boat trailer into the water. This usually meant a jackknife of car and boat, in front of a crowd who would be more amused than helpful. Mortifying.

But when we were small at Tyrella, we children were all explorers. One of our haunts nearby was an unmarked archaeological site, which must have been a 'passage grave' of some kind, a souterrain; we were sure it had some defensive purpose. After entering you had to crawl under a large slab of rock, and an intruder doing so would be easily bashed on the head by a defender. A great place for children's gruesome games.

That souterrain triggered a lifelong interest in archaeology for me. Particularly in Ireland. I am fascinated, for instance, by Newgrange, a massive construction built on the River Boyne near the border. It was built hundreds of years before the Pyramids and Stonehenge. It seems to me a common failing of contemporary archaeology that anywhere there were buried bones is commonly labelled as a 'tomb'. Imagine uncovering Westminster Abbey in a few thousand years; it's full of bones, but is hardly a tomb. There were bones inside Newgrange, but it seems obvious to me that its mysterious builders had a more serious intent than burying a few chiefs. They were building the Womb of the World. Anyone with a passing knowledge of ancient religions knows they often would see the Earth as the Mother (Gaia, if you like), the Sky as the Father. Newgrange has a carefully constructed tunnel that aligns precisely so that on the shortest day of the year, midwinter, the rays of the sun shine on the very back wall. The deep interior. The builders were ensuring that the Earth Mother was impregnated at this critical moment, promising fertility and bounty, and a rich year to come. When I took a tour underground at Newgrange, I rather alarmed the guide with this theory, but he wouldn't yield. I still think I'm right.

Anyway, back to the Standard Ten. Dad must have used it to go to work, because Mum and the rest of us got about in a donkey and cart. Ginny was our donkey: very pretty but also very bad-tempered. We'd climb on the cart, and Mum would drive

Ginny down the beach to Ballykinlar to shop for our basics at the Naafi. That donkey hated being ridden, for all that we loved her, and ejected me once over a barbed-wire fence. My left knee still bears the scar.

In the distance, dominating the view at Tyrella, were the mesmerising blue Mountains of Mourne, directly across the bay. There's something about that silhouette, graceful and balanced, that haunts me to this day. As an adult I climbed to the highest peak. It was exhilarating up there. But then the clouds came in and I got very lost and disoriented on the way down.

At the foot of the mountains is a small town with the rather pedestrian name of Newcastle. Not much of a place, to be honest, but we would sometimes go there on an outing, and as a treat we'd share in the back seat some Edinburgh rock, a sort of crumbly confection that I thought was nirvana. I tried it many years later and it was simply disgusting—sickly sweet.

County Down remains a beautiful corner of Ireland. If there is an upside at all to the Troubles, it's that for the last sixty years or so there has been very little tourism and not a lot happening in the North. Much of it is just as I remember. The Irish coast: you can't beat it.

The first time I returned to Tyrella, I couldn't find my way to the beach along the narrow stone-walled lanes. I knocked on a little farmhouse door looking for help. There I stood, a grown man, more or less, who last was there aged seven, twenty-five years before.

The door opened, a woman smiled at me, and before I could open my mouth she said, 'You are one of the Neill boys, so you are.' I have never been more surprised. It happened that we small children used to walk up there and get our milk from her, in a can. But...how on earth could she have picked that?

After Tyrella, we lived in Armagh for a couple of years,

and the Watch House was our holiday place. Dad was CO at the army depot there. Here was my first school—Armagh Girls High School. I wore a blazer that read AGHS, which I had to be persuaded stood for Armagh *General* High School, since I had such antipathy for anything to do with girls.

I should remember more than I do of Armagh. We must have been the only children in the barracks, and we had the run of the place. I knew a lot of the men—and I'd very seriously salute the sentry as I came and went through the gates. Dad had a pack of beagles I'd hang out with after school, as well as the regimental mascot—a huge Irish wolfhound about three times my size. That poor, sweet-natured animal died cruelly of distemper while we were there, which broke my small heart.

There was an old tennis court in front of our house, and my brother and I played with our toy cars and soldiers there, as well as bashing a few balls. Down the hill towards the Mall is the site of the one and only remotely sectarian memory I have. My best friend, James Morris, and I ran down to watch a parade— it must have been 12 July—that we could hear in the distance. It sounded exciting, but as we got closer it became stranger and weirdly frightening. It was all loud drums and sweaty florid faces, orange sashes and bowler hats, and an alarming sense of common purpose that I'd never seen before. We ran away.

This was a peaceful time in the North; the Troubles were still some years away. I don't believe I ever heard the words 'Protes- tant' or 'Catholic', and if I had they wouldn't have meant anything to me. At least, not until we went to New Zealand. At my school it was important that we beat St Bede's, a Catholic school a few miles away, at rugby. Other than that, I have no comprehension of any of that bloody nonsense. None of it made sense, then or now, to me.

Of course, it's possible I was simply too thick to pick up on all that, but here's a story from Mum that 'rather disturbed' her. It tells you something, particularly about her. We were still living at the Watch House.

> The sink had got bunged up, and I sent for the plumber from Downpatrick about eight miles away. I said to Helen, a girl of only sixteen who had come to help me when Madeline (the nanny) left. 'The plumber from Downpatrick is coming over, would you give him a cup of tea?'
>
> 'Is he Protestant or Catholic?'
>
> I said, 'Helen, I have no idea, he's the plumber and he's coming to fix the sink.'
>
> 'I'd like to know before he comes.'
>
> 'There's no way we can find out, and anyway it doesn't matter—and you must make him a cup of tea.'
>
> She was frightfully sulky, and when he had arrived I went into the kitchen and they were sitting as far away from each other as possible having their tea—not a word being spoken. Then as soon as he'd gone she said to me sharply, 'Was he a Protestant or a Catholic, did you find out?'

Fifty years later, the last time I was back at Tyrella, I was lucky that the owner of the Watch House was home. She and Michael had been friends as children when she lived in one of the little coastguard cottages nearby. Deirdre Dunseath was very kind, gave me tea, and over a cup told me that there were two things that Tyrella was known for.

The first was that Isambard Kingdom Brunel's grand revolutionary steamship the SS *Great Britain* beached there on her third voyage in 1846, and remained stranded for a year, not more than a few yards from the Watch House. Brunel floated her off eventually, but it meant ditching all her coal onto the beach. Indeed, I remember playing with that coal as a child; it was everywhere, smooth and benignly round, having been worn by the sea for a hundred years.

I asked Deirdre what the other famous thing was. She said, like I was some kind of a fool, 'Well. *You* lived here.' Hardly in the same league, but it did tickle me.

She sold the Watch House recently, and we all thought about trying to buy it. But I eventually decided against it. It'd be too sad without Mum and Dad there. Ghosts or something. Best left there.

Some people you miss forever.

I often think about my feeling of connection with Ireland. I feel curiously at home there, and everything is comfortably familiar—the stone walls, the trees, the gentle hills, the smell of turf on a fire, the accents. Is this just sentimentality? I think not. It is more likely that my first seven years were there and that never leaves you. Or perhaps it is all in my DNA. Thousands of years of ancestors on my Irish side. Who knows? I build stone walls around my farm these days. They serve no practical purpose at all, but they make me feel good, and that's enough.

Incidentally, I have played someone Irish on film only twice. The first was the somewhat creepy Mr Gentleman in Edna O'Brien's *The Country Girls* (1983), but he was possibly sort of British. The other was that hideous Ulsterman Major Campbell in *Peaky Blinders*. I never had more fun playing a character than him. Someone suggested I should apologise to some people from the North for that 'grotesque caricature', but I unreservedly do not.

The entirely loveable Major Campbell, *Peaky Blinders*.

What on Earth Just Happened?

YOU might well ask, but in short I am 'under the doctor'. Where does this expression come from? I think it's Scottish, but I'm open to correction on this one. Not that I *like* being 'under the doctor', but I like the term. I am decidedly a man under the doctor.

At the beginning of March 2022 I flew to Los Angeles on matters *Jurassic*. About eight of the cast had an entire three-day weekend doing interviews, photo spreads for *Vanity Fair* and all of that stuff—publicity. It was a blast to catch up with my idiot friends and goof around as per. I noticed the glands seemed to be up in my neck region, but gave it very little thought. My agent had to kill a few photographs because my neck looked lumpy. Alan Grant doesn't have a lumpy neck, it seems.

I flew back to Sydney to finish the television series *The Twelve*, but on a day off went to see my GP. I have great faith in him, but in this case he was a little conservative, maybe. I said, These lumps don't seem to be going down, and I don't know why. He assured me that my lumpy glands were due to undetected COVID, and they'd be hanging around for a little while. I went back a week later when they were even bigger. This time he sent me in to hospital for some tests.

I thought something might be amiss when a nurse was fooling around with an ultrasound under my chin. She suddenly dropped the tool and almost ran from the room. Pretty much immediately a doctor appeared and got to work with a very serious look on her face. I tried a couple of jokes, but they fell a little flat. The next day I was sent in for a PET scan. This is one of those things where they fill you with run-off from Chernobyl so you are completely radioactive, and then insert you into a tunnel.

I was not to know the results of this test just yet, because I was flying to New Zealand the next morning. At last I was going home. I'd been separated from family for far too long and I couldn't wait.

That afternoon I was at my son Tim's house and my phone rang. It was my specialist doctor from the hospital, the haematologist Dr Lavee, and she did not have good news. She told me it was serious, very serious, and I needed to get back to Sydney right away. In short I had stage III angioimmunoblastic T-cell lymphoma. (I think I have that right.) This was apparently very serious indeed, although I'd never heard of such a thing. I couldn't be bothered looking it up on the net, it might have freaked me out, and anyway I was prepared to believe her. I told her that I wouldn't come back for a few days, that I hadn't been to my farm for months and I needed to sleep in my own bed, talk to my pets, plant something, be a farmer and a wine producer, even if it was only for a few days. I really needed to do that, and she understood.

But fly back I did, and within a few days I was lying on a hospital bed having all kinds of chemicals draining into my system, killing everything aboard. For therapeutic reasons. To be cured of a thing I didn't know I had just a few days ago.

Yep, suddenly things are different—this is some serious shit. But I was, and I remain, cheerful. I'm 'under the doctor', all right. I have faith in medicine. But the world has certainly turned upside down…That is what on earth just happened.

Personally, I can't wait to see what comes next. I will keep you posted.

From the Beatles to Bill Nutt

NOT long ago, I was asked by Jim Mora on Radio New Zealand to name my favourite song of all time. I told him that was impossible. Music has been completely central to me all my life. I've loved countless songs.

But I could name the most important record ever for me.

Dad had an excellent LP collection, and was pretty sound on classical music. He loved a good orchestra and a great symphony but, oddly, I don't think my parents ever went to the Dunedin Town Hall to hear the symphony orchestra play. Mum had no real musical interest, but I was assured she was a nifty dancer in her day.

Michael, five years older, was for me more influential in this, as in so many other things. We had adjoining rooms at home, with only a curtain between us, and I'd listen to the stuff he liked. He was something of a beatnik in his early years at Otago University, wore duffel coats, affected a pipe and got as close to a Caesar cut as his wavy hair would permit. Naturally, he inclined towards blues, gospel and jazz. Nina Simone, Miles Davis, Sonny Boy Williamson, Thelonious Monk, Mahalia Jackson, Stanley Turrentine. The best. I still love all that. And one day I might make the argument that fifties jazz was the absolute zenith of American culture. Which has been in slow decline ever since.

Michael left home for Cambridge University when I was about fifteen, and I was then free to make my own collection and follow my own proclivities. He left his record player behind. The first record I ever bought was 'Nut Rocker' by B. Bumble and the Stingers, when I was maybe ten. It's a curiosity but, if you listen to it and the changes it makes, you can picture, bent over a spinning disc, a shy boy beginning to find his own taste. I also thought it was funny. I think a little humour goes a long way in life and work, and I've always tried to play even the darkest characters with some element of comedy. At least I think so.

I started reading good books as a teenager. And listening to music at the same time. I read the entire *Lord of the Rings* trilogy listening to the soundtracks of Kenny Burrell and Elmer Bernstein.

The early 1960s were a low point in rock/pop music. A lot of sappy crooners, mostly called Bobby. But then, at exactly the right time for me, something magical and transformative happened. The Beatles turned up. I was fifteen when they arrived on our radio, and twenty-two when they broke up. I was formed, grew into a man, to a Beatles soundtrack.

Of course, I loved the Stones, the Kinks, Hendrix, Cocker and many others. But the Beatles were the bee's nuts. I had my first dance with an actual living breathing girl, Julia Hall, to 'I Saw Her Standing There' in her family's sitting room, by the Avon in Fendalton.

It's hard to conceive now how important they were then. Each record they made was strides ahead of the last, and on the day of release we'd rush off to Begg's to buy it, and sprint to the bus to hear it at home. Couldn't wait. And what a revelation they'd be. Impossible, you'd think. How good could a band be? I still maintain there will never be better.

So my answer to Jim Mora was this. *Sgt Pepper's Lonely Hearts Club Band*. I was nineteen when it came out. On first hearing the title song I could hardly breathe in amazement. The *Pepper's* LP is perhaps the greatest rock record ever made and was utterly revolutionary. It looked back to the past, but propelled us into a future where anything was possible.

If proof were needed of the importance of my favourite band, almost everyone I know thought watching *The Beatles: Get Back* was their most profound experience of recent times. Everyone with any taste, that is.

How did I afford to buy records back then? I didn't get pocket money, except at Christ's College, where I was a boarder from thirteen. There we all got two shillings a week. That was enough for four crumpets with honey at little Miss Cottrell's school tuckshop. It was at College, incidentally, that some miserable bastard decided that we were not to be allowed to see the Beatles when they played in Christchurch in 1964.

Otherwise, we were encouraged to get jobs in the holidays. I was twelve when I got my first paying job. I did all sorts. I put jam into tarts in a cake shop in the Exchange Building in Dunedin. I emptied rubbish bins at the camping grounds at St Kilda. What came out of those bins you wouldn't believe. I was an assistant greenkeeper on the golf course at Balmacewen. I was a shop assistant, wearing a tie, in an appliance store. I lumped timber round in a yard near the railway station.

These and other jobs taught me so much. You have to bloody work to make a bloody quid. The world is more diverse than you'd suspect in a boarding school in Christchurch. Keep your head down, and you stay out of trouble. Humour comes in many forms. Respect the worker. Find your allies. Listen carefully to instructions. Be grateful for a pay packet.

We carried on with holiday jobs once I went on to university. For three summers in a row, initially with friends like Pip Hall and Gerse Halliday, I went to Ashburton, then a somewhat desolate small town fifty flat miles south of Christchurch. We worked at Burnett's Motors, a haulage firm that operated all over the Mid Canterbury plains. They needed students in the summer to lift hay bales and stack them with precision in sheds. It was heavy, dusty, hard work. A decent lucerne bale could weigh up to eighty pounds. As a non-sporty, weedy type, I had to toughen up fast. It took a couple of weeks for your hands to harden enough with calluses so you could get through a day's work without them bleeding. Since I have always suffered from hay fever, this was all counterintuitive. I sneezed the whole summer.

But I outlasted all my friends, none of whom did three whole seasons. I loved summer in Mid Canterbury, and I hated it too. It was flat, monotonous and bloody dry. But there, in the far distance, were the Southern Alps under a clear blue sky, a little snow on the tops and the promise of adventure. Fishing, skiing, hiking...all the things I'd been brought up to love.

Near the base of the mountains was a little town called Methven. It had two pubs—the Brown Pub and the Blue Pub. In one or the other, the old hands swore that they had a raffle on Saturday nights. The prize was a dozen beers, or half an hour upstairs with the barmaid. Apparently, if you were sensible you took the beer. I have no idea if this is true and never went there in the name of research.

The regular drivers in Ashburton rolled their eyes when a batch of new uni students arrived at Burnett's. Useless soft pricks. Bloody longhairs. You'd get picked by the drivers, rather like in games at school. Once you'd done a few weeks and had got the hang of things, you'd be first off the rank. You were useful. You knew how to make a twelve-high haystack that wouldn't fall over.

We would turn up at all sorts of farms. Some were almost landed gentry, with stately old homesteads. I'd recognise names from boarding school. You never saw the nobs; they were too grand by half for common truckies like us. Some were old bachelors whose dilapidated faces and houses beggared belief. The houses we liked the best were those where a nice farmer's wife would come out at smoko with thermoses of tea and fresh warm scones with jam. We were so starved we'd almost weep in gratitude.

Very occasionally, we'd get invited into a warm kitchen to sit around the table. This always fascinated me. I would closely observe the old drivers here. Outside these were hard men: hard swearing, hard drinking, proud working-class men. But inside a kitchen, a woman's domain, they were reduced to shy, mumbling children. They'd smoke with their tea, while silently staring at the floor, but ash their cigarettes on their trousers so as not to muck up the place. Uncle Hec in *Hunt for the Wilderpeople* owes a lot to these blokes.

You'd often be the target of ribbing from some of the old drivers and full-time offsiders. Mostly good-natured, but sometimes not. One bloke in particular, not much older than me, who could conjugate the word fuck in any number of ways, and never said a sentence without at least ten fucks in a row, picked on me for a few days. I was patient and said nothing, but it didn't abate. One day he persisted in hitting me on the back of my bare legs with heavy hay bales when my back was turned, time and again. He was throwing bales onto the truck where I was stacking. It wasn't going to stop, and eventually I'd had enough. When it happened for about the tenth time, instead of stacking the bale, I picked it up and waited until he turned *his* back. And then, with pinpoint accuracy, I hoisted the bale into the air and hurled it at his head. It flattened him and winded him at the same time.

When he stood up, I was pointing right in his face. 'Don't ever fucking do that again, you cunt!' This was language he understood. I never had a peep out of him after that.

Along with seemingly everyone in Ashburton, he had false teeth. Perhaps this was common all over New Zealand. For your twenty-first birthday, your parents would give you a free trip to the dentist, who would pull out all your teeth and give you dentures in return. This was seen as a supremely generous act of common sense. It would save you a fortune, now that you were a grown-up: a lifetime of never having to see the dentist again.

Mind you, every child in the country had suffered trauma in the past at the malicious hands of dental nurses. Every primary school of any size had one. I had a couple of terms at Cashmere Primary in Christchurch when we first arrived back in New Zealand, in the mid-1950s. There was a small wooden building which almost seemed radioactive. At playtime kids would steer well clear, for inside dwelt the wicked dental nurse. She got me in her clutches at some point. I had never had a tooth cavity in my life, but she somehow found twelve. These needed immediate attention. She had a foot-propelled drill, grindingly slow and utterly agonising. No anaesthetics.

Ashburton, dull as it was, was also liberating for university students like us. We shared flats for the first time. Freedom! We drank, smoked and ate disgusting food. It was pretty foul. Sometimes a girl or two would visit, but they wouldn't stay long. Who could blame them? If we'd had a good week and worked overtime, we'd hitchhike to Christchurch and party for the weekend to celebrate. And do the same stupid things there. When I think of our idiotic behaviour, I shudder. No one thought twice about driving blind drunk. I couldn't afford a car, so that wasn't me, but I was often in the back seat.

Not all of us made it. Here's a story I wrote for the *Press* in Christchurch about someone who didn't.

A Christchurch Love Story

I love a good love story, and this is one. It is also a true story. It's about my old friend Nigel Nutt.

We first met at school in Christchurch. We were eleven years old.

Almost immediately he became my best friend. In part I think we bonded because we were both called Nigel. It's not a great name, Nigel. So we changed our names. We liked Westerns and in Westerns people were called things like Sam. So I became Sam and he became Bill. We never looked back. What an excellent decision that turned out to be: you can NOT have a career in movies and be called Nigel Neill.

But it was far more than that. He was the funniest person I'd ever met. He didn't tell jokes—he was a joke, everyone was a joke, the world was a joke. He was fun. Everybody loved Bill Nutt. And we stayed the closest of friends right up until we left boarding school. We shared studies, I'd go to his farm on Sundays. We did pretty much everything together.

My old friend Nigel Nutt, brilliant fool.

We were in plays. He was the most naturally gifted comic actor I've ever worked with (with the possible exception of Robin Williams, but it's bloody close). He could do pratfalls and double takes before we knew what they were. We found girlfriends about the same time. Girls loved Bill. He was kind of goofy looking, but he could charm the birds from the trees. He made them laugh. And a party never really started until Bill turned up.

Then school finished, and Bill went home to the farm at Tai Tapu.

One crazy party night, another crazy party night, Bill went to sleep driving home. The car went off the road, and Bill flew through the windscreen at God-knows-what speed. And that was it for parties. That was that for everything. The life of the party was struggling to stay alive. He was in a coma for about four months, and then gradually he woke up. Very gradually. He couldn't speak, he couldn't do anything much. He was in hospital for months and months more—how he had survived at all, no one knew. Gradually he got better, but never entirely. He spoke slowly and in a monotone. He walked eventually, but very poorly. He went home and he knew he would never be the same. It was cruel.

He plunged into a deep, deep depression. Eventually he tried suicide. He failed—the bullet went the wrong way. The world was dark and very sad.

But then after a few years, he found the Laura Fergusson Home. And that's when everything began to change. His memory began to return. His inimitable sense of humour came back. And best of all, he became happy again. I'd go and see Bill as often as I could when I got back from abroad. I cannot tell you how happy I was to find him there. And how touched I was by how genuinely cared for he was there.

They loved Bill. They really dug him.

And he found a job. He was the gate man at the bridge as you cross the river to the hospital. He'd sit there all day, smoking endless cigarettes, joking dryly to the nurses, doctors and patients who had passed by. He was loved there too. To the best of my knowledge, he never turned anyone away.

And then something else miraculous happened. He fell in love. She lived at Laura Fergusson too. For me this was the best love story of all. They were utterly devoted to each other. She was sweet, he was funny; it was magic. I mean, it'd make you cry to watch it. She gave his life meaning, and he did the same for her. They only separated when Bill died. That was more than twenty years ago now.

I still miss Bill. I loved him too. We all did. And I am eternally grateful to the Laura Fergusson Brain Injury Trust—everyone who worked there, for the care and the love they gave all those years to my friend.

The B Word

I'VE enjoyed excellent health all my life. Up until now.

This hasn't been through any particularly good behaviour on my part. I've never been much of a fitness freak, and I only go to the gym under sufferance. If I have to get fit for a part, for instance. Gyms are not my idea of a good time. All that groaning and sweating. Many years ago I used to go to the City Gym in Darlinghurst. This was, for an observer of humanity like me, rather a fascinating place. There was an extraordinary mix of all sorts in there. There were obvious gangsters and enforcers, from Kings Cross. You never caught their eye. There were immense men clearly on huge doses of steroids who could barely walk because of their enormous thighs. You never caught their eye either. There were large gay guys who were dainty and muscular at the same time. They were known as Muscle Marys, and sometimes if you were on the next machine you'd hear them talking about how they would be frocking up on the weekend.

Around that time, there was a night when I felt that my future wife, Noriko, and I were under some kind of threat from a bunch of drunk people. I thought that perhaps I should learn something more than just how to stay out of trouble; something about self-defence. I found someone who could help me with that, and we would go and train in a nearby park. He was a cop who would moonlight as security in some pretty rough joints. He knew what to do under dire conditions. And so do I, now. It's a dark art. Don't cross me, that's my advice. I'm a dangerous man!

He wasn't a big guy, nor was his brother, who, like him, was a cop, Lebanese and very useful. This story about his brother has never left me. One Saturday afternoon he was, unaccountably, the only security on duty at one of those huge garden pubs in the west of Sydney. Out of nowhere, a whole motorcycle gang roared up. To the mutual horror of all the drinkers there, they sauntered into the place amid terrified silence, and ordered beers. Our friend was dismayed when management told him that they wanted the bikers to leave the premises, and that he was the one who had to tell them to do so. He pulled himself up to his full five foot six, braced himself and quietly asked them to go. This was not received well, and the next thing he knew his back was against the bar and a semicircle of hairy bikers was closing in. He was about to get the shit beaten out of him.

And this is where quick thinking and drastic measures come in. He'd already identified the leader. Quick as a flash, he grabbed him and put him in a headlock. With his other hand he hooked into one of the man's eyes, and pulled out the eyeball on the end of its stalk.

But this was the clincher. With the bikie screaming in the headlock, and the eyeball between his fingers, he looked up, and told them all to fuck off.

And laughed!

It was the laugh that did it. They were dealing with a psycho. He dropped the man to the floor, and his mates picked him up and departed.

Anyway, back to me and my health. I don't think I can be fairly accused of being a hypochondriac. No more than the next man. But at one point in the 1980s I was working in Toronto and went to the production-approved doctor on a day off, convinced I had bowel cancer and was about to die. I explained to the doctor that I'd taken a couple of decent craps that day and to my horror the lavatory bowl was bright red. It could be nothing but blood. I clearly had mere weeks to live.

The doctor asked me if by any remote chance I'd eaten beetroot lately. I thought for a second, and then I said, That's absolutely right. Some nice people had asked me to lunch and served beetroot, something I'd never liked but was surprisingly delicious. I think I'd had three or four helpings on the strength of it.

With the practised air of a patient man, he said, 'Well, that will be it, then, won't it.'

Oh, the relief.

And then he said, 'On looking at my notes, I see that you saw me last year, and at that time you were convinced you'd had a major heart attack. It was, in fact, not a coronary, but heartburn. And I prescribed Rennies.'

I blushed, muttered, 'Thank you, doctor,' and got my coat.

I have to say here that I like doctors, and I have great faith in modern medicine. It seems extraordinary, for instance, in this modern age, that you have to say you are pro-vaccination. It seems incredible to me that the whole business of inoculation has come under doubt during the pandemic when we know with absolute certainty that this side of medicine has saved countless lives over my lifetime, including, I have no doubt, my own. We don't have to fear mumps, rubella, measles, whooping cough, polio—all the diseases that could have killed or maimed us, all the diseases that petrified our parents. Simply because, since I was a kid, they developed vaccines, and these things largely disappeared.

A few years ago, my life did come under threat in the oddest way. My regular blood check detected a disease without any symptoms whatsoever. I'm sure you will have never heard of it—nor had I. It is called haemochromatosis. It's something you might inherit, and I've warned my children about it. It is found only among those, like me, who have Irish/Viking/Nordic tendencies. It is a disorder that makes your system absorb too much iron in your blood, to the detriment of everything else, and if left untreated will eventually kill your organs, and then you yourself.

Happily, it is pretty easily treated, but treated in the most peculiar mediaeval way. They bleed you. They treat you like Dracula would, given the chance. They take something like a litre of blood out of you once a week or so, and your system rights itself somehow. Don't ask me how.

The catch here is that I have always been not just blood-phobic, but needle-phobic as well. To treat my new-found disorder involved both needles *and* blood. You can imagine my cold sweaty fear.

But we did it. I trained my nice British doctor, Nigel (amazingly he was entirely at ease with his ridiculous name), to never mention what we were doing during that regular half-hour of draining. He was not to mention the blood word. He was never to mention what was happening. He was never to show me the equipment. And he was never, ever to let me see the blood that he'd sucked out of me. Never. Instead, we talked about our children and holidays on the beach at Tyrella, where, oddly enough, he'd spent some of his childhood as well.

This worked fine, until one appointment Nigel was away on leave. Dr Val, whom I'd known for many years, was filling in. We were halfway through what I would carefully call 'The Procedure', when Val said, 'Sam, this is great; the blood is just absolutely pouring out of you!'

I said, 'Jesus Christ, Val! Why did you have to say that? Please, please, please, stop!'

I was grimly silent for the remaining ten minutes, tottered out and half fainted in the waiting room, pale and sweaty, with my head between my knees. It was a good half an hour before I was okay to drive home.

And now, of all cancers, it had to be about...the B word. Cancer of the blood.

My Amazing Gaggie

I'M up here in a flat on the top of an old factory in inner Sydney. I'm up with the birds.

It can be solitary up here, lonely even, but in the mornings and evenings extravagantly coloured lorikeets join me on my balcony. They are lively companions, cheeky, demanding and highly decorative. I used to feed them porridge-textured wet seedy bread, but when I posted on social media a shot of my birds greedily hoeing into their feed, I was met with a storm of abuse. Don't you know, Sam Neill, not to feed bread to wild birds? How irresponsible can you be? You are influential, you of all people should know better!

Well, I have mended my wicked ways, and I now only give them food specially made for their breed. My sad old bread goes in the compost. I'd like to think I could feel more righteous, but I don't. People take offence at almost anything these days. Even feeding birds.

I have a thing about birds. The term bird-brain is used in a disparaging sense. But you try doing what a bird can do with a brain the size of half a teaspoon. Here they are now, wheeling around the giddying blue Sydney sky, filling me with awe and joy. The spatial skills, the acrobatics, the sheer bravado. Magpies, parrots, lorikeets, even dirty old pigeons...I love them to pieces. I even love the grubby ibis that have made their home in the city. The bin chickens, stalking around with as much dignity as they can muster. Which isn't a lot when you've got a bald back pate, your formerly white wings are covered in something suspiciously sticky and brown, and you raid rubbish bins.

I think I inherited this predisposition from my grandmother Gaggie. She loved all living creatures and was devoted to horses, dogs, cats, birds, you name it, all her life. She had a productive vegetable garden behind her house in Tenby, south Wales, much populated by chickens. And it was there that a crow fell out of the nest one day. Once a chick leaves its nest, the parents never tend to it again. Gaggie picked up the little thing, tiny and half bald, and took it inside to join the rest of her extensive rescued menagerie, where she fed it with an eye-dropper, and raised it to a full-sized bird. Being a crow, it was a bossy, dominant animal, of whom all the dogs and cats and so on were terrified. The crow ran the joint, strutting around like a little Mussolini, giving raucous commands.

The crow lived like this with my grandmother for quite some time, until, one day, again in the vegetable garden, she saw the bird eyeing off a murder of crows chatting away in a tree. Gaggie's crow flew up to them, and joined in the conversation. And then, without so much as a by-your-leave, they all flew off together. My grandmother sorely missed that little chatterbox of a bird, but was content to think it was now among its own.

But then, a year or so later, in the same garden, Gaggie heard some familiar chatter coming from the same tree. Looking up she saw two crows, side by side, staring at her. The one she recognised immediately as her crow flew down and landed on her shoulder. The bird chatted into her ear for a few minutes before rejoining its mate. The couple looked back, and then flew off and were never seen again. It was as if it had returned to tell Gaggie that all was well, and that they'd settled down happily in some big old tree. And, who knows, perhaps it'd even come to say thank you.

Back in New Zealand, on my land, I've been assiduously

planting trees for decades now. Last spring on the farm, we planted 2500 native trees and shrubs. Planting trees is about as important a thing as you can do in these times. I'd like to think we are getting as close to carbon neutral as we can be on the farm, although I've never measured that. I sometimes despair for the future of my grandchildren, and indeed the planet. But despair does no good. You have to do something. Planting a tree is a positive step every time. And trees are beautiful.

But the truth is, more than anything, I plant trees for the birds. The native birds. There are few things more delightful than a half-drunk tūī hanging upside down in a kōwhai tree drinking nectar from those strange yellow flowers. Or a riot of korimakos (bellbirds) waking you up from the native beech trees first thing. When I was lucky enough to buy the farm, twenty-something years ago, you never saw a native bird. Now there are fantails, tūīs, riroriros (grey warblers), korimakos, kārearea (falcons). We've even seen some kererū (native pigeons) once or twice. I'd like to think I helped with that in some small way.

But back to my grandmother. To say I loved her dearly would be an understatement. I doubt a kinder woman ever lived. Despite having been widowed in 1917 when her beloved Bob, Lt. Col. R. F. J. Ingham, was killed by Germans on the Western Front, she took it upon herself to care for German prisoners of war. They'd come around for a cup of tea and a meat-free pie in that same garden out the back where I played years later. This kindness, the hospitality she showed them, must have meant a lot, because some of them continued to write to her until she died.

I was sent to stay with her in Tenby for some months when I was about seven, while Mum and Dad were packing up everything, getting ready to travel back to New Zealand. Dad was posted on loan to the New Zealand army for a year, and we all had to go with him.

I don't think I've ever been happier than during that precious time I got to spend with Gaggie, just me and my gran. Tenby is a pretty little seaside town in the far west of Wales, and in those days, before Brits started to summer in Spain, they might have taken a holiday, a week or two, in a place like Tenby or Margate. But then the Costa del Sol beckoned, and coastal villages in Britain became superfluous. As a result, when you go back to Tenby now, it's as if it was frozen in time soon after I left for the other side of the planet. Back in the fifties.

We lived in Gaggie's little place, tending to birds and mammals of various kinds, pottering about. She was always busy. She had a corpulent Welsh corgi called Dorny, short for Dornier, the German aircraft that had bombed the poor animal and given her the PTSD that accounted for her obesity and fear of just about everything. The dog was far too fat to walk—they have short legs, that breed. When it was time to go to the shops, always a treat, my gran would heave this great orange blimp of a dog into an ancient black pram, and off we'd go. Most people in Tenby knew Gaggie, and we'd be hailed from all directions. But I loved it when a kindly stranger would peer into the depths of the pram, expecting to coo at a cute grandchild. Instead, they would recoil in horror at the unlikely sight of a fat ginger furball recumbent and shivering at the back.

I spent a term at a little prep school in Saundersfoot, a tiny village just down the coast, and it was fun. I had a friend called the Honourable Anthony Someone. I imagine he's in the House of Lords now. I remember standing in front of the assembled school, having been asked by the headmaster to show everyone where I was going to live on this huge world map. The map was largely coloured red, which indicated the empire. I pointed to a couple of remote islands in a vast blue ocean that I knew to be called New Zealand. But that's all I knew.

And then, when the holidays came, we went up to stay with Gaggie's sister, the terrifying Aunt Dorothy, in Kensington. She had a flat in Palace Mansions, opposite Olympia. I'd never been to London before, and I was overexcited. Aunt Dorothy's place I found a little scary, mostly because I found her so. I would stand happily outside on the balcony, staring at all the traffic grinding along Hammersmith Road. Bumper to bumper, and all uniformly black, who knows why. London was pretty dirty black already. But I wanted to see everything: the Tower, Houses of Parliament, Madame Tussauds, Buckingham Palace, the Horse Guards... and Gaggie made sure we did. We'd go all over London on a big red bus, up top, at the very front. I'd make bus noises and turn an imaginary steering wheel as we ground our way round the capital. It was thrilling.

But the most thrilling, and certainly the most memorable, visit we made was to the most unlikely venue imaginable—the Windmill Theatre in Soho.

For reasons that are unclear to me, the fearsome Aunt Dorothy Saunders, herself a war widow, adopted rather late in life a little girl, who became Josie Saunders. Josie had, it was thought, some theatrical talent, and Aunt Dorothy sent her to drama and dance school. Margaret Lockwood, a British film star from the thirties and forties, lived downstairs. Her daughter and Josie went to the same school, and were good friends.

By the time I turned up in London at the grand age of seven, Josie was now perhaps twenty or twenty-one, smiling and friendly, slim and very beautiful. She was still living at home, but was now at work as a dancer. But not just any dancer. She had a full-time job as a Windmill Girl.

Now, the Windmill was a famous, beloved Soho institution. Rather like the Folies Bergère in Paris, plus very British comedians. It famously never closed during the war, even at the height of the Blitz. It was vaudeville revue, it was Tommy Cooper, Peter Sellers, it was fabulous costumes; it was chorus girls, girls, girls. And it was tableaux vivants. Full nudity. Which was only legal at the time *if* the girl stayed stock-still. I, being but seven, had never in my life seen a naked woman before. And, I can tell you, it left a lasting impression.

Why these funny old, very proper, Edwardian grannies took me to this, with their little hats, and their handbags on their knees, I will never know. The only other people at the matinee were a few dodgy-looking geezers in their raincoats. Josie would work at the Windmill most nights. She would get home very late, and I would get up early and wander into her room. She'd open half an exhausted eye at me and say, 'Want a cuddle?' 'Yes,' would be the eager reply. I'd snuggle up, she'd drop back to sleep, and I'd drift off in the enveloping warmth of Josie's kindness. Sadly, I don't know what happened to her; she married someone 'unsuitable', I think, and the family lost touch with her.

The Windmill, early 1950s. Josie Saunders is top left, in what seems to be an Egyptian-themed tableau vivant.

Years later, I had a stand-in on many jobs named Butch, who had known Josie well at the Windmill and was very fond of her. Butch had been a hoofer in his youth. I saw him in a panto once, playing an ugly sister in *Cinderella*. His pretty days were long gone, and this camp old queen was as grizzly and funny as a good pantomime requires.

I liked Butch a lot, and often asked for him if I was working in London, but it was always a mistake to absent-mindedly ask him how his weekend was. He had a predilection for anonymous encounters on Hampstead Heath after dark. He'd be happy to tell all. I'd have to say, 'Butch. *Please*. Stop right there. I don't need to know any more, really, thank you.' Hair-raising stuff. He'd chuckle and scuttle away.

Soon after my stay in London, we sailed off to New Zealand. We moved to Cashmere, a pretty hillside suburb above Christchurch. We left my darling Gaggie behind. I often think how much that must have been a bitter loss for her. She had lost her only son John to a sniper in 1947. John was in the Indian Army and was stationed up on the North-West Frontier about the time of Partition. She'd lost her husband to shell fire in 1917. I visited his grave during the documentary I made, *Anzac Tides of Blood*. And now her last child—my mother, the dutiful wife—had gone to live on the other side of the world. With all of her grandchildren.

We sailed to New Zealand on the *Rangitiki*, flagship of the New Zealand Shipping Company. It took about six weeks, via the Panama Canal. I contracted mumps halfway there, and spent weeks in isolation in a little cabin at the back of the ship. My only companion was an albatross that seemed to like to keep an eye on me. It would glide in the wake of our vessel and drift up close to the railing outside my cabin and deliberately catch my eye and hold it for minutes on end. Then it would sail majestically out to the horizon again.

Gaggie sailed out by herself about five years later and stayed for some months. I don't know what she made of New Zealand. I was so pleased she was with us, but I probably didn't do enough to show how much I loved her. Then she went home and I never saw her again.

I still have most of my Dinky Toys, which she would send me every Christmas. I treasure them, largely because of her. She would have saved to buy them, this I know. She did the pools every week, but riches never came her way. Genteel poverty, I think they call it. She died in 1968, and I still grieve for her.

When I think of Gaggie now, rather than picturing that dotty old thing feeding the pigeons in Hyde Park at the end, I try to imagine her back when Bob Ingham first met her, before the Great War, in India. A beauty, the major general's daughter, with masses of brunette hair piled up in the style of the day. Slim waist and a bustle. A woman who could beat any man on horseback, show jumping, while riding side-saddle.

Nigel

THE one thing I resent about my parents, the only thing, is that they called me Nigel. Anything, anything at all, other than Nigel. If there is a wetter name on the planet, I've never heard it. Changing my name to Sam at the age of eleven was probably the best decision I made in my life. Sam is easy to say, sounds friendly, sounds a bit blokey, and has a touch of the labrador about it.

The name Nigel (only three people on the planet persist in calling me this: my brother, sister and Geoffrey Eathorne, an old family friend, damn them all) is indelibly tied up for me with a nervous, stuttering little fair-headed boy off the boat from the UK. To land in a pretty rough playground in a New Zealand primary school with a plum in the voice and Nigel for a name was asking for trouble.

Nigel Neill in regimental kilt. And Irish dancing shoes, by the look of it.

I learnt quickly to discard the plum. But it took another three years to shed the Nigel. Survival meant, at the very least, sounding like everybody else. And this, I think, is where acting begins for me. This was a deliberate performative act. I survived.

The last thing you want as a child is to be different. I was different in another way. I must have been teased about this by my new small friends in New Zealand, because I remember telling my mother, in extreme embarrassment, about my dick. It worked, and the next thing I knew I was waking in hospital having been circumcised. Now I know why, if you insist on circumcising your kids, it is best done before they are big enough to yell, 'What the bloody hell did you just do to me?' It hurts, it really hurts, trust me.

Anyway, I'm often curious about the backgrounds of my fellow actors. Many had parents in the services. Or the diplomatic corps. In Hugo Weaving's case, his father was in the oil business, and Hugo is Nigerian by birth. For all of them it meant a disrupted childhood: new countries, changing schools, making new friends, changing accents, learning how to be someone else, to not be different but still be yourself at the same time. In other words, fledgling actors.

I became a New Zealander as quickly as I could manage it. To a point. Dad (educated at Harrow and Sandhurst) loathed the New Zealand accent, for all that he was a New Zealander.

That is, unless it was spoken by Māori.

He would parody us mercilessly for saying, *Noey, Ded, I dudn't.* (No, Dad, I didn't.). And I get his point. The New Zealand accent can be thin soup, and a bit miserable. Like an Australian with a heavy cold. But on a marae you hear people speak as if they actually enjoy vowels.

My voice lies somewhere out in a neutral blue ocean. In England I get teased by my friends for sounding like someone from the colonies. And at home in New Zealand, some people think I sound like a stuck-up Pom. Too bad. It's my voice, and I'm sticking with it.

I am, first and foremost, a New Zealander. But having been born in Northern Ireland, I have always had a British passport as well. I like it. And for a few years now, I've also owned an Irish passport. I got one for purely sentimental reasons, because I enjoy the idea of my Irish roots. But, since the debacle of Brexit, that lovely red booklet with a harp on the cover in my breast pocket has become invaluable. I am still proudly a European, as is Ireland. I am still part of the European Union.

I am a firm supporter of the EU. Any organisation that has meant no war between France and Germany for more than seventy years gets my vote. Any organisation that diminishes nationalism is to be applauded. I think the EU is one of the great achievements of the twentieth century. It was tragic that the British chose to leave it. And what was the name of the man who was the main driver behind this madness? None other than Nigel.

Identity was an interesting question for me when I was living again in Britain. I was born there, but I am not of there. One thing that bizarrely persists in the UK is the class system. The British are very good at it. They can tell by the slightest nuance of speech *exactly* where you are on the class ladder. And they treat you accordingly. I quickly realised that my colonial accent marked me apart right away. But it confuses them; they don't quite know where to slot me, and it's a comfortable place to be. You can never belong, never, but who wants to belong to a class system?

I despise nationalism in all its forms. But if I am asked my nationality, I am proud to say I am a New Zealander. That is how I see myself. A man from Aotearoa. I always acknowledge the tangata whenua, and it gives me satisfaction that Māori and

Māori culture, as well as te reo Māori, are central to New Zealand identity.

I loathe the idea of 'race'. Culture is one thing and culture is everything. But 'race' to me is just a notion, and a pretty crap notion at that. If you accept this absurd notion of race, you also have to accept that we are all pretty much mongrels of some kind. And here's to mongrels of all kinds. My own beloved family, if you insist on persisting with this race nonsense, includes Japanese, West Indian, Celtic, African American, Anglo-Saxon and Māori. That's just my grandchildren! We are all the richer for it.

So that's my identity. I embraced it many years ago and it is very dear to me.

At the same time, and here you would need a psychologist to sort this one out, there are, if I am honest, two selves in me. My exterior is unquestionably Sam the New Zealander. You might even recognise him. But inside, somewhere very deep, there lives a small shy boy who sounds quite different, and his name is not Sam. It is Nigel. And every time my siblings use that name, that little boy squirms.

Postscript for Nigel: as you leave Sydney Airport, look left for an unlikely sight. Crossing what looks like a canal beside you, you will catch a glimpse of a bridge proudly wearing this title: NIGEL LOVE BRIDGE. I always want to stop and take a photo, but by this time you are doing eighty, and the possibilities for multiple accidents involving semitrailers, buses and so on are immense. It's a puzzle. Is this where some poor Nigel found love? And who on earth loved Nigel? Or was there a Nigel who just loved bridges—a bridge spotter? Sounds like a very Nigel kind of hobby. Or perhaps this is a meeting place for Nigels who want to find love with other Nigels? I am wiping away a sad little tear for them.

Macandrew Bay

WE spent a year in Christchurch. In 1956 we moved south to Dad's home city, Dunedin.

We bought a house in a very pretty village, Macandrew Bay, about fifteen minutes' winding drive up the harbour towards the sea. In those days, people strangely gave their houses names, rather like boats. We called ours Seaforde. It was a half-timbered Tudor-style house built perhaps in the 1930s, when such style was in vogue. The house was substantial, with five bedrooms up a bendy flight of stairs, and had a big sitting room adjoining a formal dining room. It was comfortable enough, but no one had heard of insulation back then, and in winter it was colder than Iceland.

If we left the door open on the sitting room, the only warm room in the house, Dad would bellow, 'Close the *bloody* door, boy! Were you born in a *tent*?'

The house used to be called Carnoustie. Mum and Dad both found that name unspeakably funny, not sure why. They renamed it Seaforde because our earliest known Neill forebear, John Neill, who died in 1780, is buried in a tiny village called Seaforde, very close to our old place at the Watch House. We can't find anyone further back than him. This is true for many Irish families. The Four Courts, where all kinds of records were kept, were shelled during the Civil War in 1922, and so much Irish history was lost that fateful day. I've tunnelled Mum's family back to the 1100s in some branches, but then they were, in the main, English.

I think the house was named Carnoustie because the previous owner had been a golf professional with Scottish connections. Some of his old clubs lay around the cellar where Mum would brew her explosive ginger beer. Someone said that he'd been a bit of a ladies' man, whatever that meant. My grandmother thought it should have been called 'Carnal Housie'. But it was a pleasant place when it was warm, and we grew up there pretty happily. Michael and I only saw it in the holidays as we were both at boarding school in Christchurch. We would come home on a steam train, immensely excited to be away from the shackles of school and back to the slightly feral freedom of life in Macandrew Bay.

Kids roamed free in those days. If it was fine, you were shooed outside, and it was only hunger that brought you back later. We could catch freshwater crayfish from under rocks in the nearby creek, run wild in the misty green gorse paddocks (we could even borrow Dad's .22 and shoot cans there), we could take our little boat out onto the water. We could spear flounder from Dad's dinghy, and Michael and I learnt to sail on our two-man Idle-Along gaff-rig boat. You had to be sharp on a yacht: the winds were fickle there and we'd often be tipped gasping into the frigid harbour.

If it was raining we could catch an ancient bus into town and see a movie instead. I loved going into Dunedin. There were six or seven cinemas, as well as milk bars and department stores with women wearing uniforms. The shoe shop had an X-ray machine, and you could see your feet bones wriggling around under the tube. It was still largely a Victorian city, and had been the commercial centre of New Zealand up until World War I; its former prosperity was still evident in the graceful architecture in the city centre. Dad's office was there, as well as traces of my forebears, particularly at All Saints' Church and my great-grandfather's old estate, Chingford, now a city park.

The gloss wore off Dunedin for me when I got older, and I found it small and claustrophobic. I used to say the best thing about Dunedin was the Main Road north. To this day, when I point my car in the direction of Waitati and climb the hill away, I feel a sense of exhilaration as I breathe in a lungful of freedom. One anecdote about my hometown might tell you why. In 1964, at the very height of Beatlemania, the Dunedin Town Hall was only three-quarters full when they played there. The one place in the world they didn't sell out. 'Provincial' doesn't cover it.

But back to holidays. My sister, Juliet, was more horse-orientated, and Mum would patiently ferry her about to pony club with our decrepit horse float. I would have nothing to do with horses by contrast, and it wasn't until I had to learn to ride for movies that I realised Juliet was right, and there is nothing more thrilling than being on horseback.

The one thing I dreaded at the beginning of the holidays was the arrival by mail of our school reports. These would be formally read out by Dad to the assembled family by the fireplace before dinner. I would pale in anticipation. Michael's was always fulsome in praise from every teacher, apart from Hec Mackay, the brute who taught PE. There was no question Michael was a brilliant academic student, pretty rare in a school full of future farmers. The bastard.

When I myself got to Christ's College, Hec lined us new boys up in the gym. He was a heavy-set pugilist and ex-army sergeant. As he walked past, you had to say your name.

'Neill, sir,' I stammered.

Hec stopped in his tracks and turned to face me. 'Neill? Neill? Did you have a *brother* here?'

I had to admit I had, and from that moment on I was a marked man in Hec's eyes. He gave me hell. It also didn't help that M. A. F. Neill's name was front and centre on every scholars' honour board at school.

Dad's tone would audibly darken when he opened my report. I was a very ordinary student indeed. Must try harder. A dreamer. Irredeemably lazy. I fully understand now why this would be disappointing to my parents. They gave up a lot to send us to the very best schools they could.

The house had views up and down the harbour, and across to the purple-blue hills beyond. Dunedin has a rotten Scottish-type climate, but it is very beautiful, dotted around the most lovely of harbours. I particularly enjoyed watching the old steam dredge that beetled up and down the clearway, which allowed shipping to get beyond Port Chalmers to the city docks. If you squinted your eyes, it almost looked like that strange submarine that James Mason piloted in *20,000 Leagues Under the Sea*. Only the *clackety-clack* sound from across the water gave away its true identity as an extraordinary relic of Victorian engineering.

James Mason was one of my favourite film stars when I was a kid. I loved British films and British film stars, in particular those with double-barrelled names like Wilfrid Hyde-White or James Robertson Justice. Matinees were utterly magical for me. This, mind you, was before television. The idea that that small boy would eventually *be* in the movies could not have been more preposterous. I still think it's ridiculously unlikely.

But my parents were outdoors people, and Mum liked nothing better than piling us all into her tiny car and heading for a picnic at one of the extraordinary beaches on the other side of the Otago Peninsula. No one ever actually swims at these beaches—the weather is far too brutal for that—but out there were goats, albatrosses, penguins, sea lions and all kinds of sea life. It was as wild and woolly as anything the north of Scotland has to offer. There was one big seal colony we'd often visit. It stank of old seal urine. But you could wander in among them and they didn't care. Except if, God forbid, you should get between a mother and her cub. Seals are graceful in water and clumsy on land, but, boy, they can move fast if they're angry. Mostly they basked in the weak Otago sunshine.

On the way home Mum would always stop and buy us all an ice cream in a cone. In fact, she loved them as much as we did. I inherited my incurable sweet tooth from her.

Dad drove a slightly bigger car than Mum's Fiat 500, a Ford Consul. Another crappy 1950s English car. It always gave me the shits that Dad never bought a Zephyr: not much better, but at least it had a decent-sized engine and more convincing fins. One of Dad's many eccentricities was that he would never use second gear. This meant revving too high in first and almost dying when he got to top gear, the third. Mortifying for a nascent car freak like me.

But in the summer holidays we would all squeeze into our

My brother, Michael, and me. We are proud of our new bikes.

old khaki Bedford Dormobile, a crappy English camping adaptation of a crappy English van, and head for the mountains inland. We would tow a little trailer on the back, but how we got all the camping gear, all the kids plus dog, fishing gear, food and drink *plus* a boat doesn't bear thinking about. One pre-trailer summer Dad had the brilliant idea to put the boat on the roof of the van *not* upside down. This way he could pile in even more equipment than ever, right into the boat. Although this looked precarious, it worked fine. Until we were about four hours inland and it began to rain. We kids in the back would always quieten down when we sensed something was about to go wrong. And inevitably it would. It started to rain harder. The van began to slow. The boat above was clearly filling dangerously with water. But Dad gritted his teeth and soldiered on. Until, with a long *boing*, the roof of the van bowed inwards, Dad shouted, 'Oh, Christ,' and we ground to a halt. More swearing. Michael and I were sent up to bail it out, in the pelting Southland rain. As if somehow we were obliquely to blame.

But our camping holidays were the best fun ever, despite the many setbacks we endured. Dad had a knack for finding exactly the wrong place to establish camp. It'd be a nice, clear, dry stream bed, for instance. Which would be fine until you'd wake up and find your camp bed floating away in the now flooding creek.

We learnt to fish. We caught trout, and Mum would cook them over a fire. We learnt to love canned baked beans. Mum brought a huge bag of Mackintosh's toffees, which would last us the whole fortnight; they were rationed, but no one liked the coconut flavours anyway.

We would explore and cover a lot of ground, looking for new rivers or just to see what was over the ridge. These were also known as 'Dad's Hell Marches' among the malcontents, which was pretty much all of us, except for loyal Mum. I have a clear memory of Mum getting out of the van to open a gate in her scruffy old camping shorts, and Dad behind the wheel pronouncing, 'She's always had great legs, your mother,' in an admiring voice.

What a very odd thing to say, I thought. Great legs? But I get it now.

The lasting legacy of all this is my undiminished love of fly-fishing. When I can, I walk up some of the most remote rivers in the world with a friend or two, and painstakingly stalk some of the best trout in the world. I'm not brilliant at this, and sometimes I catch nothing. Doesn't matter. There is no better day to be had. All those I do catch are released and live to fight another day. It is the most sublime thing I know how to do, and the most thrilling by far.

Every fish I catch gets a kiss, and then I return it to the river.

We loved playing what we called camp cricket. This involved most of the rules of cricket, but would be played with a good-looking stick for a bat, a round stick for a ball and a box for wickets. Juliet mostly played with reluctance. But it was the first thing, and probably the last, where it was apparent that I was better than my brother. Bliss. It really pissed him off. Especially as he was the main camp-cricket enthusiast. I think he actually invented it. Geoffrey Eathorne claims that Michael and I came to blows one summer. I don't remember that at all, but if true I must have been particularly aggravating.

Michael, all my childhood, was patience personified with his annoying younger siblings. Remarkably kind, although often distracted; his mind would be elsewhere. Somewhere brainy. While I was spending my savings on Donald Duck comics (I despised Mickey Mouse), he was analysing novels quietly in some corner of his enormous intellect.

In the holidays sometimes, if I bugged him enough, he would read me stories—more than that, actually, whole novels, every morning, in instalments. *Treasure Island*, for instance. He'd do all the different voices as well. Long John Silver was simultaneously funny and frightening. It was a lesson in how powerful story-telling is. That is art, that is culture. That is what I do now. Acting is, in part, telling stories.

That's the thing about an older brother—you look up to them, hero-worship them all your life. I saw him in school plays, I saw him in reviews when he was at university. A part of me must have thought, I'd love to do that too. So that was completely crucial to my growing up, and what would ultimately draw me to my liveli-hood. I owe him.

Michael became an academic and a scholar. He taught, in the main, at Auckland University, having done a PhD at Cambridge. He specialised in Shakespeare, the greatest storyteller of all. He also taught Irish literature and the postcolonial African novel. A colleague of his once said to me: you do realise your brother is one of the four or five top Shakespeare scholars in the world? No, I didn't know that, but I'm glad I do now. He has written or edited about a dozen books on the Bard, and is an emeritus professor. To give you an idea about how academia has been devalued, and in particular the liberal arts, there were some thirty people teaching in the Auckland English department in his day. That has been reduced to just six.

I doubt my sister looked up to me in the same way. A sibling closer in age yet older is just downright annoying. And anyway, she was interested in...I dunno...girl stuff. Mystery to me. Actually, she became a drama teacher, ran murder mysteries in big weekend houses and became a great puppeteer as a grown-up, so maybe...no, she was far too smart to be influenced by me!

Juliet abandoned horses as a teenager. I, on the other hand, grew to love riding. I've had to ride in at least a dozen movies, and if there's a horse in it, I am more likely to put my hand up and say, Yes, this film is for me. It's one skill I have in which I take some quiet pride. Actors are often terrible liars on their CVs about whether they can ride horses, and you hardly ever come across one who has ridden at all before. You need to be good to look convincing on a horse. Some never will. The chap playing King Arthur in *Merlin* couldn't even walk on a horse. In one scene, all he had to do was sit on his stationary nag and point and say, 'Camelot!' He fell off more than once. *Plonk*, sideways, into the Welsh mud.

I rode to hounds as Damien Thorn in *Omen III: The Final Conflict*, and looked wicked at the same time. More skills! I had to set my hounds on some poor follower of the Lord, who plummets to his death off a viaduct in Cornwall. In the words of the song, 'Jesus I Was Evil'. It was quite the part. I thought of Damien as the loneliest creature on the earth. I mean, just getting a date, for one thing. Imagine: 'Hi! My name is Damien.

Pleased to meet you. I'm the US ambassador, but actually I'm the Antichrist and my mission is to really fuck things up round here.' I am pretty sure that this is the sort of thing that puts women off. I had the words of the Stones' 'Sympathy for the Devil' in my head all the time: 'I'm a man of wealth and taste.' Tasty indeed.

But the best, craziest liberation on horseback was on *Robbery Under Arms*. We had that great wrangler Bill Willoughby in charge. Bill's method was ultimately ride or die. He was happy to coach you, until he wasn't. One day, if he thought you were ready, it was just flat-tack full gallop through the bush, mad helter-skelter, dodging trees: crazy, adrenalin-fuelled madness. In two days you'd see boys turn into men.

It's that full gallop crazy time on a horse for which I know no substitute. I've been hunting a few times in Australia, and I am a supporter of hunting. Forget about the fox, I've never seen one die, and nine times out of ten they get away: cunning buggers who want to kill every one of your chickens. Just for fun. When hunting, you're out there for a day of semi-suicidal, mad-as-a-March-hare race around the place, jumping fences, clearing ditches. A great day out like no other. And who enjoys it the most? Why, the horses, of course.

I expressed an anti-hunt sentiment to my mother once—she had been a keen hunter—saying I saw it as elitist and snobbish. She bristled at that, and it was one of the few times I ever saw her angry. I knew nothing. One of the reasons she loved hunting was that it was a great leveller. She was the opposite of a snob, whatever that is. The hunts she knew, everyone turned out for— the farrier, the blacksmith, the barkeep, the pig farmer and the lord of the manor as well. It was a country pursuit that brought everyone together, and she would have hated to see it disappear. That country life somewhat lost these days to rich fund managers with second homes in the Cotswolds.

Dad hunted with beagles in Ireland, and kept a pack. They hunt for hares and, as with fox hunting, a large crowd follows on foot. I don't quite see the point, but Dad loved it, and I have a painting of him with his pack up in the boggy mountains of County Down.

Which brings me to dogs. There is nothing so happy, so charged, as a pack of hunting dogs. Dogs doing what dogs should do; they are bred for it and they are pack animals. Sheep dogs love to wrangle sheep; it's what they do. The same goes for greyhounds. A racing greyhound actually racing is the happiest animal you will ever see. I got into terrible trouble with the animal rights people a few years ago by supporting greyhound racing in New South Wales. I have never been forgiven. Now, don't get me wrong, I am the first to condemn *any* cruelty to *any* animal, and I'd be naive to say all dog trainers are saints. But banning greyhounds? Cleaning up abuse, yes, of course; banning, no. These dogs love to race; you should go to the kennels, to a race meet, and see for yourself. In this case it was the Baird government in New South Wales and property developers behind this bastardry, nothing to do with dogs. You notice that, while greyhounds are the working man's sport, the same government showed no interest in cleaning up horse racing—that's the big end of town! At the same time, I applaud everyone who has adopted a greyhound; a sweeter dog you will not find.

I would like to adopt a few retired horses and ride out on my farm, but sadly I have no one here who knows anything about horses, who need a lot of pastoral care. Mum and Dad, in their retirement, lived for horses. In 1969, after we had all left home, they sold Seaforde and moved to a small farm of about thirty hectares on the edge of the Taieri Plain on the other side of Dunedin. Their happiest twenty-five years were there. I used to love going for rides with the two of them out the back on the hills. I think they understood me better now that I was on horse-back, somehow, and vice versa.

Mum was all about horses. When she left school, instead of going to Trinity College Dublin, where she had a place (she was bright), she opted to help my grandmother Gaggie with her little riding school in Pembrokeshire. They gave lessons and stabled horses, along with all their rescue dogs and other animals. Mum was quite the rider in the district and further afield, in point-to-point races, in shows and so on. Here is a newspaper clipping from the time.

The Points-to-Points: A Retrospect of the Season's Racing

MISS P. Ingham, Tenby. I put her at the top of the list for Lady Riders in the County, and I have grave doubts as to whether any of the gentlemen of the pigskin locally have a better seat, safer hands or more cunning tactics than this lady. She is a born horsewoman, and a great favourite with the crowd. Vanity and Miss Ingham form a combination which would take some beating, and I should not like to back anything I have seen this season to defeat them.

Oh, I burst with pride to read that, Mum. Safer hands and a better seat—what a woman!

Jummy

MY other grandmother, Jummy, Dad's mother, was an entirely different matter.

I never knew a grandfather. Mum's father, Bob, was killed in 1917, and Dad's father, Sid, died in World War II, in his fifties, after running up some sand hills or some such with the Home Guard. Heart attack. Quite honestly, I think I would've checked out early as well if I was married to Jummy. Sid was, by all accounts, affable and charming and very good company indeed.

When her second child, my Aunt True, was due to be born at home at Belmont, their huge house in Dunedin, Jummy went into a long labour. Sid was downstairs pacing about in great anxiety. Finally True was delivered, and the rattled, exhausted doctor marched down the stairs. 'Neill,' he barked grimly at my grandfather. 'This has got to stop!' There were no more children after that.

Jummy was a handful. She was a tiny woman, not much more than five foot two in her heels. But she had a vastly inflated idea of her own importance and allure. She was an intolerable snob. What exactly she had to be snobbish about has always eluded me. Her father had been the managing director of the Union Steam Ship Company, the most successful coastal shipping line around New Zealand, and in trade with Australia, but her family were bog-standard middle-class. Nevertheless, all and sundry were considered common by her. It is embarrassing to report.

It was said she was the first woman in Dunedin to be seen

smoking in public, and the first with a driving licence. She had been a gay young thing when she was being courted by Sid, at the wheel of a Hispano-Suiza. Sid was very handsome, unlike Jummy, who I think it's fair to say was a bit on the plain side. How my mother put up with this monstrous mother-in-law I have no idea. Mum's family back in Britain were far posher than the Neills, but that didn't stop Jummy trying to make Mum feel she was a bit lower on the stairs than her. Not that Mum gave a stuff about class.

You could see Jum had been a flirt back in the day, and this habit persisted into old age. She adored men, and was spiky with women. She also liked boys more than girls. Michael and I were well favoured, but Juliet got the short end of the stick. Jummy mostly pointedly ignored her, while Michael and I basked in her cooing affection. When Jummy came around for Sunday lunch, Juliet would slump into glum despair, which didn't help things at all. I'm sure I selfishly did nothing to help. The easy course of action.

Jummy drove, for many years, the most absurd car. It was even then very rare, but not particularly good. It was an Austin Atlantic, the sort of faux sports car that was perhaps popular in the home counties. It represented the nadir of British car design. It was essentially a two-seater, painted a rather attractive metallic green colour, with a black vinyl roof, but it was a big lump of a thing, huge and underpowered. My grandmother sat on a large cushion behind a huge steering wheel, but even then she could only just see the way ahead through the wheel.

She was never less than properly dressed when out: suit, stockings, pearls, jewellery, hat and scarf, with lipstick, make-up and hair perfect...the works. More and more make-up as the years went on. She was an avid enthusiast for du Maurier cigarettes, which did nothing for her looks later on.

She doted on me. This was both excruciating and pleasing. She insisted on calling me always Niggy Piggy Puggy Poo. (This egregious nickname is known to a handful of old friends, like Stu Mackenzie and Pip Hall, and they never let me forget it. Bastards.) I hated it, but I'd grin as bravely as I could to be a good sport. You wouldn't want to displease Jummy; the ramifications didn't bear thinking about. When young, she was very much at the centre of all things social in what passed for society in Dunedin. But she died entirely friendless. She had this terrible capacity, an urge that I sometimes detect in myself and quickly suppress: if someone crossed her over the smallest thing, she never spoke to them again. They were simply written off. In a city the size of Dunedin, you eventually run out of people to write off.

To give her her due credit, Jummy was a hugely talented gardener. The enormous garden at Belmont, where she was assisted by at least two gardeners, was a wonder to behold. I remember part of it was devoted to something you might see in Kyoto—ponds with koi fish, weeping trees in autumn colours reflected in water under a herringboned Dunedin sky. Rockeries and terraces. It was like a National Trust garden in England. The botanical gardens were a let-down after Belmont. She had huge and very productive vegetable gardens there as well, and orchards. I think there are about eight ugly houses now where her garden once was.

Eventually she had to be moved closer to us from her huge house in Belmont. How my mother must have shuddered. She moved into a very pretty cottage on Howard Street, a few hundred yards away, down the lane from us in Macandrew Bay, and created another wonder, a perfect cottage garden. It hummed with bees; the colours flowed in profusion; some scents still remind me of being in that idyllic place with her.

Anyway, I remember one particular day in her garden, when

I was twelve. I was helping her with something mundane, hedge trimming or some such. It was a hot day, and I must've grumbled. She immediately flew into a high dudgeon, sent me straight home and called my father to complain about my appalling behaviour. I was sidewinded on this. I thought I was being helpful on a day when I would've liked to have been out on the harbour in our dinghy. But there it was: I had crossed the line. She gradually forgave me. But it was a close-run thing. I might have been sent to Coventry for good. I think I only recovered because she genuinely loved me.

She was also a very good pianist, but eventually had to give that up as her hands got stiff and bent with arthritis. The radio was on all day in her sitting room with the concert program, and a lot of my familiarity with classical music comes from the days when I would have a cup of tea with her, or later a sherry, in that impeccably tasteful room. Dad popped in religiously every night for a drink with his mother. She had in her declining years a very good Chinese doctor, who insisted she drink a pint of stout every evening. I'm not sure it did anything for her iron count as prescribed, but it did wonders for her mood. She was as mellow as could be after one of those. He was smart, that doctor.

I don't really know what she ate at Macandrew Bay. I know she couldn't cook; someone else had cooked for her all her life. But she was such a tiny little thing, perhaps a slice of toast was all she needed. And maybe she cooked the odd vegetable from her prodigious garden. She did, however, make one thing every year in her kitchen: green tomato jam. Sounds awful, but it was delicious.

For all her evident ghastliness, I was very fond of her and she's someone else I miss to this day.

The Annual Purge

THE deep south of New Zealand has by all accounts some of the worst statistics for bowel cancer in the world. I have no idea why. But it certainly is worth bearing in mind, if that is indeed where you live.

For this reason, every year I go in for a colonoscopy, better known as the Annual Purge. This is common to many people of my age, some of whom rather enjoy the procedure and watch the whole thing live as the camera moves up their date, while the surgeon takes care of the coral, seaweed and other growths that have manifested themselves magically since last time he was up there. I have absolutely no desire to inspect my bowels. I prefer to be knocked out and wake up with a cup of tea an hour later.

Prior to colonoscopies you're required to purge the day before. You need to present yourself to the surgeon with a bowel as clean as Buckingham Palace. You take a lot of potions, and by late afternoon, you need to be pretty close to a bathroom. Then, at 5 p.m. on the dot, your lower half detonates in a way that is totally beyond any human control. It's like the Somme. It's a dull day prior to that, and you have to think of things to do. Putting out the rubbish, for instance.

I was doing exactly that on this occasion, taking out the rubbish as well as the recycling, like a good citizen should. Just as I popped the bags in the bins I heard the door close behind me. A sickening sound. And I realised that I did not have my keys with me.

I was locked out of the house. And I was the only one home.

At the same time, the pain in my gut was telling me with absolute certainty that I was going to explode right then and there.

At the front of our house was a low wall not much higher than your hip. It's a quiet street and I thought for a few mad moments that, perhaps, if there was no one coming, I could take an undignified crap squatting behind that modest wall. At the worst someone might just have seen my head bent in concentration above the wall. But it must have been a Wednesday, because there was an unusual amount of foot traffic passing by, people off to their boats. A front-garden crap was impossible, and I couldn't get round to the back.

Next door we had tenants. As a landlord (the one and only time in my life when I could call myself that) I made it my business to stay out of their way. Indeed, we had never met. But as I wiped the cold sweat off my panicked brow, I decided I would have to swallow those scruples and knock on the door and introduce myself.

A very nice woman answered, holding her baby, and I told her what the problem was. I asked her if she would mind terribly if I could use her phone to call a locksmith, and at the same time use her bathroom. She was kind enough to say yes with hardly a blink.

The locksmith duly summoned, the next item on the agenda was the purge in the bathroom. Now, there are certain things that, even in the most dire circumstances, are simply beyond the capabilities of an ordinary man. On the top of that list for me is taking a dump in someone else's house, even if you ostensibly own the place. It just wouldn't be in any way thinkable.

So I decided—well, it was decided for me—that I would grimly hang on, and hope the locksmith wouldn't be all that long. It took an hour, and the two of us stood around making small talk all that time. I was pale, sweaty and extremely agitated.

And then finally, as if God had intervened, the man arrived. I sprinted next door and greeted him like a long-lost brother. Hallelujah.

Cars and How I Love Them

BESIDE me here, in my study, is my prized collection of Dinky Toys, which began with Gaggie. I've added to it somewhat over the years.

This lot is mostly racing cars, miniatures of the raging beasts that tore around dangerous courses all over the world, and even

My Dinky Toys. The Ferrari is in serious trouble.

Dunedin, in the 1950s. Ferraris, Talbots, Alfa Romeos, Coopers. The drivers all stick out of their cockpits, wearing goggles and leather helmets. No roll bars, no safety features whatsoever. They had names like Fangio, Ascari, Hawthorn and, best of all, Stirling Moss. My hero was Graham Hill. What a man. In their off-season the drivers would often come out to entertain us in Australia and New Zealand. In Dunedin they roared around the streets near the harbour, the odd random hay bale their, and our, only protection.

Formula One had a high attrition rate. These were men of steely courage. They wore headgear resembling a cycling helmet and overalls that were only nominally fireproof.

Those road races in Dunedin, and at Wigram Aerodrome in Christchurch, with their phenomenal noise and petroleum smells and blinding excitement, sparked something in me that I've never lost. I love cars. My son Tim follows me in this and is even worse. He was for a while, to my great concern, a petrolhead, and drove boy-racer cars, in particular a Subaru WRX. He survived. He now drives my sedate old LandCruiser with a tribe of unruly, joyous kids in the back.

Cars meant a lot to New Zealanders in the 1950s. They drove mostly very old cars, which they would fix themselves in the back yard with Number 8 wire and an oily rag. It was like Cuba, but with much shittier cars: the Worst of British, often assembled on a Friday in various plants in Petone, around the harbour from Wellington. Hillman Minxes, Standard 8s, Ford Prefects, Vauxhall Veloxes, many more. They were slow, ugly and draughty, and they leaked.

We had to drive these horrors because no one could afford a new one, unless you farmed thirty thousand acres in North Canterbury. In the 1960s you needed 'overseas funds' to buy any new car. I still don't know exactly what 'overseas funds' are.

Nevertheless, I cannot help but have nostalgia for those ancient cockroach cars. They were cherished by their patient, loyal owners. And a couple of years ago I found a much-loved early 1960s Austin A40, and I treasure it. Granted, it is an Austin, perhaps the worst offender when it comes to downright ugliness. But someone at Austin had had the inspired idea to go to Italy, the home of automotive beauty, to get it designed. The great Pininfarina from Turin did them the favour. As a result, it is one of the first mass-built British cars that doesn't look like it was designed in a potting shed in Surbiton. It is a tiny beauty.

I also have, at my farm, a 1947 Chevy Thriftmaster pick-up truck. It is exactly as old as me, built in September. I did quite a bit to get it restored. It does zero to sixty in about five minutes. Actually, I'm not sure if it's ever gone that fast. I like having grandchildren back on the deck.

The first car I ever owned was an enormous late 1920s Lincoln sedan, when I was at university. It was decrepit, and cost me twenty-five dollars to Gerse Halliday. He got the better deal. It was the sort of car that would only go when it felt like it. Which wasn't often. One night an unfortunate woman driving an Austin 1100 failed to give way to my mammoth of a car. I braked as well as I could with whatever I had, but it wasn't enough. The front of my car had no bumper bar, just two fist-like protrusions where the bumper should have been. The left one pretty much wiped off the whole front of the 1100, engine and all. No one hurt, thank God. No visible damage at all to the Lincoln.

One of the first things I did when I earned some decent money as an actor was to go out and buy my dream car. It was 1983, and I was doing a series called *Reilly, Ace of Spies* at Elstree Studios. When I say buy, I ordered it from Stuttgart. Some months later it finally arrived, and it was breathtakingly beautiful. It was a black, all black, Porsche 911 SC. Tweed and leather

Carrera seats. It was like a mean, low-slung blowfly, albeit with classic lines. My dreams had come true.

The best car I'd ever owned before that was an old Holden HQ station wagon, which nearly killed me on the road to Melbourne. A steering arm or something broke, I lost control and the bloody thing rocketed into some poor farmer's front paddock. But at least no one hates you driving a Holden. I remember a quote from Germaine Greer: 'To drive the Hume Highway is to know true fear.' True that.

But now I felt like a million bucks owning this gorgeous Porsche beast. It wasn't to last. I felt like a wanker driving it. I would leave my flat and hover by the parked car, waiting until the coast was clear, and then jump in and roar off before anyone spotted me. Beet-red in embarrassment.

After two weeks, this terrible feeling that I was a 'prick in a Porsche' was perhaps slightly abating. Early one Sunday, driving through a wintry Hyde Park in London, I was almost enjoying it. There was no one around on this chilly morning, no one to give me dirty looks or a finger as I stopped, throbbing, at the lights. But then, as I passed the Horse Guards, I realised that the one figure visible, who was now at the pedestrian crossing ahead of me, was strangely familiar. It was none other than Judy Davis. I silently prayed to God that she wouldn't see me in this absurd car. But, no, she strode straight over to the passenger window, rapped on it and stuck her head into the car.

'No, Sam,' she said. 'No. Not you, Sam. Not you.' She turned and stalked off.

I was crushed, and not for the first time, by that formidable woman. But she was absolutely right. The next day I drove down the Fulham Road and did a deal on a rather staid BMW 5, invariably their dullest line.

The only other real sports car I've ever owned was a completely different beast. I bought a British racing-green Morgan Plus 8. No one dislikes you driving a Morgan. Instead, you often get smiles and cheery waves. It wasn't a wanker's car, but it was still absurd. The thing was made from aluminium and handcrafted in ash wood. Light as a feather. Under the leather-strapped bonnet was an enormous Rover V8 engine, so the tiny car was massively overpowered. Its steering system dated back to the early twentieth century. You had to wrestle the wheel to keep the damn thing in a straight line. It was ridiculous but, my God, it was beautiful. I miss it still. I brought it back to Sydney eventually, and co-owned it with my friend Neil Lanceley. Unfortunately, in an Australian context, it again had a touch of the wanker about it. We sold it.

Neil is another motor enthusiast. He was the first Porsche owner I ever knew, in London. He had a beautiful 1970s white 911. Sadly he had to give it up when children and marital responsibilities caught up with him. Neil and his subsequent partner, Denise, then spent many decades devoted to Aboriginal health in the Northern Territory. They were both dentists and very good ones, and they dedicated much of their professional lives to this work. Anyway, it was time to retire. And Neil, full of nostalgia for his old Porsche, decided to look for another. And there in the classifieds he saw one for sale that sounded pretty similar. He went to see it, up in the Blue Mountains, and—blow me down—it was none other than his old car. The car had made the same journey as he had, from the UK to Australia; maybe it was looking for Neil, and found him.

My love affair continues with cars, but I temper things when I buy them these days. Incidentally, I drove that beautiful black 911 SC to pick up Lisa Harrow (mother of my son, Tim) at the stage door of the Haymarket Theatre, where she was in a Shaw with Peter O'Toole. They emerged at the same time. Peter cast a baleful, jaundiced eye at me in the shiny black blowfly.

'Is that your boyfriend?' he asked.

'It is,' said Lisa.

'Hmph.' Peter gave the car another dubious look. 'He'll learn.'

I did.

Medbury School and Christ's College

AFTER a few terms at Cashmere Primary, my parents decided I should go to a prep school in Christchurch instead. Dad was about to retire from the army and go back to the family firm in Dunedin. They sent me to Medbury, all the way across town. The idea being that I could transition painlessly to boarding at Medbury once they'd gone south; boarding school, after all, never did any small boy any harm! I was eight years old.

For a term or two I was a day boy there, before becoming a full-time boarder once the family had moved.

Medbury was a pleasant enough place to look at, but grim inside. The Old Boys' Association later sometimes asked me for this or that, but I put an end to it one day, and wrote to poor Richard Ballantyne, a nice enough fellow a year older than me, who was the titular head of that organisation. 'Richard,' I said, 'you must know I absolutely hated my time at Medbury, and I have no good memories of it. I know you mean well but, please, do not ask me for anything again.' I may have over-egged the 'hate' thing, but it put a stop to the requests for favours.

While I was still a day boy, I would make my own way there from our house in Cashmere in the bright Canterbury mornings, and back home either by bus or, more scarily, on a bike that was far too big for me. It's amazing to me now that an eight-year-old boy could be trusted to make a journey possibly an hour long each way.

If I was on the bus, Mum would give me exactly the money I needed for the fare from school in Fendalton to Cathedral Square, and another one from there to the top of Cashmere Hill. Once, I rashly spent some of that bus money on sweets. It was only when I got on the next bus that I realised I didn't have sufficient capital to make it home. I started the long walk down the endless miles of Colombo Street to the distant Port Hills, and eventually all the way up Cashmere. It was getting dark when I made it. When I walked in and saw Mum's distress that her boy had gone missing, I finally cried myself.

If it was a fine day, I would wobble my way on my bike, in my grey shorts and blazer, with my grey cap on my head, across town. It must have been at least ten kilometres, pretty much an hour on a bike. The only scary bit was when I would pass Sunnyside Hospital, an enormous Gothic pile that I knew of as the Loony Bin. Sunnyside. I wasn't quite sure what that meant, but it was certainly full of 'loonies'. (The author Janet Frame was repeatedly institutionalised here in the forties and fifties.) Sometimes you'd see them in the distance, shouting at things. I would race past as fast as I could, my little feet only just making the pedals.

Many years later, in the late 1990s, when Mum was in a Christchurch old-age home, with her own flat and dog, it became apparent to the staff that her dementia was getting too much. They summarily kicked her out, and without even consulting us they dumped her in that very same bin, so ironically called Sunnyside. All my childhood fears came back, and I could not have been more angry or distressed. My mum was in with the loonies.

I got there as soon as I could, perhaps the next day. I drove to Sunnyside and found her. It was horrific. She was in a state of great distress. She was in a strange open ward with old men exposing themselves, old women curled up in corners muttering fearfully, people shouting and screaming. It was bedlam.

'Get me out of here, please,' said Mum, terrified. And we did.

Juliet found a place out in the country, half an hour north of Christchurch. It looked pleasant enough, but all the old ladies there seemed to me heavily drugged and suspiciously docile. We got her out as soon as we could find somewhere better.

Mum did need special care. The dementia was more advanced than you'd guess. She was very good at covering things up. *Oh, what a silly old thing I am. How could I have forgotten that?* But the writing was on the wall, one has to admit, back at her flat. She would run a bath, forget about it and flood the place. Or she'd have her evening gin, forget that she'd had that one, down another, and so it went on until she was blotto. All her life, she'd never have more than one drink, and that before dinner.

The trick was never to eat at Mum's flat. Always, without fail, take her out to dinner. On a low heat on the stove was an enormous pot. Everything would get thrown into it. Who knew how old that soup was? It was just a living, needy soup creature that went on and on, somehow keeping her alive. I bought her a radio to keep her company. She'd always liked the radio on, especially when she was ironing. This radio could be turned on simply, but sadly she never knew which of the two switches to turn. It remained silent until the end.

One story about Mum at that home still makes me laugh. The great Charlie Upham, the only combat soldier to win two Victoria Crosses, had moved in. At his first Friday night drinks, Mum sallied up to Charlie, who knew her a little.

'Priscilla! How are you?' he said.

Mum was just as pleased to see Charlie. 'I know you! You climbed Mount Everest, didn't you?'

The last place we found, where she died in 1999, was a dementia care home in Avonside. It didn't look much, but it was a very caring place. I liked the staff and they were genuinely fond of Mum and her eccentric ways.

It was a secure unit, so that the old things wouldn't wander off and fall into the Avon River. We could take her out for the day, which she would always enjoy, particularly the ice cream. It was like Macandrew Bay again: a good day out, followed by a cone of hokey pokey.

She became confused about who was who. Sometimes she mistook Michael for Dad. But my favourite was this. One day I popped around in the afternoon, my wife Noriko and the girls (her grandchildren) having made their visit in the morning. Mum was, as always, cheerful and pleased to see me.

'Darling, you'll never believe what happened today.'

I said, 'What, Mum?'

'It was lovely,' she said. 'A whole lot of Japanese tourists came to visit me. Can you imagine? Me! And they were quite delightful. Yes, they were.'

One evening, when she was being tucked up in bed, she told a nurse she felt tired, turned on her side and quietly died in the night. As with everything she did in her life, no fuss. None at all. Her dog died a day or two later, heartbroken, I imagine.

If there is one thing I dread, it is senility and dementia. Any sign of it, please, take me out the back and shoot me. It was particularly cruel that my mother, that cheerful, bright, vibrant, hilarious, intelligent woman, had been reduced to someone almost unrecognisable. I hope my kids don't remember her like that. She was a great woman.

When I pedalled past Sunnyside on the way to school, there was a secluded one-storeyed building nearby. It looked intriguing. I found out many years later, when I was delivering groceries in the holidays, that it was a nunnery, a closed order. Carmelites, perhaps, I'm not sure.

You would drive up to the front door, ring a bell and enter the empty hallway. At the back of the hallway was a revolving hatch. I would place the boxes of groceries in it, and ring another little bell. The hatch would revolve and the groceries disappear. But then it would revolve again, and a nice cup of tea with milk and sugar would appear. How completely sweet.

You never saw, or even heard, any sign of life therein.

Having successfully passed Sunnyside on my wobbly bike, I had another two or three miles on to Medbury School. Medbury was built along strict English ideas of what a preparatory school should be. There was bad food, there was bullying, there were prefects, there was an insufferable seniority system, boys brutalising other boys and, last but not least, there was corporal punishment. Of course. The whole British nine yards.

The rules were rigidly enforced. You were never, under any circumstances, to be seen outside the school grounds without your cap on your head. That would mean a beating. The headmaster was not a pleasant man, and he was also cunning. One deeply unhappy boy, of the name Logan, always wanted to run away. The headmaster prevented any possibility of this by confiscating Logan's cap. Each night before dinner Logan would put his hand up and ask if he could get his cap back, please, sir. No, Logan, you can't. This meant another miserable twenty-four hours before poor Logan could try to make a bid for freedom, with cap on head, still obeying the rules.

At Medbury the staff's weapon of choice was the strap. There were lashes and lashes of straps. I've always thought that the worst thing about corporal punishment is that it comes from those in authority. And somehow that very fact legitimises the idea that it is acceptable for one human being to hit another. The blows stung for a while, but the humiliation lasted a lot longer.

The one thing that garnered you respect at Medbury was

being good at sport. I was completely hopeless at it. I liked books. I could swim a bit, Mum having taken us to lessons at the Tepid Baths in Dunedin, but that was about it. I've never been able to catch a ball; the idea of being tackled brutally on a muddy playing field has always been anathema to me. I developed a special rugby skill. I could read the game, I could tell where the ball was headed. I would make sure I was anywhere else on the ground. The last thing I wanted, if I could catch the ball at all, was to be walloped by a couple of big forwards.

I think it was Barry Humphries who was asked what gave him some satisfaction later in his life. The answer was something like, 'All the First Eleven are dead.' I wouldn't go that far, but I can tell you that I've still got two hips that work, two knees, and that's more than can be said for my friends who were any good at this stuff. If they can walk at all they can be thankful they're not in wheelchairs. I, however, am proud to report that in 2020 I was able to sprint—*sprint*, I tell you—away from dinosaurs in *Jurassic World Dominion*. Try that, Hall! My very old pal Pip Hall was not only the fastest at my school over a hundred yards, he

My only sports triumph. Breaststroke, 1960.

was a copious try scorer on the left wing. I do not say this with any particular schadenfreude, but these days it takes an immense effort for the poor old bugger to walk down his short drive to pick up a copy of the morning's *Press*. Bending over to pick it up is problematic in itself; he gets the dog to do that.

I don't remember there being at Medbury any teachers who seemed to have teaching qualifications. They were for the most part retired servicemen who needed a gig. The most remarkable was a Mr Scott, who had caught something absolutely dreadful in a Japanese war camp and was, as a result, almost bent double. He had to lean forty-five degrees backwards to look straight ahead. He was also painfully thin. Needless to say, he was, from a distance, the subject of lampooning by cruel boys. But he was a pretty good teacher. He'd probably been tortured, I imagine. My heart goes out to him now, but little boys know nothing of empathy.

There was also a Major Heard, rather a nice man, and I recognised the type immediately. British Army through and through. He had some passing knowledge of geography, which he transmitted to the deaf ears of my mostly farm-boy contemporaries. His son Mike became a friend. Mike was one of the first of the people I knew who were killed on motorbikes. The only thing I have insisted on with my children is that they never, ever ride a motorbike or even get on the back. I've lost too many friends now that way.

One thing about boarding school is that you learn to make friends. As much as anything, this was self-preservation. It was physically tough at Medbury. Your friends were your allies, and you protected each other as best you could. There were bullies, and, my God, they were effective.

I don't remember anyone actually being *happy* there, and one of the saddest things I can think of is the junior dorm, where the little boys were. Boys of six or seven would cry themselves to sleep every single night, desperately missing home.

I was a long way from home myself, five or six hours' drive from Dunedin. I wouldn't see my parents for three months in a row, an unimaginably long time when you're not even ten. But one or two of my friends lived on farms, close enough for a Sunday outing, and some were kind enough to ask me out. Jim Deans, for instance. His family farmed up in the foothills, beautiful fertile country beyond Darfield. Or their cousins the Huttons, a deeply eccentric family, half wild, who lived nearby. They were the sort of people who might have a ballroom out the back of the house, and in the ballroom you might find a goat that had lost its way. We'd race around at night in an open Land Rover with a spotlight, looking for rabbits. Rabbits, the Curse of the New Zealand Farmer. We were children with guns, .22 rifles admittedly, but we were fully armed. I have no idea why there was never a fatality. They were feral out there.

I think it was here at Medbury that I probably made my first tentative steps into acting. There was a large, pleasant woman called Miss Parfitt, who taught some of the smaller boys. And on occasion, on a nice day, we'd be out on the back lawn, doing what must've been little plays, for the rest of the class. It was one of the very few things I enjoyed. I liked getting a laugh. Once a year a Gilbert and Sullivan was mounted, mainly for the benefit of parents. The music teacher, Mr Davies, who was a florid, portly gentleman straight out of an Ealing comedy, would stage these events. I desperately wanted a leading part in one of them, but I never got anywhere near that. The closest I ever got was to play one of the bridesmaids, frock and all, in *The Pirates of Penzance*.

Many weekends were spent at school. Some boys built model aeroplanes or cars in the hobby room. I didn't have the interest or the skills. Instead I raided the library, and I found myself lost in the world of fiction. Books took me away from the pain of being at boarding school: Arthur Ransome, C. S. Lewis, Robert Louis Stevenson.

Juliet was the one of us who lived at home for nearly all of her education. I think she was slightly jealous of what looked like rather more fun than being stuck at home. She has no idea what a free pass she had. Having said that, Mum and Dad did send her to board for a couple of terms at St Hilda's when she was, I'm guessing, about sixteen. They had flown to the UK (Mum always called it Home) to see family and friends. Juliet managed to get herself expelled from St Hilda's, for bunking out of school to attend, of all things, a church social! Who made that miserable

My little sister, Juliet.

decision? Instead of expelling her, they should've promoted her to head prefect, for goodness' sake.

One wonderful anachronism about Medbury was that we were not allowed to call anyone by their first name. It was Neill. Or Rutherford. Never Sam or Bill. If there was more than one Neill in the school, any confusion would be sorted out in Latin, ranked downward by seniority. I was, for instance, Neill Major, and my younger cousin Nicholas was Neill Minor. At one stage there was a Deans Major, Deans Minor, Deans Minimus, Deans Quartus and Deans Quintus.

I stayed out of trouble reasonably successfully at Medbury, to such an extent that I was made a prefect in my last year. They were scraping the barrel, obviously.

In 1961 I left Medbury, greatly relieved. I was thirteen. The next challenge would be my brother's old school. Christ's College is for the most part neo-gothic, built from igneous rock from a nearby extinct volcano, and quite handsome in a Victorian institutional way. It was part brutal, part hilarious and part survival of the fittest. After four years boarding at Medbury, I was pretty match fit. I knew my way around bullying, I knew how to make friends and I knew how to be a small target. Also, I had my friend and ally Bill Nutt, who was tougher and smarter and funnier than me. I was a wonky, nerdy, unsporty, stuttering boy, but I had support.

College thought of itself as an elite school, *the* elite school, and the fees reflected that. There was an entrance exam, but I never heard of anyone failing. There were boys there who could barely work out how to close a gate, let alone remember the names of English kings. There are still people in Canterbury today who consider it a mark of distinction that they were there. This is completely delusional; they just had four or five years of mutual mediocrity, I'm afraid.

The place was full of anomalies. The smallest building was called Big School, and, confusingly, it was just the library. The main playing field for big rugby games and athletics was called Upper. No one knew why, since there was no such thing as Lower. We wore stiff, starched detachable collars every day. If your collars were frayed, and mine all were, they would come back from the Chinese laundry with all the frays iron-hard, like a hacksaw blade. As if adolescent pimples weren't bad enough— your neck would be red raw as well. We wore straw boater hats, which were completely impractical given that Christchurch is often in the grip of a nor'wester gale. The food was both insufficient and fairly inedible. You learnt to at least tolerate foods that were otherwise unpalatable or you'd starve to death—I still enjoy kidneys, liver, tapioca pudding and so on.

There was a sharp division between boarders and day boys. Boarding was a twenty-four-hours-a-day, seven-days-a-week commitment to hell. Being a day boy meant cycling home at the end of the day to the tender ministrations and delicious cooking of your mother. Day boys, clearly, were soft. We were all divided into houses: typically seventy or so boys per house. The oldest and most prestigious house was called School House. Some boys there were from old squatter families, perhaps fifth-generation. School House was pretty easy to remember, and spell, and just as well, because many of the boys there were the product of generations of inbreeding. Canterbury farming families, for some reason, like to marry among their own. The gene pool is very small. You would think that a cursory examination of how they bred their Corriedale sheep would've been helpful in this regard. Sadly, no.

Then there was Jacobs House, which had a disproportionate number of very thick boys. Passing School Certificate was a rarity. Quite a few of my friends, therefore, were in Jacobs.

The truly eccentric boys were in Flower's House. My old

pal Gus Watson was one of these. Inspired by *The Great Escape*, starring Steve McQueen, Gus dug an escape tunnel. Like many things that Gus has done over the years, it wasn't fully thought out. When he emerged, the tunnel exit was only a few metres away from the headmaster's office. Gus's sense of direction had failed him underground.

My house was Richards. Richards was full of the boys that no one else wanted—rejects of one kind or another. I was perfectly happy with that, and there was considerably less inbreeding in evidence in my house. A couple of my older Elworthy cousins were there, Mark and Nick, and they kept a kindly eye on me. Naturally, within the house, as well as the school, there was a rigid seniority system. As a new boy you needed all three buttons

Bill Nutt and I proudly acknowledge our House of Rejects.

done up on your jacket; one button undone meant you were a second year; and finally in your third year you had the luxury of leaving two buttons undone. This absurdity was harshly enforced. Prefects pretty much ran the joint, and each prefect was assigned two fags—it sounds worse than it was—small boys who would run errands like fetching a pie from the tuckshop. Prefects enforced the rules and did most of the caning, a bamboo cane being the disciplinary weapon of choice at College.

I was okay academically, and was always in the top class, but I was never in my brother's league. I was pretty good at English and History, and perversely enjoyed Latin. I could knock out a reasonably good essay, and, as always, remained unnoticed, which was my primary objective still. I started reading good novels. It wasn't hard to be in the A-stream at College; it was a decidedly unacademic school, where the only real currency was some athletic ability. I boxed as little as I could, played rugby indifferently, and was sluggardly around the cross-country runs. Swimming, however, was my summer sport of choice—it meant time in the sun, and occasionally encountering girls at the Centennial Pool. You might even get their attention briefly if you did a decent 'bomb' from the high diving board.

Two things made life bearable at College for me. Don Hamilton, Scruff Hart and Nigel Crease, all English teachers, cast me in plays. My happy place. My parents visited but once a year, at Sports Weekend. They could be guaranteed I would never be featured in a running race or anything else sporty. But I would be in the annual theatre production on Friday and Saturday evenings. I'm not sure if I was any good, but it must've meant something to them. After my father died, I found a scrapbook in his desk. For years and years he had diligently cut out clippings from the *Press* (and later from British newspapers) that started with my acting at school and morphed into my full-time acting career. I was very touched that Dad, who never expressed much interest in what I did, would have kept this up for all those years.

The other game-changer was an activity they called Venture Group, something you could opt for instead of sport for a term, in your third year. It was a full-on Outward Bound experience—canoeing, abseiling, hiking, climbing, any number of quite challenging and often frightening things up in the Southern Alps. It was tough going, but I enjoyed it immensely. Between this and my work on stage, my sense of my own worth, my confidence, grew. And grew to the extent that, unnoticed by me, my stutter began to evaporate. I was able to talk to grown-ups. More importantly, I could talk to girls. Pleasingly, they seemed to want to talk to me too.

By my fifth year I was pretty much fully grown and reasonably comfortable in my own skin. I even made it to prefect, although just a lowly house prefect. No one gave me trouble any more, and my friends were pretty cool, but not that insufferable cool so beloved by Hollywood teen movies.

It didn't end well. I got into terrible trouble in my last term. With a number of my friends, I was caught committing the most cardinal of sins. Drinking, smoking, girls, absence without leave. In other words, all the good stuff. There were too many of us to expel (about thirty or so); instead, I was demoted and gated for the rest of my time at school. I frankly couldn't have cared less. That is, apart from the rage, the perfectly reasonable rage, of my father. My parents gave up a lot to send us to these places. I'm not sure if they got any return on their investment.

A Proper Job

I'M often asked, did you always want to be an actor? The answer is no. It never occurred to me.

I'm from a small city in a small country, profoundly isolated from the rest of the world, at the deep south of the Pacific Ocean.

The idea that I could become an actor, a screen actor, was something so far over someone else's horizon that I never gave it a second thought. There was nowhere in New Zealand where you could train to be an actor. No one was making movies, no one *thought* of making films in New Zealand when I was a kid, as far as I knew. I loved going to the films on a rainy afternoon, to lose myself in a world, in a story, that was as remote from me in my life as possible. The people in these movies were from somewhere else altogether. In British films they were better tailored and spoke better English than anyone I knew in New Zealand. With the honourable exception of my own father. Dad had perfect posture, iron upright, and was every inch the British officer. People like John Mills and David Niven played Dad in films.

We didn't get television in New Zealand until I was about twelve years old. We had an enormous wooden box, a Murphy television set in the corner of the sitting room with a tiny black-and-white screen. It took the tubes and so on about two minutes to warm up, and then another ten while my father fiddled with aerials to get a picture that halfway worked.

One channel only, for years. Anything good, and everyone

would watch it. Christchurch had issues when *The Avengers* was on. The entire city would flush their lavatories at the commercial break. We seemed to get an awful lot of bad American sitcoms after the news, and the odd decidedly ordinary Western. *The High Chaparral*, starring Leif Erickson. On balance I preferred English actors like Dirk Bogarde or James Mason, Peter Ustinov or Alec Guinness, Leslie Phillips or Sid James.

The trajectory of your life, I often think, is like a driverless train careering along. I was going somewhere, but I had no idea where. And the train would change direction from time to time, because someone would pull a lever, flip a switch, and I would head somewhere else.

As a child I imagined for a while I might become a soldier like my father. So many of my family, on both sides, were soldiers, that it almost seemed inevitable. I sensibly let this one go—I would have been a rotten soldier.

After Christ's College, I pottered around for a few years doing an arts degree, putting off the idea that I should settle on a career course. I wasted an entire year on a fruitless attempt at law; I signed up for four units and failed each and every one of them. I fancied the idea of myself as an important barrister, in a ridiculous wig. But the pressing business of doing any study proved too much. The law was never going to be for someone as idle as myself. Clicks McClelland, a famous and consummately brilliant barrister in Christchurch, took me aside once at a wedding, and seriously told me, 'My boy. There is only one place for you. The law. Criminal law.'

Alas, it was not to be. At least until we shot *The Twelve* in 2022.

The idea of joining the family firm and being a man of commerce filled me with an uncommon dread. Just the fact alone of having to go to an office every day was too horrific to contemplate. And I'm pleased to say I've managed to avoid all my life the nine-to-five business of sitting at a desk, tangling with figures. I would've been hopeless at all of the above jobs.

This dilly-dallying came as no surprise to my parents. Dad sometimes was heard to say, 'When will that bloody boy get a proper job?'

I'm still not sure whether screen acting qualifies as a proper job; it's too much fun for that. But it is a job of sorts and I'm still in a state of surprise not only that it happened to me, but that I continue to get to work in the business that I love best. It is also very hard work, in case you think it is frivolous. Somehow I muddled my way, by a series of accidents, into a pretty decent screen career.

These, I think, are the main milestones on that random railroad.

At school, acting was about the only thing that I enjoyed doing. We did three productions a year at Christ's College, and if you were any good you might be lucky enough to score a role. Acting wasn't on any syllabus in those days; it was something you did in your spare time. A hobby. Most of the other boys at school thought it was for 'poofs'. I didn't care, I enjoyed it, and it was about the only thing that I was even halfway good at. Furthermore, one of those productions would be in collaboration with St Margaret's College. Actual girls! For a fifteen-year-old, locked away in a boys' boarding school, this was a major incentive to take up acting.

It wasn't until I was three years out of school that I tried acting again. This was in 1969 in Christchurch and here was a stroke of very good fortune. I was cast in *A Midsummer Night's Dream*, directed by Dame Ngaio Marsh. I played Theseus. Ngaio was a grand dame of a very old school, and slightly scary. She drove a Jaguar XK150, smoked a pipe and spoke in a rich bass voice.

She taught you to play Shakespeare in rather a bizarre manner, the way I imagine the classics were addressed in the West End before World War I. All rounded vowels, and gesturing grandly at things.

Dame Ngaio spent every other year in the UK, and was friends with Sir John Gielgud and other thespian types. She also wrote dozens of bestselling detective stories, and was often compared to Agatha Christie. Quite a woman. The only word that seems to work for her presence seems wrong—'patrician'.

But the play was the best fun. The cast included people like Bill Stalker, Catherine Wilkin, Deirdre O'Connor, Elric Hooper; I realised I had found my people. Other People Who Loved Acting.

Bill and I kept in touch, and sometimes, over the next few years, he'd roar out on his bike to see my girlfriend Louise W. and me in Eastbourne, Wellington. Bill ended up in Australia about the same time as me, and worked happily and well out of Melbourne. I loved having an ally and rival and old friend on the same trajectory as me in a foreign land. He was living with Catherine Wilkin there, and they were a very close and contented couple. And then one night Bill lost control of his bike on a wet road, and the pair of them slammed under a car. Bill was killed instantly, and poor Catherine spent months recovering in hospital. Bill had the most infectious giggling laugh I've ever known. And a commanding presence as an actor. I'm still heartsick about his death.

But back to *A Midsummer Night's Dream*. Elric Hooper was just back from England and was an extraordinarily physical Puck, lithe and seductive, and also half naked. He had worked with Joan Littlewood, and was fizzing with ideas about new theatre. Elric took us for seminars on stage every Saturday, and they were quite a revelation. Elric had been one of Ngaio's boys, one of her famous acolytes. His approach to performance now, post London, would've been anathema to Ngaio, had she known what Elric was inculcating us with. I remember one key bit of advice he gave for anyone in theatre. He said, When you walk on stage, you need to make everyone in the audience, male or female, want to fuck you. Hmmm.

Elric soon after took over, and successfully ran the Court Theatre in Christchurch for many years.

The production, I think, was rather good. The *Press* reviewed it well. I had a terrible first night. Ngaio stormed down the stairs, looked me in the face close up, and thundered, in her basso

With Bill Stalker, in make-up and wearing garlands, for *A Midsummer Night's Dream*.

profundo, 'Sam, that was a *sissy* performance!'

A Midsummer Night's Dream was a milestone for me: my first play as a grown-up, for one thing. I wanted acting to be part of my life. There is a poster somewhere, featuring six of us: Bill, Deirdre, Catherine, Douglas Blair, Yvonne Mackay and me. We all look rather pretty. Or, I suppose, if you're Elric, fuckable.

The next play, a few months later, changed everything. It was a production of *Marat/Sade*, directed by the great Mervyn Thompson, or Proc, as we all called him.

It taught me how electrifying theatre can be. At the end of 1969, the production was taken by invitation to Downstage in Wellington. One of the actors had to drop out, and I was asked to take his place. In the asylum at Charenton, Jacques Roux was the looniest of the inmates. I played the whole thing frothing and raving in a straitjacket. Bill Stalker was a massive, dominating Marat, Catherine Wilkin a heartbreaking Charlotte Corday. And Mervyn himself a dapper, louche de Sade. Dick Nunns did the music. Dick later in life was probably more responsible than any other living being for reviving traditional Māori instruments. Aotearoa owes him a lot.

It was a short run, but I had the time of my life. Ngaio Marsh taught you to act like an Antipodean simulacrum of some West End thespian. Proc wanted the opposite. He liberated us. He insisted we stretch ourselves as performers. He pulled every possibility out of us.

It was intoxicating to work for him. The production was crazily dynamic and immensely fun to be in.

Years later, I found Proc in Christchurch, living in a small, dark flat off Bealey Avenue. Proc was in seclusion. He'd been subject to a scandal not long before: he'd been chained to a tree by some women activists in revenge for an alleged transgression in the past. As to the truth of those claims, I have no idea. He was also suffering from a terminal cancer of the face, and he was hideously and cruelly disfigured. I felt desperately sorry for him, isolated and facing imminent death. I was able, though, to thank him for the change he had made to my life, and indeed to theatre in New Zealand.

The other thing was that *Marat/Sade* took me to Wellington. It never occurred to me that Wellington might be somewhere of interest. But here it was, the capital. And culture. It was alive. In Dunedin or Christchurch, art, drama or any kind of the arts seemed to happen in spite of the place. Oddities. But here these things were part of the fabric of the city. Wellington has the most abysmal climate, whatever they tell you. It never stops blowing. But it's completely beautiful, with one of the most spectacular harbours in the world, and charming wooden houses that spill down steep hills to the water. And it's also like a basin, with the city centre at the bottom. And all the energy, all the creativity of the place, drains into the city itself. This is a very good thing.

I decided I wanted to stay, and to transfer to Victoria University for the last unit in my Bachelor of Arts, the slowest degree in the history of education. Someone had switched the points on the railway and here I was.

I shared a squalid flat with an old friend, Tony Denniston. Tony was at this point waiting, bowtie and all, at one of the very few restaurants in Wellington that had any pretensions at all. Toad, as he was known, was a sort of sleepy, amused chap, who seemed to have no idea what he wanted to do. Just like me. It was a tiny, freezing, third-floor, two-bedroom flat in a large blue concrete building, up the laughably named Oak Park Avenue, a grubby, treeless alleyway off Buller Street. Toad might have seemed the slowest, laziest fellow on the planet, but he had a knack with women. Bafflingly, he always had more than one on the go. You never knew who you might run into at breakfast.

Unwisely, he was having an affair with the boss's wife. This is never a good idea. One night I was woken by screaming and shouting and the sort of commotion that was clearly no business of mine. The next morning I asked Toad what had happened. The boss had somehow got into our flat, flung open Toad's bedroom door and there they were. In flagrante.

He was understandably apoplectic with rage, screaming at his wife. I asked Toad, What did you do? I imagined that perhaps he might have got up and asked the boss to kindly leave the premises. Something in gallant defence of the naked woman beside him. No, he said, I just pulled the eiderdown over my head until it all went away. I still find this arrant cowardice completely hilarious.

Victoria University was a sprawling campus about ten minutes' walk up a couple of very steep hills. And there I spent a year, mostly in the cafeteria, but also doing drama again. I played

Toad and me, debating team. I doubt we were any good.

Macbeth himself in a production of the Scottish play directed by Phillip Mann. Phillip was a little bit like Mervyn. He wasn't interested in niceties, or gentlemanly acting. He loved extremes. I'm not sure if I was any good, but I gave it a crack, and to my astonishment more or less got away with it. The worst thing was that I had to lie dead at the end, after an exhausting and dangerous sword fight, trying desperately not to breathe, while everyone else took a curtain call. Ngaio came to see a performance. She didn't come backstage to say anything afterwards, and I never saw her again. I guess she thought I'd been a sissy again.

Later in the year I got a part in another play at Downstage. This was the first time I'd ever been paid to act: thirty-five dollars a week, with a free feed thrown in at the end of the night. Every night the food was the same, lasagne. Downstage was dinner and theatre. The actors got to eat whatever the audience left. Being excessively poor I was only too grateful to eat the same awful lasagne night after night. I think this is where my lifelong affliction of heartburn began.

But it was professional theatre: paid acting. This was Euripides' *The Bacchae*, and I was playing Pentheus. An immensely impressive actor from Wales, Ray Henwood, was playing Dionysus. We all were dressed in sheets of one kind or another. Things don't end well for Pentheus; it is, after all, a tragedy. Dionysus turns him into a sort of drag queen, I think, but this newly acquired femininity doesn't save him from being physically torn apart by a chorus of dangerous women.

I did, in fact, complete my degree, such as it was, that year, thanks to the great John Clarke. All I had left was one small unit in philosophy and I was done. I thought philosophy would be a doddle, and possibly even interesting. Wrong—not a doddle. Of course, again I did no work. One paper was logic—rather like pure math—all e = f + g. Double Dutch to me.

John Clarke I knew a bit about the traps and from drinking hilariously with him at crap parties in mouldy flats. He was a regular star in late-night revues at Downstage with Ginette McDonald, John Banas, Paul Holmes et al. There was no one like him, a total original. In various sketches you could see the prototypes of Fred Dagg; Dagg in embryo. He was an acute and fond observer of all things New Zealand. I thought he was amazing.

Anyway, it was a week or two before exams, and we were queuing for a pie in the university cafe. He asked me what was wrong, and I told him I was rooted—there was no way in the world I could possibly pass logic. Another wasted academic year.

John said, 'No worries, son. Give me a couple of hours in the library, and you'll be right.'

And that's exactly what I did—John spent two or three hours talking to me, the moron, and I passed the damn thing. Miracles happen when you know someone like Clarke.

We became friends thereafter, and he was a great ally when I got to Australia. John's wife, Helen McDonald, is Australian, and they had settled in Melbourne. Here he carved out a career as Australia's greatest satirist. Bless him. When he left New Zealand he was probably the most famous person in the land— our first big television star.

John told me a story about how, returning from the UK after a year of Overseas Experience, the plane he was on had an almost fatal mishap. The pilot, Australian, and very dry, announced before landing that one wheel was stuck. And they would have to plummet a few thousand feet and try to shake the bastard out. This they somehow managed to do after several tries. John along with everyone else onboard was traumatised.

Later he took a long course to overcome his fear of flying, and claimed he was cured. But he can't have been because for decades he refused to fly again, especially to the land of his birth. Everyone missed him.

Back in 1972, my next gig of note was travelling the length and breadth of New Zealand for a year with the New Zealand Players Drama Quartet, taking Shakespeare, Shaw and the like to mostly ungrateful schoolchildren. Again the pay wasn't a lot, but there we were, two men, two women and a Kombi van. We mostly got on well, with the occasional flare-up. There was an altercation once between John Banas, the leader of our band, and Kate JasonSmith. Kate was a strong woman, and John was a very slight man. John had angered Kate to the point where she picked up a whole school desk, raised it above her head and threw it hard at John. John might have been slight, but he was also nimble. He dived sideways and the desk smashed into the wall behind him, leaving him unscathed.

We travelled like this for a whole year, playing to intermediate and high schools. The worst audiences we had were private schools. They were too good for us, it seemed. The best audiences we had were in remote Māori communities. The kids there thought we were great, and believed every second of what we did on stage. I loved them. They particularly loved Shakespeare.

I was pleased to be on the road, just to get away from things. All the year before I'd been hopelessly in love. The object of my desire was one Jenny Lindsay. She'd been a witch in *Macbeth*. I followed her around all that year, pathetically panting like someone's stupid lapdog. She seemed to like the attention, but it was not ever going to be good enough. She was engaged to someone else, someone in Indonesia, someone better. At the end of the year she went off and married him, leaving me desolate and entirely unrequited. Oh, well.

Both her parents played in the New Zealand Symphony Orchestra. Her father was, in fact, the leader and the first violin. So I saw a lot of classical music that year; I even saw the remarkable Jacqueline du Pré perform. Who knew the cello could be so damn sexy? Their circle included all sorts of people in the arts: poets, painters. I was both intrigued and daunted. None of them paid me any attention, but I didn't mind. It was apparent that Wellington had much to offer. The world of art seemed to open up. I got interested in the visual arts and developed a fascination for New Zealand painting. That has never left me. Colin McCahon, Ralph Hotere, Toss Woollaston... these were my new heroes. Up to this point, I think we were persuaded that the only living heroes we had in New Zealand were All Blacks. For heaven's sake.

That year on the road was immensely educational for me. We saw our own country, from Kaitaia to Bluff. We met all kinds of New Zealanders. It afforded me an opportunity to become familiar with my own country in a way that I couldn't have hoped for otherwise.

We were once having a beer in far north Kaitaia. I was with a bunch of amiable Māori guys. The bloke next to me was particularly friendly, and after a few drinks he leant over to tell me something quietly. He pointed out a white fella over the other side of the bar.

The man was hideously marked, with what looked like a vivid dark red birthmark taking up the whole of one side of his face. The story was this—there are caves up in the hills that are tapu (forbidden, sacred). He'd been told, Don't go near them, dangerous, there are ancestors' bones there.

But he said, Bugger that, and went up and had a poke around anyway. Came back and bragged about it. The next day he woke up and his face was ravaged.

At the end of 1972, I turned my back again on acting. There was no way in the world one could expect to make a proper living as an actor. A freelance actor had every opportunity to starve, unless you were one of the half-dozen favoured actors who could scrape by doing some radio drama. No, I would have to follow my father's constant refrain and get a Proper Job. And so I joined the New Zealand National Film Unit.

Stories from the Front

Sexy Whales

IN about 2008 I was shooting a television series called *Crusoe* with Philip Winchester and Tongayi Chirisa. We found ourselves filming at the far end of South Africa, on what's known as the Garden Route. The production rented me a house on the sandhills overlooking the most beautiful bay. The calmest place imaginable. Except it was shagging season for right whales.

Look away now if you're squeamish. The right whale is a big fella, and a promiscuous one. The males are equipped for this; they have a manoeuvrable four-metre penis, a joystick if you like, which is pretty handy under the circumstances, and each ball weighs a tonne. If you're going to be at it for days on end, and they are, it clearly pays to be well endowed.

The thing is, not to put too fine a point on it, these animals are into group sex. A female swims into the bay and indicates that she is up for it, in season. Immediately she attracts up to six males, and then it's party time. The males crowd around her and take it in turn. When she's had enough, and I imagine that wouldn't take too long when you are being shagged by up to six huge whales in sequence, she turns upside down so her genitals are unavailable. Poor thing. That often annoys the males, who simply refuse to stop partying. These randy buggers are known to co-operate: two of them will tip her over and there will be another bloke underneath, ready to seize the advantage.

All the time we were there, there were whale parties all over the bay: by my count, six on average. They just go on and on. You can see a whale party from some distance—the sea around them is an alarming shade of white, which one can only assume is gallons of surplus seminal fluid. Ghastly. Sea birds are having a ball, eating up said white matter.

This is no silent sex; on the contrary they are very, very noisy. They moan, scream, splash about, clack, groan, hoot... They make a whole variety of whale bedroom sounds that carry well across and under water. Enough to wake the neighbours. In this case, the neighbours were us. I'd wake at four in the morning to a cacophony of noises seemingly just outside. I'd walk out in the moonlight and find a big whale party just fifty metres away, at the edge of the surf. They get so engrossed they forget where they are, and often come close to getting beached mid-shag.

I've had some noisy neighbours over the years, but these whales took the biscuit. I actually shouted into the dark a few times, 'Keep it down out there!' but to no avail.

Ten years later I was in Tonga filming the television documentary series *The Pacific: In the Wake of Captain Cook*. While we were there we trumped up a flimsy excuse to swim with the humpback whales that are around the islands at that time of the year. This was the single most exhilarating experience of my life.

We were alongside a young adult male when the guide told me to jump in. When I orientated myself I realised I was floating right above this most immense creature; he was maybe twenty metres below me, and he was twice the size of the motorboat I'd just left. I felt like the tiniest living thing on the planet. He was staring at me, and I was hyperventilating through my snorkel. He swam off a little ways, and then came back again. He did a few rolls for our benefit. He was showing off. Look at me, look what I can do. Acrobatics. Then he came up, and eyeballed me. No more than five metres away, and checking me out. Then he lazily rolled sideways, and this huge flipper passed me, mere centimetres from my face.

Eventually he left us, after corkscrewing, tumbling, playing for a good twenty minutes. He'd probably heard a female turn up, and, entirely reasonably, went off for something more interesting.

Happily, humpbacks are a tad more discreet than their orgiastic right cousins.

No judgment from me, though. Whatever floats your whale.

Love Birds

Of courtship, the right whale knows naught.

By contrast, the male weaverbird devotes his life to it. I was shooting a film called *Skin* with the marvellous Sophie Okonedo and the equally fabulous Alice Krige. This was also in South Africa, and we were shooting in a vast valley not that far from Pretoria. Curiously, it is one of the spots most hit by lightning on the planet, and every day you could set your clock to it—a big storm would roll in from nowhere at about 5 p.m., and it was like being in the washing machine that was sparking all the fuses. Terrifying.

Alice Krige and I were playing the white parents of a child whom the authorities in apartheid South Africa deemed to be black. A true story, but a most peculiar one. Anything was possible in that bizarre and cruel time.

Anyway, we were staying at a kind of game lodge, except no one hunted. It was right under a bluff where, famously, the Boer army had escaped the British forces, who'd had them trapped at the edge of the chasm and would've massacred them. The Afrikaners stealthily and silently climbed down our cliffs in the dark, and slipped away.

We would eat breakfast and dinner outside on a large veranda overlooking the valley. The bush was alive with animals and birds.

It was nesting time for the weaverbirds. One brave chap started to weave his nest, a most beautiful construction, right beside the spot where I would have my breakfast. I followed his progress for weeks.

It's a heartbreaking business. It takes days and days to painstakingly weave together this exquisite nest, which hangs like fruit—some trees would have twenty or thirty such nests. Once he's finished the shell, he collects little feathers, fluffy bits of grass and so on to make a comfortable bed inside, fit for a princess. After what seems like quite a few days he emerges satisfied that he's achieved something brilliant. He jumps up onto the nearest branch and sings and sings. He's singing to tell a female, any female, that he's the man—he's built something beautiful, and it's just for her.

I watched this for quite some time and no female turned up. Then after a couple of days one drab little bird made an appearance. He was quite a pretty, well-dressed, colourful fellow. She was positively dowdy. She sat on the branch close to him and looked dubiously at what he considered a great work of art. Finally, with immense reluctance, she flew down and entered the nest from below. You could see him holding his breath. We were holding our breath too. Would she, could she be the one? Or would it fall short of all expectations, his highest hopes?

She eventually emerged. She flew up to the top of the nest and sat there for a few minutes. He was hopping around his branch in eager anticipation. Then she pecked at the thing, discarding sticks and a few bits of grass. The message was clear: it was not up to snuff. I looked up at him and he was utterly crestfallen, deflated and defeated. It was the saddest thing I ever saw. She flew away, leaving him disconsolate and silent.

And then the really sad stuff. He flew onto his own nest, and completely dismantled it. It took him ages, but there was nothing, nothing left at all. It all had to go. I'm not sure who was more gutted, my little bird or me.

And then after a day or so he started all over again, from scratch. With tremendous energy and tenacity, stick by stick, blade by blade, he began to build another beautiful nest *identical* to the one that had suffered rejection. It took days and days, from morning to night. I could not admire a bird more.

There is a happy ending to this. Just before we left, another drab and dreary female turned up, and grudgingly condescended to nest with him. You could see how completely thrilled my little chap was.

Me too.

Animal Amour

More on the subject of love.

I was in Montana in the late 1990s filming *The Horse Whisperer* with Robert Redford, Kristin Scott Thomas and Scarlett Johansson. I had a lot of days off and we'd explore, trout-fish, river-raft and sometimes I'd even paint.

One day we were filming at a ranch at a high altitude. Outside a giant barn, standing side by side, watching our crew in action, were an enormous red bull and an almost equally huge stallion. I thought nothing of it for a minute or two, and then I went back to look again. Why were these two tremendously different animals so close and so clearly attached?

I discovered that they were orphans and had been reared together. They became friends as they grew up. So much so that now they were completely inseparable. If they took the horse away to do whatever it is that horses are supposed to do, the bull would simply bulldoze down any barriers between them to get back to his friend. Similarly, if the bull was taken away to perform his bull functions, the horse would jump any intervening fences until they were reunited. I'm not sure if you call this love, or just companionship…It doesn't matter. It was clearly deeply felt. I found it very touching.

About ten years ago, in one of the newer subdivisions near Queenstown, an enormous ram turned up, running helter-skelter and half crazed around the beautifully paved streets. It was enormous because it hadn't been shorn for years. If ever. It was like a mad woolly blimp. Finally someone caught it, and the question then was what to do with this crazy animal. Lauren, my wonderful PA, who was living there, called me and asked if it would be all right if the sheep was put out to graze on our lower paddocks. I said that would be absolutely fine, as long as someone shore him and kept an eye on his welfare, given that I was often away.

At the same time our friend and neighbour Mel had been grazing her pony Woody for quite some years in the same paddocks. Woody was an amiable enough horse, but I always felt rather sorry for him, as he was so solitary. He looked lonely to me. I asked Mel about this, and indeed she had tried to move one or two other ponies in at various times to keep Woody company. The problem was Woody just hated other horses. Loathed them. There was nothing that could be done about this; he would bite them, kick them…do anything to get rid of them.

I was curious about how he would get on with the sheep. Initially they kept their distance, but there was no hostility. Gradually the atmosphere thawed, and they became friends. Unlikely friends. And then inseparable. If Mel moved Woody to the next paddock, the sheep would be right beside him. If the gate was closed, the horse would jump the fence to get back to his sheep friend. Lionel and Woody, best pals. They were never more than ten metres apart from each other. More than that, they were demonstrably affectionate. Woody would lean down to Lionel, and Lionel would crane up so they could have a good nuzzle together. I swear they'd kiss. Two funny old boys. If it rained, the ram would take shelter under the horse to keep dry. They were together for four or five years until the old ram finally died. Woody is still there, nearly thirty years old now. I'm sure he misses his old pal.

You can indeed find love in unlikely places.

I am not sure if this counts as *love* exactly, but there is this about my pig. My adorable ugly white Kunekune named Angelica. He is not transitioning or anything—he has that name from a little girl who owned him before me, and the poor old bloke is stuck with that heavenly moniker. He is rampantly heterosexual, despite the name. I just call him Pig when we hang out—it seems more dignified.

For some three years we provided him with a wife, a ginger Kunekune with an overshot jaw. She was not a pretty pig. Not at all. This didn't slow him one bit, and he was on her day and night. On and on they went. Rams climb on a ewe—blink and you miss it. A pig just grinds on and on and on incessantly. She was always grumpy, and one can understand why.

No manners, that fella.

Some years later we had Saddleback pigs, rather beautiful in a porcine way. Our sow we kept a long way from our boy, since we knew she would cycle any day. We were saving her for a handsome Saddleback boar, a near neighbour. Everyone went away one weekend and when Mike Wing, who manages the farm, got home, the two were caught red-trotted, shagging in the vineyard. It seems that *both* had broken down their respective fences in pure unbridled lust and been at it all weekend. I told Angelica sternly next time I saw him, 'You really let yourself down, mate.' We got her over quick smart to her *real* boyfriend, hoping it wasn't too late.

Some months later, instead of the ten cute Saddleback piglets we were expecting, she gave birth to four hairy little mongrels. They all had the unmistakable Angelica stamp about them.

First Love and a War Hero

My first girlfriend is still one of my closest friends. Not many people can say that.

In fact, it's pretty unusual for me too. I think most of my exes probably loathe me, with very good reason. Let me take this opportunity to apologise for being, you know, a dickhead. Causing pain. Letting people down. It wasn't all one way, though, I have to say. I've served my time for the suffering statistics, don't worry. But I think of my exes fondly. With gratitude. And with considerable nostalgia from the perspective of this end of my life.

Lou and I met at a dance in my second-last year at school, and we were boyfriend and girlfriend on and off, mostly on, for about five years. She was at another boarding school a hundred miles away. You'd meet a girl hurriedly in the holidays and get officially appointed Boyfriend. Then not see each other for another twelve weeks of term. She would write every day, which was exhausting, as it was considered poor form not to reply. We pretty much got through all of our lessons in adolescent stuff, fumbled around, grew close and enjoyed ourselves. We skied, went to parties and hung out. She was and is a beautiful person, generous and affectionate, and I am godfather to her second daughter, Caroline. That tells you something.

Lou came from a farm not far from Culverden in North Canterbury and I loved going up there to stay. I slept out the back in the single men's quarters, which suited me fine. The only television they had was also out there. Her father, Dick Ormond, was a splendid fellow. Dick was Māori, from the Māhia Peninsula near Gisborne, so he was a long way from home. He had a good farm, mostly sheep. Terraced land, with views west towards the Southern Alps. Exhilarating. He'd give me work to do and I drove the tractor, worked in the woolshed when the shearers

Lou and me, Cathedral Square, Christchurch, 1965. She is in school uniform; I am in my best Mod gear.

were there, all sorts. Quiet and gentle, he was endlessly patient with a pretty inept town boy.

Dick had served in the war, and his best and closest friend was another Canterbury farmer, Charlie Upham, VC and Bar, whom my mother met in the old people's home. Dick and Charlie both ended up war prisoners, and I think that is where they made an unbreakable lifelong bond. They were quiet men, but their wives, Jenny Ormond and Molly Upham, were garrulous in the extreme. The Uphams would come for Sunday lunch sometimes, and the two women never paused for breath, sitting between these two completely silent men. After pudding, with no perceptible signal, the two old blokes would quietly slip away from the table and disappear.

I wandered after them one day, curious as to what came next. Typically they would find a gate and lean on it together. They might roll a cigarette, but generally they just leant in companionable silence; once in a while Dick would sigh, 'Ah, well.' That was all the conversation they needed. There was nothing else to be said. They had heard enough noise in their lives, enough bangs, enough explosions, enough yelling. They had served, and a little calm and peace was all a man needed, as well as a mate who understood.

Charlie had three beautiful daughters, very beautiful. He bore a lifelong grudge against Germans and everything remotely connected to Germany. If a young farming prospect turned up at the Upham farm driving a VW Beetle, hoping to woo one of these beautiful girls, Upham would tell him to fuck off. He was scary as hell, and you didn't hang around for a second warning.

Luckily, Dick chose to be a lot more tolerant when it came to his two daughters. I think he turned a blind eye at such times as I would sneak over to the house after dark and climb in the window for a bit of a cuddle. The silence out there in the country was deafening; for all my stealth, I must've been detected at some point. Bless you, Dick, for everything.

And bless you, Lou, for all the times. I am so glad we are still pals.

Young Love

I was once home at my parents' farm for a few days. They had a charming guest.

My parents often had young people passing through, children of their friends back in England, who were making their way around the world. Quite often they were chinless wonders with so many hyphenated surnames it made you wonder how they got around at all, let alone around the world.

But this one was different. She was about my age, twenty-two, and stunningly beautiful. I developed a crush immediately.

She was rather posh, and extraordinarily confident and self-possessed. I was way out of my depth. She was breathtaking on horseback. She was elegant and captivating.

On her last night there, my parents both went to bed, leaving me alone with her. I plucked up my courage and sat beside her on the sofa, making conversation that I was fairly certain was both witty and entertaining. I thought I was doing rather well, until she cut me off mid-sentence.

'Nigel,' she said, using the name my parents still insisted upon. 'Nigel, do you know something? You are the slowest person I have ever met. The slowest. You talk slowly. You move slowly. You think slowly. You are just…slow.'

Clearly, I was also the most boring. I was crushed, and made my way to bed as soon as possible. And that was that.

I'm not sure I've ever fully recovered.

The Road to the Coromandel

I got my proper job at the National Film Unit under completely fraudulent circumstances.

Life, I think, is often as much about the people who say no to you as the ones who say yes. I once applied at New Zealand Broadcasting to be a trainee news reporter. I was given a flat no. Just as well. Once I was working part-time in the Wellington post office to earn some money to keep me at university. Mail sorting. Absolutely mind-numbing. My supervisor called me over at the end of the first week. He said, not unkindly, 'I don't think this is for you, son.' He was right. I left immediately.

I needed a job. An old friend, John Laing, was working as a director at the New Zealand National Film Unit at Miramar near Wellington airport. John had always been interested in film, and we'd often go to the flicks together in Dunedin. As soon as he left university, he had the gumption to go to Wellington and apply to be a training director at the unit. I had no interest in becoming a filmmaker, but John was doing it, and I met a few of his friends out there at Miramar, like Philip McDonald. My Canterbury University pal Cathy Isaac was working there as a film editor, the best they had. They all seemed to be having interesting fun. So one day I went out and got an interview with Ron Bowie and David Fowler, the producers. John had trained me about what to say—that I had a long, a lifelong, interest and passion for documentary film, and the only thing I wanted to do in life was to make documentaries. The truth was I'd only just considered it the week before. But somehow I must've been convincing enough, and I found myself with a job. I think I started on a wage of $3200 per annum. I was a government servant and that was that. I considered myself fortunate.

I was a phenomenally lazy young man. Eventually, however, after a couple of years of editing, laying soundtracks and so on, I became a director. It sounds important, but it wasn't. Unless you made something of it, and I didn't. Far too idle for that. Paul Maunder, who not only worked for the NFU but in 1971 founded the radical Amamus Theatre Troupe, made something of it, and created original, exceptional documentaries and dramas that eclipsed all else. I was something of a follower of his for a while.

I did a couple of plays for Amamus. One was about the 1951 waterfront strike/lockout, from an entirely wharfie viewpoint. I think it was rather good. I got to play a number of parts, including Sid Holland, a man who had been the right-wing prime minister during the strike. We thought Sid was a buffoon.

One of my first jobs at the National Film Unit was editor on a little ten-minute drama, written and directed by Maunder, called *Seals*. We showed it at the Wellington Film Festival later in the year. Behind me in the theatre were a couple of drunk guys, one of whom yelled, 'Aw shit! Don't tell me this is a *New Zealand* movie!' And you know what—he got a big laugh. The times.

I pulled away from Amamus and Maunder soon enough. It was starting to feel a bit weird for me: slightly clammy. My fellow actors seemed to have turned into disciples of some kind, as if thinking that the sun shone out of Maunder's bottom. To this day, I've never met a man who can convincingly shine a sunbeam from his arse. The idea of self-appointed leadership gives me the creeps. As is so often the case, what had started as a sort of co-operative had turned into a cult.

When at the NFU, I wrote and directed a couple of things that remain not altogether excruciatingly embarrassing. I was an admirer at the time of another radical theatre group called Red Mole, which was led by the poet Alan Brunton. And, predictably, Red Mole became a cult as well. But at about this time, 1976, Red Mole were at their height. If they were political at all, they weren't left-wing like us; they tended towards anarchy. On a good night, their blend of satire, music and knockabout circus skills had to be seen to be believed.

I persuaded the NFU to allow me to make an hour's documentary about them on tour: *Red Mole on the Road*. A road movie. *Close Encounters of the Third Kind* came out about that time, and the surreal elements in our film owe much to that. I thought there was a touch of psychedelia in what Red Mole did; I wanted to reflect that in the structure that I built around them.

We toured New Zealand together, we filmed their shows, and between gigs we would shoot some of the stuff I'd scripted. Brunton, who was a brilliant but arrogant son of a bitch, soon

Directing, 16mm, NFU.

found this work for the film, despite their being paid for their trouble, a bit of a drag.

One day in Nelson they didn't turn up at the agreed meeting place—not just their usual lateness, but not at all. I decided to see what was up. I knocked at the motel door, and walked in. In the kitchenette there was something boiling on the stove. I lifted the lid. It wasn't breakfast. In the boiling water were three syringes busily disinfecting themselves. I carried on to the bedroom, and there, all comatose in the same bed, were Brunton and his wife plus A. N. Other. Smack. Suddenly this explained so much. They didn't work, needless to say, for the rest of the day. I was quietly furious. They were a prodigiously talented but very strange tribe.

The NFU was the least cool place in the film world in New Zealand. The coolest of all were the Blerta crew from Hawke's Bay. Blerta stood for Bruno Lawrence's Electric Revelation and Travelling Apparition. Also, in the slang of the day, blurter was a term for your arse. They were musicians and actors and could turn their hands to pretty much anything, and lived communally at a time when communes were as cool as it got. The leading lights there, apart from Bruno, were Geoff Murphy, cinematographer Alun Bollinger, and my old friend Bill Stalker. It goes without saying that their long-suffering wives actually made the place work. They started making little films, comedies, largely with equipment and even footage that they would nick from places like the NFU. They epitomised the New Zealand do-it-yourself aesthetic.

We didn't know much about what was happening up in Auckland, so next down the rank were people like John Reid and Barry Barclay at Pacific Films, an independent outfit founded by John O'Shea in the fifties. They made shorts that would be played before the movies, and then documentaries for television, when we finally got telly in New Zealand in 1960. John O'Shea was a splendid figure, a large florid man with a stammer that was even worse than mine when I was small. It would get exacerbated when he got excited about things, which was often. John was much admired and was a great pioneer in New Zealand film. He made three features before anyone else had even thought of it.

Third in line for coolness was TVNZ, whose new head-quarters were out in Lower Hutt. They had a purpose-built office block and even film studios. They started making dramas: nothing terribly interesting that I remember, but it was a start. Definitely cool people out there, and most people on a Friday night drank at the Duke of Edinburgh, a pub on Willis Street. Pretty much everyone was in there: actors, musicians, filmmakers, artists of one kind or another. The occasional weed dealer. One of the latter was reputedly a guy with curly ginger hair called Fat Charlie. Charlie started going around with one of my friend's sisters. I told my friend of Charlie's reputation; I thought it only fair that he should know. While I was waiting for a drink at the bar one night I felt an odd sensation right above my left kidney. It was a knife. Keeping still, I turned and it was Charlie. He was red with rage. He knew what I'd said. I never spoke ill of Charlie again.

It was at the Duke and our other watering holes that it was clear that we humble workers at the National Film Unit were the least cool of all. The rest could barely give us the time of day. I'd like to think we didn't care. But we must've, because I remember it.

There was another pub in Cuba Street, incidentally, that Toad and I would go to once in a while, because we found everything there fascinating. It was extremely rough. There were hookers who specialised in fishing boats from Asia. There were criminals of all kinds. And, most fascinating of all, drag queens. Big tough Māori drag queens. Toad and I were fish out of water, but for some reason the drag queens were protective of us. We were safe with them, and they were hilarious, camp as hell and didn't give a flying fuck what anyone thought.

Further up Cuba Street, where the massage parlours were at their thickest, was Peter McLeavey's gallery. They should have knighted Peter—he did more for New Zealand art and artists than anyone I can think of. He had a small gallery up some stairs where he showed pretty much all the best artists of the day. Don Binney, Robin White, Bill Hammond, Toss Woollaston, Richard Killeen, Gordon Walters and New Zealand's greatest painter, the legendary Colin McCahon. Peter had immaculate taste. I'd get invited to openings there, where he'd give you a glass or two of terrible wine. Of course, I never had the money to buy anything, but I was learning. Peter was happy to talk to you about what you were looking at. He was an education. He was a small man, always elegantly dressed in a dark suit and tie, with a quiet, studious manner and round spectacles. The only time I ever caught him out of sorts, flustered even, I turned up a little early from overseas, 9.45 a.m. perhaps, just before opening. Peter was rolling up a sleeping bag and a camping bed. I didn't like to ask, but it looked like maybe he had done something very wrong and been expelled from the family home. Perhaps the smartest thing about Peter was that for all those years you were bludging wine, he must've suspected that one day you might just have some money in your pocket and you could buy something good. And on this occasion, now I had an international career, I did indeed have some money. And I was able to say the unthinkable. 'Peter, I'm back and I want to buy a McCahon.' Well, that felt good.

Some years later, a few of us were out to dinner after a spectacular and successful Bill Hammond show at Peter's gallery, with Peter and Bill himself in attendance. Everyone agreed it was a masterful display, with Hammond at the top of his game. At one point I piped up, 'Peter, this is all very well. But what about controversial art shows where people argue, take sides, disagree.

Ever had any of those?'

Peter thought for a moment. 'Well, Sam,' he said in his quiet and refined way, 'as a matter of fact, I do remember one. We were having a Woollaston show and a book launch at the same time. The gallery was full of people from the art world, as well as the literary set. After a few drinks, one of the art types turned to a literary type and asked, "Does your wife like it up the arse?" Without another word the literary type plucked a Woollaston painting off the wall and smashed it over the head of the arty chap. That was controversial.'

One of the reasons this still cracks me up is that proper Peter was the *last* person you would expect to tell a story like this.

For most of my time at the NFU, I lived at Eastbourne, on the other side of the harbour from Miramar. It was a long drive to work in one of my crappy old cars. I had a Morris Minor for a while that had a rusty floor beneath the driver's feet. On a wet day I would roll up my flared trousers to drive, because the water coming off the motorway through the floor would completely drench them and I would be wet at work all day. Better a wet leg than wet jeans.

Louise W. and I had bought a house there together. It was reasonably sized, dating from the 1920s, best guess. Pretty shabby, and full of dry rot, but we gradually fixed it as well as we could afford. From upstairs you could see the wind-blasted harbour all the way to the capital on the other side. Eastbourne was a very pleasant place to live in those days, despite the extremely windy climate, and not entirely inhabited by the rich as now. A lot of our friends gravitated there: Nigel Hewat and Yoko, Darryl and Jane Watt, Simon Walker and Mary Strang and more. It was a sociable bunch and particularly on the weekend we had good times. We smoked dope and drank dreadful wine. But it was also quietly engaging too—everybody liked gardening. We crocheted bedcovers. Well, not me exactly. It was half hippy, half suburban. I grew vegetables in the back garden and planted out the front with native trees. There was a beautiful kōwhai tree there, and the tūīs would fly in when the flowers were full and drink themselves stupid on the fermenting nectar.

We had a cat called Frank. Frank was an independent soul, but liked nothing better than a dinner party. He would insist on jumping up to a kind of top window to join the band. Mostly he wouldn't make it and would hang there for ages by his front legs,

Louise W. and our house, Eastbourne. Long hair and flares were never a good idea.

then land in an undignified way back on the windowsill. This, right beside the dinner table. We tried not to laugh, but it was his own fault. He could have come to the door like everyone else. I loved Frank.

Louise and I lived in quiet domesticity in our ramshackle house on Marine Parade. She was kind to me, cooked better than me and was a better person than me. It was clearly doomed. She worked in promotion for EMI, and this meant she brought at least half-a-dozen albums home every week. I was absolutely in love with music of all kinds in those days, and I bought a couple of really good speakers with a powerful amplifier you could crank up to good effect: the Stones, or the Allman Brothers if you'd shared a joint. Bloody bliss.

She also knew all the promoters who brought an extraordinary array of international acts through Wellington, and we saw them all. We would get free tickets to anything we wanted to see, something we would've never been able to afford on our combined small income. One of the greatest nights of my life was when we had tickets to *both* the five o'clock and the eight o'clock performances at the town hall of my favourite band of the time, the great Little Feat. (As soon as you say something like that, a voice inside you says, what about the Beach Boys, what about the Beatles, what about, what about...) Lowell George, that fat man in the bathtub with the blues, that genius, front and centre. To my dismay, when they got to the encores, it was apparent that even at the last show they were not going to play the greatest Feat track, 'Willin''. This was completely unacceptable to me. I rose to my feet and bellowed as I have never done before or since, 'Willin'!' They were gracious enough to come back yet again and do as asked. Wellington should thank me for this if for nothing else. The great Lowell George sang 'Willin'' in Wellington, because I made it so. Score.

It was the sort of place where you knew all your friends' business. Mary and Simon were trying very hard to have a baby. It took ages. And then miraculously Mary fell pregnant. One couldn't have asked for better news. They had a small, needy Boston terrier of whom everybody was very fond. But when the baby arrived, the terrier took it hard and had a complete breakdown. Poor thing would shit all over the house. They took it to a vet who prescribed the little creature a heavy dose of Valium, of all things. After six months of banging into doors and falling off beds stoned, the dog improved, thank God. Sometimes it can be hard to find yourself down the ranks in the pack order.

It could be pretty wild out there in a roaring southerly. You could almost see the spot from our house where the ferry had sunk coming into the harbour back in 1968. Mac McDonald, a wonderfully droll and witty friend, was renting a cottage on the rocks at Days Bay. I believe the house had once belonged to Katherine Mansfield's family and she had set one or two of her wonderful stories there. It had a huge window that looked directly south towards the heads, towards Cook Street. In a big storm it could be spectacular. Mac and his mate used to like to smoke a joint and watch the waves roar onto the rocks below. It was better than television. One night, however, it was better than even that. A huge wave broke over the house, smashed the big window in and swept them out to the back. Bummer.

It was a rare experience for me; I lived in a real community. Our friends were close friends, and we all lived close by. It felt comfortable. And it's a beautiful place. There is bush up the hills behind, loud with native birdsong. But that comfort meant I couldn't be there forever. Unthought, and unstated. But there. We've all scattered now. Many are still friends; some have died. Like Gerse Halliday, who was as close to a genius as anyone

I've ever known. He was a friend at school, and became a stellar economist for the Reserve Bank of New Zealand, and later the World Bank. Ironically, he failed school certificate, because of (compulsory) English; he couldn't quite get it over the line. He was a lovely, gentle bear of a man, devoted to his family, and he had an outstanding career. He was also capable of dicking things up in a big way. Like smoking forty cigarettes a day. Of course, it killed him long before his time.

The atmosphere politically in New Zealand then was increasingly strange. The Vietnam War was still on and we'd march sometimes. I think the first time I ever saw Simon Morris, one of my best music mates, was at a protest, singing 'Street Fighting Man'. None of us was fighting. But we were angry.

Norman Kirk was elected for Labour in 1972 and withdrew our troops, putting an end to all that. Kirk was also angry about another issue that concerned us deeply, the French exploding nuclear weapons not far from us in the Tahiti islands. It was to his credit we sailed a frigate up there in protest. I think Norman Kirk, who died in office at only fifty-one, was as great a prime minister as we've ever had.

He was soon followed by the appalling Piggy Muldoon of the National Party. Muldoon was an arrogant, nasty man and he cast a gloomy pall over our country for far too long. He was an authoritarian in the mould of what we are becoming used to today. New Zealand was still a deeply conservative country, but for all that a decent one. In the National Party there were still decent men, like Marshall, Talboys, MacIntyre, McLay, who believed in social security, public housing, good health, good schooling. The things that my parents paid a lot of tax for, and we took for granted as the measure of a civilised society. (This was pre-Thatcher and the grim idea that the market, a dumb greedy beast, knows best. And before even Labour shamelessly flogged off our best national assets, that eighties madness, with the deluded rationale that everything should be run by anything other than government.)

That decent society: Muldoon did much to change that. He was one of those leaders who brought out the worst in people. He was divisive and cruel. He poisoned the atmosphere, and it was one of the reasons I was relieved to leave New Zealand in 1978. He was responsible for the infamous Dawn Raids of the 1970s; these were crimes committed by the police against our Pasifika people, many of whom are still in trauma. He refused to stop the Springbok tour of 1981. And, apart from the recent disgraceful, shameful anti-vax nonsense, the country has never been more divided. And violently so. I was glad I wasn't around for that.

I was around, however, two or three years ago, when the prime minister Jacinda Ardern ran a referendum on the question of whether to legalise the recreational use of cannabis in New Zealand. Former prime minister Helen Clark talked me into publicly supporting this. The referendum was narrowly defeated. It was a loss for us all. Prohibition doesn't work. I tweeted: 'Decriminalise it, regulate it, tax it…the whole community benefits, not just gangs. The police have better things to do, they have enough on their hands already.' Plain common sense. One day, a majority will see the logic of this.

But back to the 1970s. Barry Barclay was one of the cool guys at Pacific Films. I barely knew him. He was a quietly spoken, erudite, good-looking Māori guy. And he was the next one to flick a switch, and make my train change course. He was going to make a short film, forty minutes, about spirituality and people, *Ashes*. He asked me to play a part in it, a young priest. I was kind of playing Barry, really. He'd spent some years in a seminary training to be a priest, until good sense made him see otherwise. He was also quietly a bit of a libertine, so just as well. The film is a sort of documentary, although my presence in it makes it a drama too. I was acting. And it was my first decent role on film. I must've been reasonably convincing in it, because some friends of mine from Christchurch caught it on television; they hadn't seen me for a few years, and were puzzled that I seemed to have turned to God. Not me at all. That's acting. I have absolutely no idea why Barry chose me, but he did. And changed my life. He died a few years ago, long before his time, so I guess I'll never get the chance to ask him. He was a great pioneer for films from Aotearoa, and for Māori film.

I enjoyed it, forgot about it and went back to work at the NFU. A couple of years later I got a letter out of the blue, an aerogramme, from Hong Kong. It was from someone I only knew by reputation, Roger Donaldson. Roger was also called Roger the Dodger because he had sensibly fled to New Zealand from Australia to avoid going to Vietnam and all that bloody mess. After a summer in Nelson photographing people on the beach for a dollar a pop, he went to Auckland and invented himself as a filmmaker. He became successful directing commercials. But he had wider ambitions and wanted to make movies. He teamed up with the esteemed Ian Mune, a terrific actor, stage director and screenwriter also from Auckland. The idea was, I think, that Roger would look after the visuals, and Mune would look after the performances.

They had made a series for television, and a very good one, called *Winners and Losers*, based on famous New Zealand short stories. But now they wanted to make a feature film. No one had made a feature film in many years since the last one O'Shea had made. It was going to be called *Sleeping Dogs*. Furthermore, it was going to be in colour, a first for New Zealand! But far more surprising was that, having seen me in *Ashes*, they wanted me to play the lead. Me!

I wandered around the house in a daze. For the second time in two years my train was changing course. Of course I was going to say yes, terrifying and all as the prospect was. How on earth could an untrained, inexperienced boy be a lead in an actual feature film? And who was to say I'd be any good? Certainly not me. Somehow people had confidence in me, which I didn't have myself. Their certainty didn't make me any less scared about what I had to do over the next eight weeks.

I got to Auckland and met everybody. Roger was a handsome, amiable Australian, comfortable in his own skin, and comfortable with his own talent. Mune was energetic, ebullient and charismatic. I couldn't tell if he had the same faith in me that Roger did. He'd never seen me on stage, for instance, the testing ground, really, of any actor.

The gloomy one in the room was Michael Seresin. Michael was the only person in the entire cast and crew who had made

Roger Donaldson prepping me for *Sleeping Dogs* in 1977. Damn, he was handsome.

a feature film before. He was also very clever. He'd shot *Bugsy Malone*. We were all immensely impressed. At this point he was the most famous New Zealander in the international film industry. He was also very grumpy. As soon as he arrived, I imagine, he looked around the room and thought: What a lot of amateurs.

And he was right. This was all new to us. For all that, *Sleeping Dogs* remains one of the most noted and best shot films ever made in New Zealand. It was based on a novel by C. K. Stead and imagines New Zealand as a police state in which members of the resistance confront government forces.

At the time I was sporting an enormous beard. So the first things we shot were with beard, from somewhere in the middle of the story. It was a shock to me as an actor that you didn't shoot films in story sequence. You just had to know where you were in the story, if you could. My character Smith has been arrested and jailed, and then makes an escape. This involved a stuntman rolling out of a van at the lights, and me sprinting like hell down a crowded lunchtime Queen Street in Auckland, trying to go as fast as I could and not knock over old ladies. No one had heard of security, crowd control or even telling the police. Or extras. It was all completely illegal, not to say a little dangerous. And that went for pretty much the rest of the film. The poor stuntman actually got wrestled to the ground by a diligent member of the public who thought he was a prisoner trying to get away from our (fake) police. He wasn't a stuntman, anyway; we didn't have such things in New Zealand. He just gave himself that title. Yep, we were amateurs.

After a week we all decamped to Coromandel, a ridiculously beautiful village at the top of the peninsula. We filled the only motel, and spilled over into the camping ground and anywhere else people could find a bed. We also used the motel as a location, and half blew it up with our amateur explosive effects, courtesy of

Geoff Murphy from Blerta, who was normally a trumpeter and film director, and hardly knew a thing about SFX or explosives. At the end of the film Smith gets shot; Geoff strapped a big bag of what may have been sheep's blood with a detonator behind it to my back. I had a wire that ran down my left arm for the switch. In other words, I had to shoot myself. We had no access to the approved blood bursts that you might find in a normal film. No, this was the kind of detonator that they use to blow up canyons for hydro dams.

I asked Geoff if he was certain that I was safe. He paused for what seemed like five minutes. His answer was 'Yeah. Probably.' With Geoff you never knew whether this might be understatement or a true evaluation of the situation. Either way I was fully expecting, if not death, at least a major injury. Just as well it worked—we only had the budget for one exploded jacket.

The main income generator in those days in the Coromandel was growing marijuana. There were a lot of hippies around who were more prosperous than they should've been. Some of them were helping out on the film. This made for a happy crew. And

A Man Alone in *Sleeping Dogs*. The Coromandel.

a very happy Warren Oates. Everyone was amazed that Warren came out from Hollywood and did our film, just a week or two, for peanuts. We loved Warren, and we loved his work—*The Wild Bunch*, *Two-Lane Blacktop* and so on. Somewhere in his contract I think it insisted that he be supplied with dope, and they grew really good stuff in the Coromandel. Even while we were shooting, he'd have a joint in his hand. They'd say, 'Turnover, Action,' he'd take a toke, and turn to me and give me his lines with the joint behind his back. Then cut, and another puff.

He could tell great stories about films, and was a good-natured and generous actor. He was also the most realistic thing in the whole film. Effortlessly. I learnt a lot. The last thing he said to me, out the window of his car as he pulled away, was 'See ya, Sam.' He winked. 'See you in the movies!' He died only a few years later, and I never got a chance to thank him for the kindest thing he could possibly have said to me.

As for me, I was doing my best. In my defence, when I think about it, Smith was a difficult part to play. He's a man who vacillates, is drawn into the resistance against his better nature. His mentor and ally, Mune's character, is assertive and something of a bully. Something to play there. Big and loud. Smith, on the other hand, is quiet and passive aggressive. Mune likes to tell the story that initially he found me frustrating. I didn't seem to be *doing* anything. It took about ten days for the dailies to come back from the States. We all went down to look at them at the cinema in Thames, me with some trepidation. Mune apparently looked at me on the screen and realised I actually *was* doing something. It just wasn't obvious, but it was clear enough on film. The character had an inner life. That story pleases me; I knew a little bit, at least.

In 2020 in Auckland, the day after I got out of two weeks' quarantine, I was delighted to present Mune with an Equity New Zealand Lifetime Achievement Award. It's hard to think of anyone more deserving, anyone who has contributed more to theatre and film in our country. Roger, meanwhile, went to Hollywood and has had a stellar career there. *No Way Out, Cocktail, The World's Fastest Indian*...It's a very long list of very good and successful films. We've been friends for life, and one of the best things about going to Los Angeles is going around to his place and chewing the fat. Or, to be completely correct, eating one of Roger's delicious dinners. He's also a very good cook. We grow wine side by side in the Gibbston Valley.

God bless them both for completely changing my life.

While Roger and Ian were casting *Sleeping Dogs*, we somehow had access to TVNZ's casting files. I was curious to see what was in my file. Every actor in New Zealand had one, with a photo and a summary of what TVNZ thought of you: important, as whatever little work there might be for an actor on film would be at TVNZ. I'd auditioned for a couple of productions there to no avail, and indeed there I was under N. The summation on me was brief. 'Sam Neill. Could be all right in homosexual roles.' Hmmm.

So after *Sleeping Dogs* I thought, Well, that'll be it. And I went back to work at the NFU. I made a film about my favourite architect, Ian Athfield. I've long been an architectural enthusiast. And Ath was the most exciting architect at the time in New Zealand. He'd won an international competition, a scheme to transform the biggest slum in the world, the Tondo in Manila. It was all designed so that everyone there would have the capability to build their own structure, and live well. We went to Manila for a chaotic ten days, and we were supposed to meet Mrs Marcos herself. She was the weight behind the weight. When the big day came, we were instead marshalled in to meet a general of some kind. There was a formal ceremony, and Ath was presented with a prize and a cheque. And that was pretty much it. The best thing in the film, the saddest, is the look on Ath's face when the penny drops. Nothing would be built. They'd simply bought him off. It was the damned Marcos era after all, and she probably spent the rest on shoes.

A year or so after we shot it, *Sleeping Dogs* came out. It's hard to describe how excruciating I found it to watch myself on the big screen. It only confirmed for me that, as far as screen acting went, this was the end of the road. The film review that mattered most at that time was in the *Listener*, the only serious magazine we had in our country. While it was generally favourable about the film, and very encouraging for Roger and Mune, it did not give me a good review. Nor did it give me a bad review. It made absolutely no mention of me whatsoever. Disheartening. New Zealand can be a very discouraging place.

And then, surprisingly, the film was invited to all the film festivals in Australia. And that's when someone threw another switch and the train took a different direction again.

I Discover Australia

SLEEPING *Dogs* had some kind of a release in Australia. I was sent over to do publicity for it. I'd never done anything like this before in my life, and I found myself, at one point, on Australia's most watched current affairs program, talking to Mike Willesee. Boy, was I out of my depth.

This was in Melbourne, and it was here that the distributors called a press conference. I imagined myself being grilled and photographed by a raft of eager journalists. Alas, no. Only one journo turned up, and he had made a mistake. He was a sports reporter. We abandoned the idea altogether, and he and I got half cut at the bar.

I'd never been to Australia before, and like many New Zealanders I had strange ideas about our much bigger cousin across the water. I'd never had any interest in going there, none at all. It looked boring, arid, hot and full of people I wouldn't like. The one thing that intrigued me was the nascent New Wave Australian cinema. I'd seen some new Australian films in Wellington: *Newsfront*, *The Chant of Jimmie Blacksmith*, *Walkabout* and so on. These films were good, they had something to say, and were not a little encouraging to up-and-coming filmmakers from New Zealand.

Finished with Melbourne, I took a train, a sleeper, to spend a few days with my friend Alan Galbraith in Sydney. I love sleeper trains. I feel like an infant being rocked to sleep as we go. I woke early and pulled up the blind beside my bed. That simple action changed my life. I could not believe how beautiful, how different, this land was. Green gum trees receding towards gentle blue mountains, a radiant cobalt sky, strange animals lolloping past, unknown to someone from across the ditch. Simply breathtaking. Unimaginable. I fell in love with Australia then and there.

As a result I have spent a lot of time in Australia, lived there a bit, worked there a lot, brought up children there. I enjoy the business of being more or less from both countries; I enjoy leapfrogging from one to the other. I am very grateful to Australia for the rewarding work I have done there, the friends I have made there and its glorious, unearthly beauty. The great thing about filmmaking is that it tends to cart you around the place. There is no state I haven't worked in. I know the red centre, I've swum on the Great Barrier Reef, walked the Bungle Bungles, bodysurfed at Bondi and haunted rock'n'roll joints in Brunswick. At home on my farm in New Zealand I can be agrarian; in Sydney I can be cosmopolitan. Bless you, Australia.

When I got to Sydney, I found an azure harbour crisscrossed by ferries, a brilliant white opera house that only genius could have dreamt up. You didn't need to wear much; the climate was as different from Wellington as you could imagine. It was still and warm and smelt of peppermint gums. The women in Kings Cross seemed so extravagantly friendly. 'Come on up, darling. Have a good time!' What generosity! To a stranger! I was so naive I had no idea what they were talking about.

I somehow heard about people auditioning for a new film, something called *My Brilliant Career*. They contacted me, who knows how, and asked me to come in. It was a casting agency, another concept entirely foreign to me. I did a little acting there, perhaps on film, I'm not sure, lines on a page with Julie Hamilton, who was already cast to play Sybylla, the lead. They were looking for a Harry, and it seems that neither Gillian

Armstrong (director) nor Margaret Fink (producer) could find exactly the person they wanted. They were both delightful, Julie seemed nice, and I gave it my best shot. I left thinking, Well, that's never going to happen.

To my astonishment, the phone went a day or two later and they told me they wanted me to play the part. I was stunned. I was told I would need an agent, whatever that was, and they recommended me one, with an address, and said I should knock on his door.

I walked up to 72 Queen Street, Woollahra, climbed a flight of stairs, knocked on the door, and behind the desk was a good-looking man in his thirties.

I said, 'Hello, my name is Sam Neill. I'm from New Zealand. I seem to have landed a good part in a film here. They tell me I need an agent. I'm embarrassed to say I don't know what an agent is. But I'm told I need one to look after me.'

He smiled and asked me to sit down. 'Hello,' he said quietly. 'My name is Bill Shanahan. I am an agent. And I will look after you.'

Bill was the sweetest man, and he took diligent care of me until the day he died, in 1992, so young like so many, from AIDS. Bill made an enormous difference to my life. He gave me confidence. He believed in me, which was more than I did. He left his excellent agency in the capable hands of Ann Churchill-Brown, who has looked after me very well ever since.

Bill had a stable of the most exciting actors in Australia. He had a big board in the office with all their headshots. There was Mel Gibson, Wendy Hughes, Johnny Hargreaves and so on. It was a very impressive bunch to be associated with. Bill was kind, and incredibly thoughtful. He also made me realise what a good agent does. For one thing, he asked for far more money than I would ever have dared to consider. For my first film in

Australia, I wasn't paid a lot by any standard but it was about three times what I would have been paid for an entire year at the New Zealand National Film Unit. I could not believe my luck.

He sent me out to get a headshot done immediately, by his favoured photographer. I'd never been photographed before by someone like that, and I rather liked the result. I thought I looked moody and broody. Mel Gibson, whom I got to know later, spotted it one day when we were in the office at the same time. He pointed to it and said, 'You look like you haven't had a good crap for a few days.' Harsh, but probably fair.

I found Australia so exhilarating that I decided to resign my job at the NFU and move to Sydney. Louise and I had lived together for four or five years, but the relationship was not to last. We sold the house on Marine Parade, and we were on our way. I am always grateful she was generous enough to give me that time, her time. The truth is, she deserved better than me, and I believe she found it.

*

So, with Bill's help, in late 1979 I found myself playing Harry in *My Brilliant Career*, opposite an actor called Judy Davis, who had replaced Julie Hamilton in the role of Sybylla. Judy was interesting. More than interesting; she was beautiful, extremely gifted and whip smart. She also seemed deeply unhappy.

I myself was as happy as the proverbial Larry. I was in the hands, mostly, of some extremely talented women. The wonderful, acute Gillian Armstrong was directing. Margaret Fink, all enthusiasm and exquisite taste, was the producer. Luciana Arrighi and Anna Senior created for us the best wardrobe of any film I've ever been in. Jill Porter (make-up) and Cheryl Williams (hair) made us look a million pounds—it is, after all, a period film set in 1897. The script was written by a woman (Eleanor Witcombe) adapted from a novel written by a woman (Miles Franklin). Luciana's design was a wonder; she absolutely knew and understood the aesthetics of these people. The cast was equally full of great women: Wendy Hughes, Patricia Kennedy, Julia Blake. I thought this preponderance of great women might be normal on Australian films. Sadly it was not to be. It should be.

To be fair, we had a few good blokes to make up the numbers. The peerless Don McAlpine shot the film. Robert Grubb, as the singing delusional other suitor, was hilarious, and so was Max Cullen. Max quietly closing the dunny door, in which he is abluting, to avoid trouble is the moment I most remember from the film. The very experienced McAlpine gave me the worst acting advice (at least for me) over a barbeque one night before we began. 'If in doubt, mate, do nothing,' he said. The theory is, I think, that the camera will do it for you, and the audience will read whatever they want in you. I see a lot of actors 'doing nothing', and I find it dead boring. And lazy.

None of the above seemed to make Judy happy. I was perplexed by this; it was clear to me, even before we began, that this would make her a star. But the whole process seemed agony for her, and she would talk wistfully about being on stage, which she regarded as *real* acting, and about actors like Robert Menzies, with whom she had just graduated from drama school. I hadn't been to drama school, so I was clearly inferior.

She has never looked so stunning on film, and that is largely because Jill and Cheryl left her to look pretty much herself; almost no make-up, allowing a few light freckles to show, and her hair remained its natural auburn, and was allowed to go wild. Sensational, but she hated it. I think this, in large part, accounted for her extreme discomfort, her prickliness in dealing with other actors (mostly me) and in taking direction. She was bloody difficult, but I was okay with that, since she was also bloody good. In addition, if I'm fully honest with myself, I was probably ever so slightly in love with her. Fat lot of good that would do me.

Some ten years later we made a film together called *One Against the Wind* in Luxembourg. My character, a British Army major, is parachuted behind enemy lines in occupied France to join Judy's character, a British aristocrat who is fighting with the Resistance. We rehearsed in London, and it was there that we nearly lost our director, Larry Elikann. There was to be a scene where our two characters kiss—the only time in the story. The sexual attraction has been building, and it culminates in this kiss.

Judy's idea was that we should *not* kiss, and the scene would be much sexier if we played it not just apart, but from opposite ends of the room. Larry was enraged, and Judy was adamant. I was just perplexed. I was, not for the first time, the peacemaker. I had worked with Larry before, and I called Judy to say he was fine. I called Larry and gave him the line I was so used to giving: 'Look, Larry, yes, she's difficult, but you know, it's worth it.' And difficult indeed she was. Somehow the next day, the kiss was agreed to and later performed, with very little pleasure. She got a Golden Globe and an Emmy, so she must have been worth it.

There was one fine summer's day in Luxembourg when Judy and I were waiting for a delayed action in a classic French car in a bucolic green landscape. I was perfectly happy, but I noticed Judy was in a dark mood. I imagine being stuck in a small auto with me, being nice as always, was an insufferable trial for her. I heard her muttering to herself what sounded like words of encouragement to see her through this misery. I leant closer to hear, and she was saying over and over: 'Think of the money, think of the money, think of the money...'

Five or six years later I was in *Children of the Revolution* with Judy, Geoffrey Rush and a very young Richard Roxburgh.

It might have been almost the most interesting film made in Australia, but somehow it isn't. It was predictably awkward as hell working with Judy, but as always I told myself it was worth it. Towards the end, I realised that for some reason she wasn't talking to me. Not even 'good morning' in the make-up trailer. I'm often slow to realise these things, but I reluctantly came to understand that it really wasn't worth it at all. Not at all. Her last faithful supporter iced. We have never spoken again. I sometimes spot her in a foyer, and I see her sharply look away. I have nothing to say to her anyway.

But back to *My Brilliant Career*. Our roles demanded that we know how to ride. Judy and I were given lessons by a big bloke, footy player–sized, who had some land near our location at Camden Park, south of Sydney. He was an ex-cop, still young, and I asked him why he'd left the force. He'd been on highway patrol for some years, and one day he had a full-scale breakdown—he said he could not take one more car accident, one more scene of carnage on the highway to Melbourne. These days my heart goes out when I see similar accidents on the news; it's

Keeping calm on my crazy horse in *My Brilliant Career*.

easy to forget the PTSD that goes with being an ambo or a cop on the wilds of country roads.

They gave me a thoroughbred racing gelding from Victoria with very little brain, totally untrained for film work, but he looked handsome. I handled him reasonably well. The horse was really only capable of turning left, as that is how they run in Victoria—anti-clockwise round the course. While we had our riding lessons, Judy still had some grudging respect for me, I think. I was marginally better than her. It was not to last. The respect.

Aside from all that, *My Brilliant Career* is a very good film indeed. It was a joy to work on. Not least for the beautiful landscape we moved in, that same enchanted eucalypt-blue land I'd spotted from the train. Camden Park, belonging to the delightful descendants of that dreadful old villain John Macarthur—he of the Rum Rebellion and the Merino sheep—is as elegant as any house anywhere. The crew, the cast, the food, the friends I made, the sublime direction from Gillian—damn, it was good. It was also something of a game changer for me. The film did extremely well, especially at Cannes. Finally, I realised, at the advanced age of thirty, I could become a full-time professional actor. A late starter if ever there was one.

Another Purge

I was thinking rather wistfully about the Annual Purge the other day. It's hard to imagine such a horror show being remembered with nostalgia, but I was afflicted for twenty-four hours by the Worst Constipation in the History of Mankind. It was extremely painful and not a little humiliating.

As a result of the treatment I'm undergoing at the moment, I was awakened in the middle of the night with a terrible pain in my lower stomach area. I realised I needed to void myself immediately. Parking myself on my very own lavatory, I breathed a sigh of contentment in expectation of the Relief of Mafeking to come.

To my surprise, there was no result at all. I tried again ten minutes later: close, but no cigar. This went on all night. Walking around, doing squats, drinking hot things: nothing helped. My bitter disappointment began to turn into something like fear. There was a time when I thought perhaps I should go to the ER. But I knew that was impossible; I would be laughed out of the hospital. So I might as well die on my own because that would be the outcome anyway.

I got maybe one hour of sleep as the pain grew worse. By morning I was exhausted and writhing in agony.

As soon as the chemist opened I bought anything and everything that might alleviate matters. I took these things fast and at great volume, and waited. And waited. Again, nothing to show for it. The pain increased and the despair with it. There was a period in the late afternoon when, having nothing left to lose, I went full Catholic and was praying to the Virgin herself. *Please release me, Mary, Mother of God. Have mercy on this poor sinner. I swear, dear Mother Mary, whatever it was, I will never do it again.*

And then, at 5.13 p.m., finally a result! I was relieved of some great and heavy burdens. If ever there was divine intervention that was it. These immense beasts, which had been a good week in gestation, left me with extreme reluctance. And inflicted as much injury on the way out as possible. One particular enormous gnarly bastard sat at the bottom of the bowl, glaring baleful-ly up at me, looking as if I had betrayed it in the most callous manner. It refused to flush at all, and sat there darkly brooding and sulking, determined to grimly hang on. It was family. Why should it have to leave home? Finally, thank you, Mother Mary, the sewage system swept it away to a better life among friends. I hope it's happy.

I Loved Bali

I loved Bali.

I had two or three months there by myself in 1979, living in what was then quite a remote village up towards the mountains, Peliatan. It was completely unspoiled, one scruffy little dirt road running through it. A bike or two or perhaps an open taxi might have weaved past once in a while, dodging potholes, but mostly nothing. Just a few houses dotted around in compounds with gardens, temples and lush jungle. It was the closest thing I've ever seen to Eden.

Life was quiet and slow, and lived along entirely traditional lines. I would go for weeks and never see another foreigner. An enormous banyan tree dominated the village, and in the cool evening the men would gather there and smoke and chat. Sometimes, you'd hear a gamelan orchestra practise somewhere in the distance. Chickens ran the place, along with scrofulous yellow dogs that barked manically as you walked past their formal doorways. It was said that God made Bali, but it was too close to paradise so he made the yellow dogs to take a bit of the shine off.

I had a little bure of my own, living among a large, happy extended family, children and grannies in abundance in their extensive compound. They were by all accounts semi-royalty in Bali, and the head of the household was called Prince Kaleran. Kaleran was a handsome, affable man who took a kindly interest in me. I had sensibly read the seminal text on Bali by Covarrubias before I got there, and was very interested in finding out all I could about Balinese culture and history. Kaleran was an authority and immensely helpful on all of this during our long chats in the morning over my black rice porridge. He found me somehow amusing, and was happy to indulge my endless curiosity.

The people were quite simply the most beautiful I'd ever seen. Kaleran's wife, the princess, looked like a goddess, and in addition had a formidable presence and intellect. She was also a famous dancer. Later she became a politician and would travel to Jakarta to represent her people there in parliament.

Life on the compound was lived as I imagine it had always been lived. Apart from the occasional white formal shirt on the men, everyone wore traditional dress. I myself wore a sarong the whole time, and learnt how to tie it so it wouldn't humiliate me by falling off my non-existent bum at critical times. The sarong also denoted a measure of respect for the locals. I got to know a lot of this very big family, and they were happy for me to drink my tea and watch these lovely, graceful women teach their girls the exquisite dance that is unique to Bali.

I lived there for the grand sum of three dollars a day, and that included a simple breakfast, which would be brought to me on my porch by some of the children, who took this task very seriously. The rest of the time they were a giggling, riotous, happy crew. In the evening I would wander over the road to a little outside restaurant of sorts, and for a dollar I could get a great feed of satay and vegetables, and a beer. If you haven't tasted goat satay, you haven't lived.

I would go for walks in the surrounding countryside. Sometimes I would cross a high rickety bridge over a dark green gorge, and far below I'd see the women gossiping and laughing while pounding the laundry on the river rocks. One morning, one of the kids followed me out into the paddy fields, and following him was a flock of maybe a hundred ducks. He had a long bamboo stick with a little white flag on the top. He would plant the stick into a muddy field, leave it there and run off to school. Somehow the ducks knew to stay close to that flag, their flag, feeding and doing duck things. In the distance you could see other flags in the paddies and palm trees, with their own flocks of ducks in attendance. At the end of the day the kid would come back and pick up the stick, and the ducks would all follow him back to the compound for a safe night's sleep.

Some days Kaleran would be kind enough to tell me what was going on somewhere else, something I might enjoy. He'd suggest a temple festival, for instance, in another village close by. Once he suggested that I might like to join a big family ceremony not far away, an important rite of passage for a child. A baby in Bali is always carried around for its first six months, and is never on any account allowed to touch the ground. You cannot risk the spirits that might come out of the earth to harm the baby during that period. So, after half a year, the priest comes to the home and, in the presence of the whole family, the child is ceremoniously lowered onto the earth, onto the planet, for the very first time. Quite a moment.

Another time I was invited to a tooth-filing ceremony. This happens when you become an adolescent. Those pointy eye-teeth that most of us have are thought to be those of the devil, and they have to be filed back by a priest with an implement that looks like you could use it in the construction of a steel building. This sweet girl lay unflinching and uncomplaining on a dais in a pavilion, around which we all crowded, while the priest sawed away on her jaw. I can only think it was agony. I was very touched to be allowed to be part of it. As in so many of these things I was the only foreigner at all.

Another time Kaleran suggested a very important ceremony

at a large temple quite some distance away. This, I think, was the principal temple connected to the most sacred Mount Agung, the live volcano that dominates Bali. The Balinese regard Bali as the Navel of the World, and Agung is the epicentre of that navel. And it is vital that the sacred mountain is placated and worshipped to keep the Balinese safe, and, more than that, to keep the entire world secure. This was the most important ceremony of the year, and thousands were there. I zoomed off on my trusty 50cc Honda moped, and this time Kaleran joined me for the day.

The most dramatic part of what I think was a three-day ceremony was a kind of trance dance that all the young men joined, stomping and singing around the huge temple complex. The choking dust, the noise, the frenetic gamelan music—all of this was overwhelming.

I would always ask if it was okay to take photographs, and Kaleran would tell me yes or no. On this particular day, the one day of the year, in an inner sanctum of one of the temples, the carved image of a god would be revealed. Elaborate carved doors were opened and inside was a colourful deity, something that looked vaguely tigerish. Riveting. I asked Kaleran if a shot would be in order. He thought for a little while, and finally said, Absolutely fine, go ahead. I took three shots on my Pentax 35mm. When I sat back down next to Kaleran I was ebullient at having taken what I thought would be beautiful photographs.

Kaleran smiled gently and said, 'Good. That's good. But don't be surprised if they don't come out.'

Of course, I knew better, and in those days rather fancied myself as a pretty good photographer. When I got back to Australia, I got all my film rolls developed and to my surprise in the packets of prints there were no shots of the god image. I took out the negative of that roll and held it up to the light. Every one of those thirty-six shots was perfect, except for numbers twenty-seven to twenty-nine, which were absolutely blank. Make of that what you will.

I travelled for a couple of weeks, first to the top of the island, very high up. I spent the coldest night of my life shivering under one blanket in a hostel above a crater lake. Bali lies just south of the equator, but it still freezes at altitude. Then on to Java, crossing the short strait by ferry. Java was, on the surface, culturally similar to Bali, but in other senses a world away. The warmth and the friendliness were absent. This was a shock.

I filmed there, out of Bondowoso, twenty-five years later. The atmosphere had further chilled, and it was no surprise to me, when it became apparent even later, that a radical Muslim movement in Indonesia had its roots in East Java.

I took an old bus up to the top of Mount Bromo, a spectacular multi-cone volcano; the mountain retriggered my obsession with volcanism, something that dated back to a film I directed at the NFU in 1976, which involved skiing down the perfect cone of Ngauruhoe, at the time very much alive and belching smoke and fumes.

I spent the night in a very basic hostel, and the next day everyone there had got themselves pre-booked with a local, along with his pony, to go across the vast crater floor to the live cone. The guides turned up in the dark, the idea being that you arrive at the cone rim as the sun comes up. My guide was the only one who didn't arrive, so I set off on foot after the others. After a while I heard a clattering behind me on the steep path. It was my guy, plus pony, spouting what could only be apologies. I was furious with him and waved him away, shouting 'No!', but he wouldn't take the hint. He stuck with me persistently, trotting alongside me, hoping I would give in. I wouldn't, and strode on all the way, grim and silent. After a truly magnificent sunrise above the boiling caldera, I came down and he was still bloody well there, waiting. I ignored him again, and walked myself doggedly all the way back. He finally left me at the end, with no satisfaction. I know I was stubborn, pathetic and petty, but I'm still angry at him! Just turn up for work on time, mate!

Anyway, it was back to Bali and Peliatan once more, and all that green quiet, before returning to Australia. I will always be thankful for that calm, peaceful time I had among those most gentle people.

Years later, I took the family to Bali on holiday. Everything had changed. Those little dirt roads were now freeways. There was traffic bumper-to-bumper. The place was entirely devoted to commerce. It was jammed with tourists, and we, of course, were part of the problem. It was kind of heartbreaking.

We went down to Jimbaran Beach near Kuta, where all the restaurants are on the sand itself. We had dinner while it got dark. A good enough experience, even if the food was pretty ordinary. Exactly a week later to the minute a bomb went off right there, killing and injuring multiple people. I suspect the terrorists were there at the same time as us, perhaps rehearsing what was to come. I wondered if these terrorists had been radicalised in East Java, where I had felt that chill, that unstated resentment.

More recently, I went back to Bali, to Ubud. I took an afternoon off to try to find Peliatan if I could. That peaceful, meandering village was now more or less a thundering commercial neon strip along the roaring road to the interior. But I did find what looked much like the gates to Kaleran's place. There was a very old man sitting outside. I said hello, and told him I was looking for someone called Kaleran. He smiled and said, 'I am Kaleran.'

I was delighted to see him and told him so. I told him about my time with them, and how much it meant to me. He was pleased to hear that, but he said he couldn't remember me at all.

To be honest, I was slightly disappointed. But why should he? I said thank you. And I meant it. And said goodbye.

Poor Choices and the Kindness of Strangers

AFTER my extreme good fortune in co-starring in *My Brilliant Career*, I almost immediately joined a film called *The Journalist*.

Sod's Law. Wikipedia says it has the reputation of being one of the worst Australian films ever. It was entirely forgettable, proof being I remember almost nothing about it. From one of the best films ever made in Australia to one of the worst. Should have learnt something. But it was not to be the last crap choice I was to make.

Before we started to shoot, Michael Thornhill, the director, took Liz Alexander and me to have lunch with Jack Thompson, so the main cast could get to know each other. It was a sunny day in a garden restaurant in Double Bay. The waiter had only just taken our orders and conversation was beginning to warm up when Jack excused himself for a moment. I spotted him over at the bar chatting to two good-looking girls. Ten minutes later they were still at it. Our starters arrived and we looked for Jack. He'd disappeared, and so had the girls. He never came back. He was a charmer.

Soon after that I went to Melbourne to do three months on the most popular soap of the day, *The Sullivans*. Rather a miserable job, if I'm honest. They always had some guest stars like me, and indeed I had replaced none other than Mel Gibson as Kitty Sullivan's new love interest. Kitty (Susan Hannaford) was Australia's sweetheart. My character was something of a cad; it turned out he was married. The relationship climaxed in Kitty running away to Sydney with my bounder. Dave Sullivan put an end to that quick smart by catching the train, punching me on the nose and whisking Kitty back to Melbourne, with her honour thankfully still intact.

It's hard to credit how much work went into a soap like that. They produced five episodes a week of *The Sullivans*. It taught you to learn your lines quickly, and make acting decisions on the fly. Not bad training, when you think about it. Guest artists were treated rather like second-class citizens by the main cast; they barely spoke to us, but I was fine with that. Michael Caton was an honourable exception, and we are still friends. We made *Rams* together not long ago.

Melbourne had the worst climate I'd ever worked in, and that included Wellington. I got to hang out a lot with John Clarke and his wife, Helen McDonald. John was establishing himself as a performer and satirist in Australia, and they were bringing up two small girls in the suburbs. There was a solidarity between us, two expats trying to make our way. I was lucky to know John. If you

Rams with Michael Caton. Old buddies.

say he was a remarkable man, you haven't even touched the sides.

We made John Ruane's *Death in Brunswick* together in the 1990s. It remains one of my favourite films, not least because of the partnership between John and me. The graveyard scene, I am told, is once seen never forgotten. The fart from the corpse was my idea, by the way. There is a shot where you can't make out what I'm up to—supposedly recoiling in horror at John's crushing of bones in Maria Di Marco's grave. The truth is I was crippled with laughter at John. I think my portrayal of Carl—the half man, half child—was pretty decent, if I say so myself. John was superb as Dave, Carl's only friend, the gravedigger. The film stands up well.

John Clarke died about five or six years ago, and we are all the poorer for it. I am still in shock.

Another expat I ran into was Mike Rudd. Melbourne had a very lively music scene, and Mike was part of it. He was at my school when I was there, rather older than me, and far cooler. When we could, my friends and I would put on our mod gear and go see his band The Chants in a basement club near

Carl and Dave, post-graveyard, in *Death in Brunswick*. John Clarke could just stand there and be funny.

Cathedral Square. They were incredible, and played all the stuff we loved. They covered the Stones, the Kinks, all R&B. He left New Zealand soon after that for Australia, and I followed his career with interest. He became quite a success in the music scene over there, with his bands Spectrum, Murtceps and Ariel. And one night, in a Melbourne pub in 1979, there he was. I couldn't believe my luck that he was over the other side of the room, having a quiet drink on his own at the bar. I almost ran over, fired with enthusiasm.

'Hi, Mike. I'm Sam Neill. You don't know me, but I've always been a great fan of yours. We were also at school together, but that doesn't matter. I think you're an amazing musician.' And more of the same drivel.

He put this beer down, turned slowly towards me. After a brief pause, he said, quietly but with purpose, 'Look. Just fuck off.' And so I did. I don't blame him.

Which puts me in mind of other musicians I've run into over the years. I suppose I am a bit of a groupie, but then music's been such an important part of my life.

I was in Washington once for a weekend with my son Tim, who was perhaps fourteen at the time. We were having lunch at the Four Seasons, when I became aware of an enormous man standing beside our table.

He said, 'Mr Neill?'

I said, 'Yes,' rather nervously.

'Mrs Springsteen would like to invite you to the show tonight.'

'Mrs *Springsteen*?'

'Yeah, I have tickets if you like.'

'Wow, sure. Thank you!'

There we were, with two primo tickets and backstage passes. I couldn't believe my luck. I said, 'Tim, can you believe it, we're going to see Bruce Springsteen tonight!'

Tim looked a little blank, and said, in a voice that was still breaking, 'Who?'

This was something of a blow. I had to explain that Bruce Springsteen was The Boss, and he was the biggest thing in America, and...still blank. Poor Tim. It was a generation thing.

So we find ourselves in this enormous stadium, and it's the last of five gigs The Boss is playing in DC that week. Bruce and his fantastic band play for two and a half hours. The audience is on its feet the whole time; they know every word of every song. It is Sunday and it is like being in church. What a show. Even my adolescent son is blown away.

Then we went backstage. To my surprise, the green room, rather than a big party, had only one other person in it, at the bar. We went over and said hi, and she said, Hello, I'm Emmylou Harris. I was weak at the knees. I'd been a fan for thirty years. Then Mrs Springsteen, Patti Scialfa, appeared and the four of us chatted for a while. Both these women were delightful and put us at our ease. I was still buzzing from the most extraordinary show.

Finally, The Boss turned up. Very pleased to see us. Lovely guy. And what completely charmed me was that he took the time to talk to Tim; really took an interest in this gawky, hilarious, goofy kid. And he told us about their own kids, who were around the same age as Tim. They hadn't seen their parents play live, since Bruce took quite a few years off touring while the children were small. To see not one but both parents rocking out on stage they found mortifying and embarrassing beyond measure.

While I'm at it, many years ago, another musical encounter. My agent told me that they were casting for someone to play opposite Barbra Streisand in a period movie that would be shot in Europe. I thought I was unlikely for it, but since they were going to fly me to New York to meet Barbra, I thought why not. So I find myself at the door of a grand suite in a grand hotel, and her partner Jon Peters answers the door. He invites me in, introduces me to Barbra and leaves us to it.

I spend a few hours with Barbra chatting about this and that. She's a charming woman. She grew up, she tells me, across the river, but didn't come to Manhattan until she was about twelve. This was dreamland, if you like, right where we are now. She tells me about the movie. It's called *Yentl*, and the more she tells me about it, the more unsuitable I realise I am. Nevertheless, it sounds very challenging, and a great part for her.

Now, I'm of the view that Streisand is a really good actor, and very capable of comedy. That's quite rare. But her music is another thing altogether. I am not a fan, although I know millions adore her singing. There's a lull in the conversation, and here's where I make a mistake.

I say politely, 'Barbra, is there any music in the film, any songs?' It doesn't exactly sound like a musical, but you never know.

She says, 'Yes, there are. Would you like to hear one?'

Of course, it would be rude to say no. We are sitting at either end of the sofa. She is about six feet away from me. And suddenly, she lets rip with 'Papa, Can You Hear Me?' at full volume. I am stunned like a mullet, and I can feel my smile beginning to freeze as the song goes on. I cannot believe this is happening.

She finishes and we both take a breath. I'm relieved, but then she says, 'Would you like to hear another?'

Again, politeness gets the better of me and I nod enthusiastically. Oh, dear God…Yes, folks, two songs from Streisand just for me. I love telling this story to my gay friends, who go green with envy. They want to kill me.

Needless to say, I wasn't offered the film and Mandy Patinkin played the guy. He's a musical kind of actor, so all this would've been perfect for him.

But back to 1979. After *The Sullivans* and then two or three months in Bali, I was offered a film that would be shot in Taiwan, directed by Phillip Noyce. I knew Phil's work from *Newsfront* and I thought him brilliant. He was a considerable figure in the New Cinema that was alive and cracking in Australia. He called me and said, 'We're gonna do a film called *Z Men.*' (Ultimately it would be called *Attack Force Z.*) 'Don't worry about the script, we will change it. And we'll have a great time.'

Mel Gibson was on board, fresh from *Mad Max*, and that was a real incentive as well. It was action, it was Phil, it was Mel—what's not to love? Well...not the script. But not to worry, Phil knew what he was doing, and we were in safe hands.

Mel and I flew in together, and had an interesting day or two in Hong Kong on the way. We were looking forward to it—exotic locations, new horizons, a new script and Phil. This was all very well, but Phil got himself fired the day before we were due to shoot in Taipei. Phil wanted to change the script, and the producers wouldn't have a bar of it. At least, that was our under-standing—no one bothered to explain it to the cast. So he was on the next plane home. Good Lord. We found ourselves in a weird state of limbo while we waited for a new director.

Finally, Tim Burstall turned up. Nice enough fellow, but not my first choice of director. Tim was famous for sexy comedies of variable quality, the most famous being *Alvin Purple*. All success-ful, but of no particular interest to me. Anyway, nothing for it but to get on with it, albeit with the script Phil had promised we would not be doing.

Taiwan was kind of a wild west, and in a state of great flux. Chiang Kai-shek had not long died, but his authoritarian finger-prints were over everything. A tightly controlled place, apart from the nightlife, which was wild indeed. The place had become much accustomed to servicing US armed forces personnel, and where we were in Taipei was like an eastern Kings Cross. You could get yourself into terrible trouble.

Chris Haywood was in the film as well, and he was trouble in himself. The headliner was an American actor called John Phillip Law. I don't think it's unkind to say he wasn't the greatest actor in the world, but he was very handsome. He carried a mirror in his top pocket and checked that everything was just so before every shot. We tried but we couldn't take him very seriously. They put him up in the poshest hotel in Taipei, a sort of red and gold palace up on the mountain. I'd like to say we didn't resent this, but we probably did. We also found out he was being paid five times more than us. Ah, well.

We were, by contrast, put in a dingy, damp hotel which seemed to double as a kind of informal brothel. Again, trouble, if you weren't careful. We got to be very good at Space Invaders. All the Australians would be out and about of an evening. The food was delicious, sushi as well as the street food, the clubs were amazing, and it was the first time I had ever been to a Japanese bathhouse. I was beginning to experience the world, and it was a far more diverse and interesting place than a boy from Dunedin could imagine.

Mel was extremely good fun. He's a funny guy, a natural comedian. He's also an immensely gifted actor. He effortlessly fits the description of leading man. You can have an opinion about Mel, go ahead, but we had fun. I see him every now and then, and I avoid any topic that might drive a wedge. He makes me laugh, but we don't agree on much. I tend to avoid judgment about others, but on the other hand I am not an apologist for Mel...All right, call me an idiot. And you will.

We had a few days of rehearsal, which didn't lead to much, but we did have a couple of days' training with the Taiwanese army. That meant handling guns, running around and, in my case, falling into a trench. My knee was painfully sprained. This, two days before we started to shoot. I was on crutches, and I faced a flight home. There didn't seem to be much in the way of western medicine available, and I was sent instead to see a venerable old man with a long wispy beard and a long Chinese traditional robe. He seemed like he was from another century altogether. He was an acupuncturist, and none of us had ever heard of acupuncture. I just had to trust the process when he started to stick long pins into me all over the place: my head, my feet…you name it, anywhere but my knee. We had no language in common and, since I thought he was making a big mistake, I gestured wildly at my knee. His shook his head in a venerable old way and so I stuck with it.

After an hour I walked out of there with no crutches. Two sessions and it was as if it had never happened at all, and on Monday I was running with a gun. That incredible old man.

The lead Taiwanese actor in the film was Ko Chun-hsiung. We were fascinated by him. And also rather scared. He clearly had some dodgy connections, shall we say, and was always

Ko Chun-hsiung in Taiwan. I am right to look a little apprehensive.

accompanied by some bruiser bodyguard types. Who never smiled. The bodyguards would always check for bombs under the big vehicle they drove him around in, before he was ushered on board. That's how we knew he was no ordinary actor like us. He once took us all out for a big night, and everything became much clearer. We got home in one piece, but only just. Terrifying. By contrast, the great Sylvia Chang was in the film as well, a model of decorum, but sadly I wasn't in any scenes with her.

Taiwan was filthy—so polluted that, even on a fine day, you couldn't see the other end of the street. But there were pockets of beauty, particularly in the mountains, a reminder of those beautiful rice terraces that curve elegantly around the mountainsides in Bali. Towards the end, we shot in a national park at the far south of the island that was not unlike the wind-blasted nether regions of Wellington.

We got through it okay, but sadly it never got any better than the script. We did our best, you can't ask more than that. We loved the Taiwanese crew. We had no language in common, but it mattered not. Good will and good humour go a long way.

We got back to Australia, and I went straight into an ABC drama being made in Melbourne called *Lucinda Brayford*, starring my pal Wendy Hughes. Melbourne, with Sod's Law as per, was too hot already. I got to wear a nice white suit and played a rejected suitor one more time. Wendy was completely delightful and utterly brilliant. There's nothing more comfortable and rewarding than working opposite someone you know well, who trusts you, and you just get along. You can make the page sing.

And then somebody switched the points on my railway line again. Luck was on my side, and I have no idea why. We were shooting on an ABC stage when an assistant director crossed the floor with a message for me. 'There's a phone call for you, Sam.'

This was in the day of landlines, and no one ever called you on set. 'It's from Switzerland.'

I picked up the phone, very puzzled, and a strangely familiar voice said, 'Hello, this is James Mason. You don't know me, but my wife and I watched your film *My Brilliant Career*, and we think you're good. And, what is more, we think you should be working beyond Australia. So I'm sending you an air ticket. We would like you to come and stay with us in Switzerland, and then go on to England and meet my agent. What do you say?'

You already think I'm an idiot, but I'm not *that* big an idiot. The kindness of strangers. A few weeks later, I was on my way.

Gielgud

IN 1984 we shot *Plenty*, directed by the brilliant Australian lout Fred Schepisi. We shot it in both London and France, in an unusually benign northern summer. It was my first film with Meryl Streep, of whom I was terrified, and my first with Charles Dance. And my first with Schepisi. Fred was to become a close friend. It also featured Sting, the divine Ian McKellen, Sir John Gielgud and Tracey Ullman. My God, *she* is a force of nature, and funny as a fight.

Meryl and Charlie loathed each other. I like both of them, but Meryl seemed to take a violent dislike to Dance virtually at first sight. It was reciprocated. Charlie was a newly arrived star; he'd recently had a big success in *The Jewel in the Crown* on the telly. Brand New Stars can sometimes appear a teeny bit up themselves for a while. Privately he was probably quaking with fear, as a big movie lead opposite the formidable Meryl Streep. He's fine now, by the way. Delightful, in fact. People usually get over themselves in time.

It all started without me, but in week one I thought I'd drop by the set, in a mansion in West London, and make myself known. And familiarise myself with how things were, now we were shooting. Observe. Watch Meryl work.

A strange thing happened as I pulled up in my BMW 5, the car that had rescued me from my Porsche error, in Holland Park. Over the road I spotted Sir John Gielgud talking to some crew, having just got out of a car. He was eighty by now, and the grandest of grand among British actors. I felt a little shy—I'd never met him before—so I dawdled and pretended I had a few things to do in the boot of my car.

Michael Stevenson, the greatest second assistant director of all time, was looking after Sir John along with a new and nervous runner, or some kind of assistant, called something like Sebastian. His parents were clearly well connected in the film business. He looked white as a ghost standing in the diminutive shadow of the great Sir John Gielgud.

According to Michael, Johnny Gielgud spotted me across the street, momentarily froze, then turned to Stevenson. 'Michael,' he said with a smile. 'Who *is* that *interesting* young man over the road?'

'That's Sam Neill, Sir John. He is also in the film.'

'Oh. Oh, Sam Neill,' said Gielgud, turning to the unfortunate blushing assistant. 'Sam Neill. I hear he's fucked absolutely everyone in London.' He paused. 'Has he fucked *you*, Sebastian?'

Sebastian looked suitably aghast, and stammered, 'No. No, Sir John,' several times.

I found this story pretty unlikely, if very funny. I thought it beyond probability that Gielgud had ever heard of me. I was hardly a West End star, and to this day I have never even stepped foot on a London stage. Nor had I fucked everyone in London. Not by a very, very, very long shot. On the other hand, Michael had no reason to make it up. Slanderous, really.

But then, years later, I met Michael Caine at a film festival in Toronto.

I admire Michael perhaps more than any other screen actor alive, not least because he tells the best stories. He was giving a talk at the festival. I got a ticket and he was wonderful. He told this story (try to hear it in the famous Caine voice):

'When I was a young bloke, I was once staying in a hotel

in Bristol. I came out of my room. And ran straight into Cary Grant. Cary Grant!

'I said, "You're Cary Grant!"

'He said, "I know!"'

Caine took questions at the end, and I couldn't help but stick up my hand. I asked him about tips for acting in cinema. Mainly because I wanted to hear his famous advice about love scenes. To wit—before a love scene, *always* suck a mint, and kindly offer one to the lady with whom you are playing. He recognised me, and chuckled, which was flattering. And duly gave the mint advice.

Afterwards he asked me to dinner, with a bunch of important film-type people. I sat beside him and was in stitches to the end. At one point he turned to me and said, 'Sam, have I told you my Sam Neill story?'

'Well, no, Michael. We only just met tonight.'

'Well, Sam. John Gielgud. Funnily enough, I only met Gielgud a bit later on in life. First thing he said to me. He said, "Hello, Michael. Now, Michael, are you like that Sam Neill? Have you fucked everyone in London?" Just like that.'

I mean...bloody Gielgud. There are thousands of Gielgud stories. That's mine. Years after that we shot *Merlin* in London. Gielgud had a day or two only on the film—sadly without me. He was ninety-four at the time. Our lovely director Steve Barron asked him why he kept working when he could so easily have retired decades ago.

'My boy,' Gielgud said. 'I have a *very* expensive boyfriend.'

I'm sad that I was in two films with Gielgud but we were never in the same scene. I am also sad I have never worked with Michael Caine.

That night Michael's wife, Shakira, was also at dinner. It's commonly agreed she is perhaps the most beautiful woman who ever walked the planet. I named one of my beautiful cows after her. Lady Caine. If she ever heard that, I hope she took it well. It's as great a compliment as I can bestow. Helena Bonham Carter, similarly divine, has also been so honoured. Helena has had some nine calves to date and is still going strong. Helena (human version) has been a pleasure to work with—twice—and is going stronger than ever. I have known her since she was a kid, really. She has become the most accomplished clever actor imaginable. She is also a very dear friend.

But back to that posh house and the *Plenty* set. Gielgud, Streep and a few others were sitting around on these plush sofas chatting a trifle stiffly between shots.

Now, David Hare had written the play *Plenty* for his then girlfriend Kate Nelligan, who'd enjoyed a triumph with it on the West End and Broadway. She was, I'd imagine, miffed to not be playing the same role in Schepisi's film. And I'd also hazard a guess that Meryl might have been a little tentative about taking it on, when the part was so closely associated with Nelligan.

During a temporary silence, Gielgud, who was famously gaffe-prone, was heard to announce to the assembly, 'Of course,

Helena Bonham Carter, mother of at least nine calves.

Kate was *simply marvellous* in this part.'

All eyes on Meryl, who visibly stiffened. The silence that followed was deafening. On day two of the shoot this would have been a crusher for a lesser actor but, predictably, Meryl was simply marvellous. Of course.

No one ever knew which of Gielgud's gaffes were deliberate and which were simply ingenuous. That's what made them so delicious.

Morning Walks and Loved Ones

I'VE started to talk to strangers on the street.

I make myself walk every day, even if I don't feel like it. I'm always glad that I've made the effort. But it is an effort sometimes, and one of the things I notice about what I'm going through at the moment is that just walking up to Crown Street can sometimes feel like Everest. I can hear Ed Hillary whispering in my ear, 'What the hell would you know, sonny, did you ever beat the bastard?' But in my own small way, I am attempting to conquer a bastard right now.

I do enjoy wandering around Surry Hills. It is a maze of alleyways, old factories, charming old working-class terraces and a lot of entirely necessary but ugly public housing. It is surprisingly leafy, and it's always easy to find a good coffee and sit under a tree somewhere in the sun. It's the place where I bought my very first house on my own, a tiny terrace on Bennett Street. It's a considerably safer place now, but it is still lively, and everywhere you get a sense of its industrial past and its criminal history. The notorious Tilly Devine, madam, and sly grog and cocaine dealer, lived just around the corner between the wars. She had blokes with razors to enforce her rules and collect her debts. Nearby there's a plaque that marks the spot of the last outbreak of bubonic plague in Australia, as recently as 1921. I myself live in what was once a suitcase factory. Here they made portmanteaus and lunchboxes for Australians of another time.

But it does feel a little solitary up here, living on my own. So I've decided to just stop and talk to people if I like the look of them. This morning I noticed an old woman across the park who looked even more solitary than me. I walked over and asked her if she was okay. She said, Yes, I'm okay. I said that I only asked because she looked a little lonely. She looked up then, gave me a small wan smile and looked away. I left it at that.

Yesterday I was wandering down an alley I hadn't explored before, and outside one of the minute houses was a woman about my age, tending to some flower pots. I said, What a lovely little laneway this is. She smiled and said, Isn't it. I've lived here for forty-something years and, you know what, I bought my house off Wendy Hughes.

Wendy Hughes! My new friend was an old friend of one of the first people who made me feel at ease and welcome in Australia. She was on *My Brilliant Career* with me. We took a shine to each other, and she was outrageous fun. She was also a comfort, when working opposite Judy Davis became difficult for me.

Wendy was generous and warm. There was never anything remotely romantic between us; she was just a really good friend. I loved her.

She was an old-fashioned true beauty. She had movie-star glamour, like Lauren Bacall. Breathtaking. She was also an immensely good actor, versatile and magnetic on the screen. When I met her she was with Chris Haywood, and things didn't look very happy to me. Later she was with Patric Juillet, who could carelessly flick his wavy dark hair out of his eyes with a grace that only a Frenchman could muster. Patric had a fancy French restaurant at the posh end of Oxford Street. Noriko and I saw a lot of both of them in Los Angeles years later. It was Patric who told me, with forceful authority, that there was no reason not to drink red wine with fish. I'm not sure if this was good advice, but I still pass it on with a similar sense of absolutely knowing what I'm talking about. In fact, I stand by it as far as pinot noir goes, that most versatile of wines.

Wendy could also be a very naughty girl. She drank for Australia, and was pretty much a chain-smoker. She was one of those people who could make smoking look glamorous. Inevitably it got her in the end. But the drinking was interesting, not to say downright terrifying.

In 1980 a bunch of Australians plus me, maybe thirty of us, were invited, for reasons that eluded all of us, to the film festival at Sorrento in Italy. There were people like Barry Humphries, Thomas Keneally, Bruce Beresford: all kinds of louts. This was an important time for me, because one of those louts was Bryan Brown. This was where I first met Bryan, over beers. We clicked,

Wendy Hughes. So beautiful.

and ever since that time he has been my closest and most loyal friend. For that alone, I express my thanks to those worthies who organised that peculiar film festival on the Neapolitan peninsula. They hadn't a clue as to who any of us were, but they were immensely hospitable, as only southern Italians can be.

One night we were presented with mysterious awards on stage at Teatro di San Carlo in Naples. It was televised nationally, and I imagine the Italian public were as puzzled as we were. All of us got a prize for something. I was awarded, and graciously accepted, a statue for an Australian film that had been made in 1936. We were all wearing the best clothes that we had, but we were an extremely scruffy-looking bunch. In the wings I spotted an immaculate Marcello Mastroianni, dressed in a three-piece white linen suit. I thought, This is too good a chance, and I should take the opportunity, so I sauntered over and introduced myself, and stammered the usual fanboy stuff. Embarrassing. Marcello glanced sideways at me, took a drag on his cigarette-holder, muttered *grazie* and turned away.

My friend Wendy was among us, and one night as we were all in the bar, she turned on me. Just like that. She gave me the most humiliating dressing-down of my life. It was blistering. She mocked me as a little, little man. I was speechless; I had done nothing to deserve this. I went to bed very upset and genuinely astonished.

The next morning I was still feeling desolate. Kind Judy Morris, a contemporary and a very good actress, came up to me. She said, 'Sam, I'm sorry about last night. It's happened to all of us, and you have to understand that if you want to be Wendy's friend, it'll happen to you too. It's the alcohol and that's what happens.'

I took that on board and, when I saw Wendy again later in the day, it was as if nothing had happened. She was just as warm and delightful as ever. Nothing had changed, nothing at all. From then on, I could recognise The Switch, just before she would turn. And I knew it was time to make myself scarce; it was a bit like being under machine-gun fire, and I never wanted it to happen again. Disappear, that was the trick.

As my work took me away around the world more and more, I saw less of Wendy than I would've liked. One of the last things she did as an actress, and with me, was a short film that Bryan himself produced, one of the *Twisted Tales*. This was not long before she died. She was still beautiful and still delightful, but it's fair to say you could tell she'd partied hard. It's a sadness to me that she kept her illness a secret, telling only a very few people. I was not one of them, and I was gutted to hear she died in her house down on the south coast. I do wish I'd had a chance to say goodbye. I loved her.

Brutal Brilliance: *Possession*

ONE of the best films I was lucky to be in is *Possession*. This is by no means a universal view. Not many people have ever seen it and, of those who have, it is true that many loathe it. I myself regard it as a masterpiece, albeit a very flawed masterpiece. I am not alone in that view.

We shot it in the summer of 1980, in a strangely empty Cold War Berlin. The director was a crazed, dangerous Polish genius, Andrzej Żuławski. Żuławski was a handsome, charismatic and wild filmmaker. I didn't like him much; what he saw as direction often was just downright bullying. But he had vision, he was a true cineaste. And they are rare.

I was starring opposite Isabelle Adjani. This in itself made me somewhat apprehensive. I had admired Isabelle's work from a distance: she was a force to be reckoned with in contemporary French cinema, immensely talented and heartbreakingly beautiful. And I was just an ordinary bloke from Dunedin.

Isabelle was a curiosity to me. Tiny, bird-like, almost invisible; if you saw her on the street, you'd barely notice her. But there was something about her, something chemical, something *alchemical* about Adjani combined with celluloid. She was mesmerising on screen. They shot the infamous subway scene before I began shooting, and I went to see the dailies. Just her, a shopping bag, some soup and a frightening, giddy commitment to madness in an empty subway tunnel. A crazy woman miscarries, and that miscarriage becomes a monster. It is visceral, disgusting and terrifying all at the same time. I'd never seen anything like it, and I still haven't.

I was playing a spy (Mark) who on returning home from a mission finds his wife (Anna) wants a divorce. Isabelle and I worked in a close partnership for eight weeks, very close. She was immediate, and in the moment, and electrifying to be with in the same room, in the same scene. She was intensely collaborative. But I cannot say that I knew her any better at the end than I did at the beginning. She was completely mysterious and unknowable. But that was fine by me. This film was so all-consuming, there was barely anything left of either of us to offer. It just ate you.

At the end of the day I would go back to my hotel, utterly spent, and run a bath and listen to music (Genesis) as I tried to breathe normally again. It was an exhausting process.

Żuławski asked more of you than you could possibly give. There were times when he would scream, bellow at Adjani right in her face. It was distressing to see. You thought you yourself couldn't be crazier than you were, but you were mistaken. You needed to triple that. Nowadays I doubt you'd get away with it. But with Żuławski, you would do whatever it was he wanted. And although that makes me sound like a classic victim of abuse, which in a sense I think we were, it was more than that. We had complete belief in him as an artist, and we wanted to make this thing, whatever it was. We really wanted to be in This Thing. We were making something bigger than ourselves.

But this one day was worse than anything else. There's a scene in the kitchen where Mark (me) slaps Anna (Isabelle) hard on the face. Now, I have never raised my hand in anger or in any other way to any other human being in my life. In the movies you pretend these things. You fake it, but you can sell it: make people believe it on film. Movies are fake; hate to tell you so. But no, Żuławski wanted the real deal.

I couldn't believe what I was being asked to do. Not just slap Adjani, but slap her hard, more than once. I cannot tell you how distressed this made me and I refused. But then Adjani herself came to me and said, 'Sam, you must do this. You must.'

Christ almighty, now I had no choice. Rightly or wrongly, I did as I was told.

Inevitably there were multiple takes, at least three, of this real violence. Adjani took it much better than me. She was tough. And there is a close-up of her that is indelibly imprinted on my mind. She reels away from the blow, turns her head back towards Mark, wipes the blood from her mouth and laughs in contempt at him. The shot and Adjani are so powerful—I don't know, maybe it was worth it.

When the scene was done, I found some fire stairs where I could shakily be alone. I put my head in my hands and wept for ten minutes. I was convulsed with shock and sadness.

Another time, I was the one who took the beating.

In this scene, Anna enters the Cafe Einstein to see an enraged Mark, who starts throwing tables and chairs around. At least three burly waiters wrestle Mark to the ground. Again, it had to be for real. We had these mad guys from Hungary, who were ostensibly stunt people. That meant that they were willing to do any kind of crazy shit that Żuławski asked them to do. In this case, it was to beat the crap out of me. Given that we had no common language, my screams of agony just looked like good acting to them.

One reason some find the film problematic is that it bestrides a number of different genres. Or arguably falls between a number of stools. It is on the one hand a dissection of a painful marital break-up. Żuławski was going through the same process back home in Poland, and the story is in some sense autobiographical. It is also a kind of monster movie. The monster is in Mark's head, but none the less real for that. Or surreal. I love the way the film is permeated by some kind of existential dread, something we could palpably feel as we filmed in Kreuzberg, in the shadow of the Berlin Wall. I could see armed East German guards walking up and down No Man's Land, with us in their binoculars. The strip was supposedly mined, and the crew claimed they'd often see rabbits being blown to smithereens after making the wrong bunny hop. The Cold War was very weird, certainly in Berlin.

Another thing I was obliged to do was drive an immense BMW 1000cc motorbike. The largest thing I'd ever been on before was my 50cc moped in languorous Bali. I had two lessons to graduate to something immensely more dangerous. This consisted of having to plunge myself into full traffic on the autobahn, with a German instructor bellowing Teutonic instructions into my helmet speaker. *Rechts! Links!* Blinker! Blinker! *Blinker!*

When the time came to shoot the motorbike stuff, it was pretty much all me. Riding full tilt behind a handheld camera,

Taking direction from Andrzej Żuławski when I really should have known better.

seemingly centimetres away, weaving in and around Berlin. Utterly insane. I did my best to hide my terror. Mark's accident, where he rockets off the bike across the road, scraping himself all the way, was one of the completely nuts Hungarians. It was twice as dangerous as even Żuławski would ask for.

For all its crazy shit, I still think it's amazing. It is the stuff of legend that Adjani had a shattering breakdown in the wake of the film. I entirely understand. But we took it to Cannes, and after wrestling through a frenzied mob of photographers (security was much less controlled in those days) we showed the film. It had the most extraordinary reception. It enraged half of the audience, the other half of which was enraged by them, because they themselves thought it was brilliant. When Isabelle and I left, it was like being in a maelstrom. We were separated, losing our footing, and were borne away by a mad crowd of continentals. And I never saw her again.

Isabelle got Best Actress there at Cannes, and she deserved it.

Flats

I'M a crusty old bachelor now, and not afraid to admit it. It's a conundrum that a lot of people come across at some point. Where does the line lie between solitude and loneliness? And does there come a point in your single life where you are not only reluctant to live with someone again, but you strongly suspect that no one in their right mind could put up with you? You're just an unbearable old bastard. That old bastard is fighting cancer now as best he can, up here in his solitary flat. So far, so good.

I do like flats, though. I like the way you can walk away with the door closed behind you; you don't have a lawn to mow; someone else cleans the downpipes. And when you come back, nothing's changed; it's just a dustier version of what you left. When you've lived an itinerant life as I have, that's a strange comfort. Something has a small sense of permanence.

For anyone of my age, flatting comes with all kinds of connotations. Flatting meant freedom, it meant squalor, it meant sex if you were lucky, it meant freezing cold and bathrooms green with mould.

Some people near me in Central Otago had a son at Otago University. His mother was vaguely concerned for his welfare, so they went down to check on their nineteen-year-old boy. Eventually they found the grim place in which he was flatting. The toppling piles of empty pizza boxes at the front door did not bode well. Inside, the kid looked sickly ill. They hurried him off to a doctor, and the diagnosis was scurvy. Scurvy is not something you hear about much these days, even in the Royal Navy. But that is hardcore flatting. I have a grudging admiration for that young man.

Flatting also meant companionship. I've flatted with some great blokes. In Ashburton one summer, and I'm not entirely sure how we did this, we rented a huge homestead that was nevertheless close to the middle of town. The grounds had gone wild and were so extensive I can only believe they now are covered by a housing subdivision. The house itself was wooden New Zealand Victorian Gothic, complete with turrets and witches hats. No one had lived in it for years, and there was a good half-inch of dust over absolutely everything. Not that there was anything much in there. It was empty, and felt, after dark, a bit haunted.

· My room wasn't a ballroom, but it was at the very least the biggest drawing room you ever saw. Total contents of said vast room—one mattress, one pillow, one sleeping bag. There were no curtains, of course, so I would wake up at first light looking at the dust motes floating in the summer air. This was the first place I ever experienced asthma. Asthma was something that happened to other boys at school, not me. But one night on that mattress I woke up and found I couldn't breathe, and as I gasped for air I plunged into panic. Thankfully, my girlfriend Lou was with me. She told me to lie on my side, and calmed me down. She saved me.

We lived there in squalor, despite the grand surroundings. After a day's hay carting you are completely filthy. But the plumbing, such as it was in the old place, only allowed for one bath a day. We had to take it in turns. One of us had a girlfriend somewhere else in Ashburton, and he'd go round there and clean up. Lucky bastard. The rest of us looked like street people.

The house was called, of all things, Bleak House. This has always puzzled me. I mean, even the most diehard Dickens fan

Flatting, 1969.

would surely not go that far, to build your dream house and give
it that extraordinarily stark name. No wonder it was abandoned.

In 1969 I flatted in Hereford Street in Christchurch, in an Art
Deco icebox, with Pip Hall, Stu Mackenzie and Pete Steel. This
one was not so squalid. We were all still at university and very
good friends, but we were already going in different directions. I
was dipping my toe into drama. Pip, who was never particularly
academic at school, was doing well in his law studies, on his way
to an outstanding career as a barrister and QC. Pete Steel was
shining at accountancy, which was double Dutch to me. And Stu

Mackenzie already had a faraway look in his eyes; soon he would leave New Zealand for good and have an extraordinary life as an international polo player.

In this flat there was a surprising amount of discipline. Needless to say, this was not my idea. But everybody had to do their bit to keep the place clean...well, more or less. And once a week it was obligatory to shop and cook a dinner for your flatmates, plus the occasional guest. I had to learn to cook, because anything less than a decent meal meant getting a heap of shit from your friends. Lesson learnt. So, to this day, although I have never had any pretensions to being any kind of a chef, I can at least cook a foursquare meal. And here, in my single old man's life, I know how to keep the place orderly, and I can drum up a decent feed. Thanks, Stu, Pete and Pip, for that.

*

The best flat I ever had was in Kentish Town in London. It was a whole top floor of what had been a piano factory. It wasn't as big as it sounds, but it was light and airy and had a small roof garden with a view as far as Crystal Palace. I bought it about three years before I got married to Noriko and we moved back to New Zealand. We would stay there if I was working in London, or I was on holiday, or just in London to see my son Tim, who lived there with his mum, Lisa Harrow.

I loved that place. Kentish Town wasn't exactly Holland Park at that point; it was pretty rough. Someone got murdered in the pub around the corner while we were there. And at one point, in my absence, some lads from the nearby estate tried to burn our building down by posting burning fuel-soaked rags through the front-door letterbox. And when you'd park your car on our little street, you were always thankful the next day that no one had broken in and stolen your radio once again.

I never rented the place out when I was away, but I would instead allow friends and family to stay, particularly those who couldn't afford to live in London, ostensibly to look after the place. No one ever took the last part of that seriously. Hardly a week goes by when I don't run into someone who will say, 'I went to a fantastic party at your flat in Kentish Town. Best bloody party ever!' Needless to say, I was never myself the host of any of those wonderful parties, or even there to clear up the bloody mess.

Being a fairly rundown area, it was inevitable there would be a few actors in the vicinity. Tom Bell lived around the corner above a shop. Further down the road were Bill Nighy and the glamorous Diana Quick. I was pleased to get to know them a bit. At that time, as is often the way with couples, Diana was busy but, unaccountably, Bill often seemed to be out of work. This was a puzzle, as among my peers he was very highly regarded. Bill was a gentle soul, quiet and sweet. Diana by contrast was lively and vivacious. Bill could drink and smoke like few I've ever met, and yet always remained completely civilised. This is not easy to do. Eventually, though, he gave all that up, and has worked absolutely nonstop from that day on. He is one of nature's gentlemen, the most dapper man in London, and a very good actor indeed.

I sold the place in the 1990s because we needed the capital to buy the cottage next door in Sydney. I couldn't have timed it worse. A matter of weeks after it went, the London property market, which had been pretty level for decades, suddenly went into overdrive. Some people have the knack for these things, and I don't. Sometimes the kids will look at me and say, Why did you sell that flat, Dad? They loved it. And I ask the same thing of myself. Why? Bloody thing would be worth millions now. The answer, of course, is that I bought the cottage next door largely for them. Children, my children, don't think I don't regret this. And please, for the love of God, don't ask me that question ever again.

*

At the Kentish Town flat, something remarkable happened that I've never quite understood and certainly not forgotten.

Somewhere around 1990, I got a call from Michael Foster, my British agent, who said that Dennis Potter wanted to meet me. I couldn't have been more surprised. Dennis Potter was arguably the most exciting writer, certainly for television, in Britain during the seventies and eighties. I remember seeing *Those Blue Remembered Hills* and being swept away. More recently he'd become famous, very unusual for a television writer, for the great *The Singing Detective*, with Michael Gambon, and *Pennies from Heaven*, with Bob Hoskins. No one had seen anything like these before, and indeed no one had been so bold or innovative with the telly. He was a phenomenon. Both Gambon and Hoskins sealed their reputations as screen stars with these works. Potter was the hottest writer in Britain by a country mile.

I got a further call from Michael to say that not only did Potter want to meet me, but he would come to me, rather than the usual business of making your way to Soho and having an awkward conversation over a casting table. His coming to me instead was in itself flattering.

So not long after that, the bell went, and I opened the door and there was the famous Dennis Potter. A small, bespectacled man, slightly stooped and very unassuming. I invited him in. And here I did something that I've always regretted. I took his hand and shook it. This sounds prosaic enough, mannerly even, but I should've remembered about his debilitating condition, his painful psoriasis, combined with some sort of arthritis. *The Singing Detective* is largely about this. But he held out his hand and I took it. I hope I didn't see him flinch as I gave him my usual New Zealand farming shake. His hand was not so much a hand, more a tiny claw. I felt terrible. But I sat him down and made a cup of tea for us both.

We made some small talk, but it was clear he wanted to get on with discussing the script he'd sent me. I wanted to talk about it as well, because I just didn't get it. I didn't understand what he was trying to realise. And it was apparent that this would be a very personal project, because he was going to direct it himself. It was also going to be a movie, not something made for television.

But I wanted to clarify something first. I asked him, Why me? Why, of all people, did he want *me* to be the lead in what was his first time directing a feature film? I couldn't believe it.

He blinked at me a couple of times, and looked at me through his bottle glasses. And he said, 'Because I think you are the world's most underrated actor.'

I questioned for a second, did he really say that? But yes, he had, with the utmost sincerity. No one has ever said anything so generous to me.

I enjoyed his company, and I was honoured that he'd come to see me. But I still didn't understand the script. And it seems implausible to say now, but I turned down, of all people, Dennis Potter. I felt rotten about it.

Ultimately it was the right decision. It was one of the rare things he did that was, by all accounts, an absolute stinker. Shame.

*

At the Kentish Town flat, I would walk around to the Pakistani shop on the corner, and buy my morning *Guardian*. And it was here that the greatest gaffe of my life took place. Still today I blush and sweat to think of it.

We are all of us prone to the occasional gaffe, and I am no exception. Not at the Gielgud level, you understand, but there have been one or two doozies.

One sunny morning on the way back to the flat I ran into June, an ex of my old friend John Hay. I liked her a lot: she was Irish and fun; all three of us had gone on a road trip years before, up to Queensland in my disgraceful old Holden station wagon. We drank, we smoked some dope, we threw ourselves into the surf. It's what you did in Australia back then.

With June on this lovely morning was a young mother, her best friend, also wreathed in smiles. As well she might, because she was pushing a double stroller in which sat the most beautiful identical toddlers. Now, I *never* coo over babies; as a rule I find other peoples' babies not merely uninteresting, I actively avoid them like the plague.

But these two were different. They were utterly irresistible. I leant over them, gushing like a mad granny.

'Well, look at you two. You are so completely gorgeous and completely beautiful. And so *cute*, and who knitted your wonderful, hilarious, cute jumpsuits? They make you look like your little legs are on back to front. Adorable!' I chortled.

I looked up. The smiles had vanished. The air was suddenly chilled. There was an ominous silence.

I stood up. What had happened?

June was stone-faced. She cleared her throat. 'Well, Sam,' she said. 'As a matter of fact, they are going into hospital next week. For that very problem. A major operation.'

They strode off, leaving me speechless. If the ground could have swallowed me up right then and there, I would've given thanks to a greater power of any kind.

Bloody Bryan Brown

AFTER my first chemo, it took only a little over two weeks for the hair to disappear completely from the top of my head. My brother was unkind enough to say, as we FaceTimed, Black men look cool bald, but white men look like some giant's thumb. I am no exception. I look like a boiled egg that's been sitting around in the pot long after the water has dried up. Someone has peeled that egg, but not very well.

At the same time, immediately after I'd undergone my first treatment, my friend and nemesis, Bryan Brown, made a good attempt at setting himself on fire.

You would think throwing petrol on a bonfire would be the kind of error a grown man of his standing, someone who's been around the block once or twice, would avoid. Alas, no. This enormous bonfire was sulking with only diesel as encouragement. So Bryan sloshes on the gas. Silly bugger caused an explosion that blew him back off his feet, scorched all the hair off his head, and inflicted quite major burns on his face, arms and hands. Bryan was screaming and writhing on the ground. His wife Rachel, unfazed, emerged from the house and tipped a saucepan of cold water over him. To not much avail. Bloody painful, poor old bugger.

He spent some days in a burns unit somewhere in North Sydney, after a dramatic flight courtesy of the flying doctor. As I write he is now in a surprisingly quick recovery, but for a couple of weeks he was quite unrecognisable, puffed up like a red Michelin man. He's still red and sore, but he does at least look like Bryan. More than that, he looks like me. We look like two weird old duck eggs, from the same use-by batch. That this should happen at exactly the same time beggars belief.

Laura Dern was hilariously appalled. 'This was supposed to be *your* time, Sam!' she said. 'And he has to go do this! How far does this competitiveness need to go? I mean, really, the *narcissism*.'

None of it is attractive, none of it. And I made it worse two nights ago. My beard has been under attack for a while now, at least the last ten days. And then in the hospital the other night, and when I woke in the morning, my pristine white pillow was covered in beard. Like an old spaniel had moulted on the bed. It was definitely on the way out, but it was worth hanging on to the vestiges for as long as I could.

I woke up a couple of nights ago, stumbled into the bathroom, and noticed that my moustache was weirdly black, while everything else on my face was ghostly white. I meant to trim the moustache, but mistakenly buzzed it all off. In the morning I realised my error, since the remainder of the beard was like a white fringe around the face. I had turned into an unwitting Quaker Oat. I decided to dispense with the rest of the beard altogether.

Big mistake. I've had a beard for quite some time, and this has meant I haven't seen my own face for many years. Fifteen years, I'm thinking. And here was my face, now entirely unadorned. This was no small shock. Time has not been kind to it in the meantime. I'm not just wrinkled in the space where there formerly resided a beard, I am positively wizened. Three or four strokes of my trimmer and I had aged twenty years. Just like that.

And then today another setback, this time at the hands, once again, of Bryan Brown, Esq. I took my daughter Maiko, her partner, Sly, and baby to visit the great man in residence on the other side of Sydney. He was as pleased to see us as we were delighted to see him. This was our first in-person contact after my news and his pyrotechnics. We spent an afternoon in amiable chat, telling jokes, swearing like troopers…the usual nonsense.

But I was eyeing him suspiciously all the while from across the table. The first thing was, to my intense irritation, his hair had begun to grow back. Not only that, I suspected that there was more hair on the way than he had had before.

The second thing, again to my dismay, was that he looked as if he'd had an amazing facial. Even at the worst of the injury, he'd say, 'Mate, people pay thousands for the facial I'm getting!' The idea that this would all be free, absolutely no charge at all, was completely thrilling to him. All the sunspots, the warts, the moles, the gnarly growths…all magically gone. His skin looked great. Even his burnt hands seemed rejuvenated.

You can understand my mixed feelings. My friend was much better, almost all healed, and therefore I was very pleased. But he was much better looking than before, and certainly much better looking than me, which put me into a state of quiet disappointment.

What a complete bastard. Not only had he gone to all the trouble to outdo me in the sympathy stakes by blowing himself up, but he'd had a cunning plan underneath it, all the while. It was, of course, a plot to make him not only more handsome than before, but to out-handsome me by a factor of a hundred. And, what was more, it had succeeded on both counts. I feel a little bitter just writing this.

This is not the first time he's attempted something like this. Bryan has always been twenty times more sporty than me. He surfs gracefully and effortlessly, for instance. It's horrible going to the beach with him to see how bloody good he is. He's a pretty ordinary horse rider, but then again he wasn't brought up with horses, so I overlook that.

But I noticed with grave suspicion some twenty years ago that he had started to ski, at least to learn to ski, with great diligence. This went on season after season, Bryan and Rachel heading typically for Italy, and the boy was enjoying himself immensely. Now, skiing is the one thing, the one solitary thing, that I knew I was better at, better by far than Bryan. I started skiing when I was about ten years old, best guess. And for me it's like riding a bike. I'm not saying I'm a brilliant skier, but I'm a pretty good one. It is the only athletic activity that I can pull off with some flair. The idea that Bryan could be better at this, this particular thing, the only thing I'm better at than him, was simply unbearable.

And then after about ten seasons of Bryan learning from the very best, in all the very best ski resorts of the world, we finally got to ski together. We were ascending the mountain in Deer Valley, just he and I on the lift. I was in a state of quiet apprehension. Would I have to ski my arse off to keep up with the bastard? Would I be able to keep up at all? I had absolutely no idea.

We arrived at the top, and I let Bryan go first, and he skied away to find somewhere to pause and get our bearings at the top of the run. As soon as Bryan left the lift, the second he pushed himself away, my heart lifted in gladness. My prayers, if I actually prayed, had been answered. In spite of all the tuition, in spite of all the naked ambition to be better than me, as soon as I saw his arse forty-five degrees up in the air, I realised none of it had worked. He looked like a goose. And there was no way in the world, none under God's creation, that he would ever be as good as me. I wanted to shout, 'Hallelujah!'

So then, back to today at Bryan's house. I was balefully eying up the newly minted spring chicken across the room. Another blinding success for Bryan. He'd gone to immense trouble for this, almost killed himself. And, dammit, it had worked.

But then I noticed something else. Something else altogether.

I sat up, newly optimistic. I'd overlooked something. Yes, on closer inspection, what I thought I'd glimpsed looked as if it was real. Eureka.

It was true that Bryan had a brand-new head. But his neck was older than ever. It looked ancient. He'd forgotten to burn his damn neck! Rookie error.

I walked over to look close up. Yes, the adolescent head was atop a neck that was positively reptilian. A dinosaur would be ashamed to sport something so wrinkly and wizened.

Perhaps this was proof that there is a God in heaven. I'm not sure.

But what I do know is that Bryan is not nearly as clever as he thinks.

Trieste, 1946. Dad on his purloined Austrian cavalry steed. I should have *Made in Italy* stamped on my backside.

Above: Tyrella beach, 1948, the Mountains of Mourne across the water. Dad leans into another leaky boat.

Right: Mum and Dad, Michael in uniform, myself in non-disposable nappy, with my adored Gaggie.

Above: my brother, Michael, with an undersized fish. My sister, Juliet, and I are fishless.

Right: Lake Sumner. The greatest thing in my childhood was camping in an otherwise empty New Zealand.

Left: my terrifying and always immaculate paternal grandmother, Jummy.

Right: I loved my other grandmother, Gaggie, to death. She has neatened my hair for this street photo.

Dad with the Queen, Guard of Honour, circa 1953. Group Captain Peter Townsend in the rear, which might explain the Queen's grumpy expression.

A Zoo and a Safari

AROUND the turn of the century I was working very hard on a film called *The Zookeeper*, based in Prague. It was shot half an hour out of town, in the arse end of a miserable, freezing-cold Czech winter, primarily in a rusty, derelict old Soviet military base. We were sure it was full of corroding asbestos. It was a desolate place, perfect for the setting of the film.

The story was set in a fictional Balkan city, in the recent wars, and was based loosely on a true story. The war roars through the place, leaving the zoo isolated and the zookeeper (me) completely on my own to look after all the animals. Not much of a zoo, but a very conscientious, silent zookeeper. Gina McKee turns up at one point, a traumatised woman accompanied by a small child. Reluctantly the zookeeper takes them into his care as well. And a sort of romance ensues.

But for most of the film it was just me and an assortment of unlikely animals. These were rented from, you'd have to say, a slightly dodgy eastern European circus. We had a caged bear, and the poor thing clearly had PTSD and major stress. It walked back and forth in its horrible cage all day long. We had a lioness, who had cubs while we were there. It was the first and last time I got to cuddle several little lions at the same time. There was a dazzle of zebra, who were completely unbiddable, maybe not even right in the head. I understood why you never see anyone riding a zebra. They look like horses, but they are nuts. There was one wildebeest who was in a constant state of rage. Terrifying.

But the one animal who did become a friend was an enormous chimpanzee, whose name I've sadly forgotten. He took a liking to me after a while, and would make agreeable noises when I entered his building. Then he'd turn his back to me against the bars of his cage. I was happy to scratch him for as long as he wanted. I hate seeing animals in cages. And he obviously hated being in one. At one end of his enclosure was a concrete wall on which he would smear his shit. He was very creative. It was hard to know whether this was a protest or an art installation. I've seen worse at the Tate Modern.

All these animals belonged to a rather dubious type, who was the circus owner, and I imagine the master of ceremonies when they were on tour. The chimpanzee was his best friend. I was reliably told by people he worked with that he was fond of a local country brothel and had become a regular while we were shooting the film. The circus owner would take the chimpanzee in there with him after work, who would drink beer with the girls in the lobby while his friend, the boss, was upstairs with the girl of his choice. He certainly liked his beer, this chimp. They both came to the wrap party, and the chimpanzee downed one Budweiser after another with no detrimental effect. As a footnote, it should be known that Czech Budweiser is entirely different from the American Budweiser, and much superior. I am sure my chimp friend wouldn't have been seen dead with the pallid Yankee version.

This chimp was a very amiable chap, and I could see how the brothel girls would enjoy a drink with him between clients. The only thing he hated was children. Apparently he'd been tormented by some in years past, and had never forgiven any of them. No one was to know that. That is, until we had a set visit from the American ambassador's wife, their small daughter and some of her friends. They were ushered in to see my friend the chimp. The highlight. They were having a great time, until suddenly he seized a child's hand, pulled it through the bars, and bit her finger so hard that he almost severed the digit altogether. Well, that rather put a pall on the day, and with much screaming and wailing the whole party was rushed away to hospital in Prague. Oh, dear me.

*

A few years later I was filming in north-east South Africa, Richards Bay, on a BBC project with Benedict Cumberbatch, Jared Harris et al. *To the Ends of the Earth* was an adaptation of William Golding's trilogy.

Elena had school holidays, so I flew her out to keep me company for the last bit of the shoot and have a break together afterwards. At this time she was about fourteen years old. I don't know any fathers of daughters who have had an easy time during their adolescence. And Elena's teenage years were, to put it mildly, turbulent. Much as I love her, she knew how to put me through it and back again. At this point she was not at peak trouble. That would come two or three years later. She was somewhere between a child, and a sweet one at that, and a volatile, emo teenager. Half monster, half baby. There was a lot of eye-rolling and groaning at my obvious stupidity. She was suddenly an expert, it seemed, at everything. But she still had that curious, inquiring mind, and much of this strange, beautiful country fascinated her, in spite of the teen ennui.

We headed out on safari. We camped, albeit very comfortably, at the edge of the river in the Okavango Delta in Botswana. We saw lions, hyenas, baboons and even a leopard up a tree, eating its prey. The water, the deep river outside our tent, was full of hippos. At dinnertime, a tall warrior with a long sharp spear would collect us and see us safely to the dining tent. We trailed, secure in his wake, on the three-minute walk in the gathering twilight, the air full of strange animal noises and unfamiliar insects. When we were leaving the place, I asked as a matter of interest whether, if one of these hippos had come tearing out of the water to attack us, the warrior would have been much of a hindrance? The answer was he would've been completely useless, but at least he would die before we did. Ferocious things, hippos.

We stayed at a hotel in Livingstone in Zambia, beside the Victoria Falls. You're right there, in the thunder and the mist coming off the immense cascade below. We took a little expedition out into the middle of the river to some tiny islands at the top of the falls. And right at the lip, at the very edge of oblivion, was a swimming hole perhaps ten metres by ten metres. And one or two metres deep. We threw ourselves in happily, in all that dense African heat. In the distance we could see elephants wading around upstream, hosing themselves down with their massive trunks at the edge of the jungle.

There were three or four other young people swimming as well. Elena plunged into their company right away, as is her wont. The next thing I knew she was perched on the very edge of the Victoria Falls, sitting in the current, 885 metres above oblivion. Laughing and kidding around with her new friends. I was horrified. One slip, one simple mistake, just a tilt backwards and she would never be seen again. Without making a scene, I told her through gritted teeth to please, right now, come away from the edge. Listen to me. Come away from the edge right now. Elena, one more time. Come. Back. Here. And of course she completely ignored me. Blanked me. I was now furious. But, because I thought anything could tip her over the edge, I restrained myself from any further action, fearing she might do something even more stupid, showing off. Eventually she did come back; I got her out of the water immediately, and made no mention of it until I'd calmed down back at the hotel.

You couldn't ask for a better metaphor for Elena's life. Fearless, always on the edge of something, full of bravado and fun, contemptuous of authority...Oh, boy.

We were lucky to stay on an enormous privately owned game reserve right next to Kruger National Park. Thousands of acres. On the first day out in our open Land Rover, we saw the big five (lion, leopard, black rhinoceros, African bush elephant and African buffalo) in one day. The guide said that was the first time he'd ever experienced it. We were even lucky enough to see a white rhino, very rare indeed.

The nice couple who were part-owners of this amazing place had a compound of five or six huts, and a living–dining house in the centre. It was all very new, but somehow it looked as if it had always been there: grass thatch roofs, mud-brick construction and so on. Wild dogs, monkeys, giraffes, gazelles: all kinds of animals, including lions, strolled past, barely noticing us. At dinner, or brai, around the open fire, you could hear the lions too, growling and grumbling. Elena had her old favourite sleep cuddle toy with her—her Jarf (giraffe)—and, when a real giraffe ambled past, I took a photo with Jarf in the foreground.

Elena and I had a hut each to ourselves, and on that first night, as we were heading for bed, I asked her if she was going to be all right. She rolled her eyes, clicked her tongue and looked at me as if I was an imbecile. Aw, Dad. Duh. Of course I will. She marched into her hut, and with a curt good night slammed the door behind her.

I retired to mine, and fell asleep over a book.

An hour or two later, there was a bang on the door. 'Dad! Dad! Let me in please, Dad.'

I ran over and she rushed past me, terrified and white as a sheet. 'Dad, I am so scared. Those lions! Can I sleep in your room? Please?'

I said, 'Of course, darling, of course you can.'

I made her a little bed on the floor. She curled up there, and went straight to sleep. I got into bed chuckling, and listened to those lions; they did indeed sound like they were just outside. But I went to sleep with a big smile of contentment. There are moments when parenting can give you some wry satisfaction.

It was a great time.

Hitchhiking

NO one hitchhikes any more. I'm not sure why. Maybe too many creepy Hollywood movies? Overprotective parents? Who knows?

I spent years hitchhiking. I didn't have a car. Trains were boring, and buses worse. Besides, they cost money and I didn't have any.

Hitchhiking was more interesting. There was the element of uncertainty. You were never entirely sure whether you'd get there. But you almost always did. Sometimes it would be five rides to travel fifty miles, sometimes one ride would get you two hundred miles and all the way. But the best thing was the company. Because the sort of people to pick up hitchhikers are kind people, and you learn a lot from kind people. Not least how to be kind yourself. Sometimes people just wanted someone to talk to. A small price to pay, and I had conversations with people from all walks of life. Life lessons.

I once was picked up by a lovely ancient couple in an ancient American car just out of Christchurch. You'd expect them to be going twenty miles to Amberley. But, no, they were going to the West Coast, like me. Not just the West Coast, but turning right at Westport. And not just to Granity, north of Westport, but up a winding switchback to an obscure village called Millerton, like me. Couldn't believe my luck. Took us all day, and we were happy all the way, talking all the while.

In the early 1970s four of my hippy friends and I had gone in together to buy an old miner's cottage in Millerton. A hundred bucks each and the house was ours, freehold. It was wild and woolly up there on that plateau high above the Tasman. On a good day you couldn't beat it for views. But it is the West Coast there, and if you didn't like lashing weather you were never gonna be happy. I liked both weathers. My friends were musicians, and they'd take out their guitars and drums and practise on the veranda surrounded by native bush. The two or three remaining old miners in the village thought we were freaks. We were perfectly happy with that judgment. The local doctor had lived in the cottage once, and the only cooking tool we had was an old sterilising implement. We'd boil our eggs in it.

My mates were good, relaxed company, and very talented musicians. They smoked dope, of course. People inevitably change as life goes on, and one of those hippies, Tim Groser—in all fairness, the least talented of them—ended up holding various ministerial positions in the right-wing National Party government. Ain't life strange. As for the others, they disappeared and

Millerton Cottage, the owners. I am looking with scepticism at the future National Party Cabinet minister.

I have no idea what happened to them. Somehow, still, the local government up there used to send me rates bills from time to time for a place that none of us had visited for years. I wrote back and said the house was theirs and they were welcome to it.

Many years later I took a trip with my daughters down the West Coast, and drove up that impossibly winding road to Millerton to try to find the old place. I had good memories of a few summers there with my laid-back friends. The village was still semi-abandoned, but instead of a few peace-and-love hippies living here and there, hostile squatting ferals with alarming haircuts had taken it over. I found the house and it was changed. The veranda was gone. Someone had obviously ripped it off and burnt it in one of the freezing winters up there. A danger-ous-looking man emerged and asked me what we wanted. I explained I kind of owned the house he was living in. He had a strange expression as he advanced on me, and he started breath-ing weirdly, way too much white in his eyes. And then he said in a very quiet voice, 'Just fuck off.' I took his advice quick smart, bundled the girls back into the car and was never seen again.

Back to hitchhiking. One year at university, I realised that I'd done absolutely no work at all and exams were looming fast. Most of the year I'd spent in the cafeteria doing crosswords, getting slightly involved in politics, doing plays, finding a girlfriend or two. Anything but what I should've been doing. Ironically, most of it turned out to be the useful stuff later on. Anyway, the shock of truth suddenly became apparent and caused me great stress. I decided I needed a little comfort, a little soothing from my mother. I hitchhiked home again, back to the farm near Dunedin where my parents now lived. I got there mid-afternoon, and Mum was at home. She sat me down and asked me what was wrong.

'Mum,' I said, 'I'm not doing too well. Not at all well. I think I might be having a mental breakdown.' I suppose I imagined that

Mum would make soothing noises, stroke my head or something like that. What was I thinking?

Mum took a sip of her tea, put the cup down on the saucer and looked straight at me. She said, 'Well, darling. You'll just have to pull yourself together. Won't you?'

I hitchhiked back to Christchurch and pulled myself together.

Mum always picked up hitchhikers, all her life. Even as an old lady she would stop and say, Hop in. I have to admit that that worried me, this frail old thing, just as generous as ever. I asked her if this was wise. She said, 'Oh yes, darling, of course it is. In fact, I usually get them to drive.'

The Hitchhiker, 1970.

I said, '*What*? Mum, are you serious?'

She said, without a blink, 'Well, yes. I mean, what can they do to me if they've got their hands on the wheel?' I sighed and left it at that.

Sometimes she would drive her pony and trap into Mosgiel, do her shopping and drive home again. One day the Hells Angels were in town, and she stopped to admire their bikes from atop her cart. Mum loved motorbikes; she had ridden one in the war. She was also fearless. She spotted the leader. She said she'd love a ride on the back of his Harley, and in return she'd give him a ride in her buggy. The bloke, amazingly, said yes, she jumped on, and they roared off through town, a big hairy bikie with an old lady clinging on behind. And then, when they got back, he got onto the trap and, giddy up, off they went around the block. Clip clop. Oh, dear God, how I would have loved to see that.

Mum was made of sterner stuff than me. Just before I was born, her brother, John Ingham, was killed in India. John was her only sibling, and she was devoted to him. My second name is John, after him. So it was just Mum and Gaggie left. She was, of course, stoic. A friend was worried for her—she didn't seem as emotional as one would expect. Mum's reply: 'Oh, if one were to let oneself cry, it would never stop.'

To the End of the World and Back

THIS is a fact that I wish wasn't one.

I've worked with some formidable directors over the years, but rather too often in their less memorable films. Perhaps it's my fault. People like Claude Chabrol, François Ozon, Chris Columbus, Sally Potter…

Until the End of the World is not Wim Wenders' greatest movie. It is, however, easily his most ambitious. It was a road movie—but futuristic, visionary even, and it took us all around the world for seven or eight months. The film has its detractors, but admirers as well. There is an undeniable dream-like quality that could only be Wenders'. It may be cinematographer Robby Müller's most beautiful work. (Then again, I always think, as a rule of thumb, that if you are noticing the photography, someone isn't telling the story right.) Look, whether or not it's good I will leave to the critics; it is not my job, don't ask me again. Grumble, grumble.

It was the nearest thing to the ideal adventure movie to make: I think we shot in some twelve different countries, and this in 1991, when the world was being tipped upside down. The Cold War was finished, communism was done for, and everything was in a state of flux. Not least in Wim's own Germany, where the Berlin Wall had just been torn down. Anything could happen. Particularly so given the very international cast that Wim had assembled—a mixed bag of lollies if ever you ate from one. While

I'm at it, two years prior, I was in an even more multinational cast in Paris—the official bicentennial anniversary film about the French Revolution. The cast was pretty much from anywhere but France. Absurdly, I was playing Lafayette, in bad Kiwi-inflected French. Ridiculous.

We arrived in Paris for Wim and rehearsals. The main stars were William Hurt and Solveig Dommartin. Hurt was relatively new to the world of sobriety. This didn't make him any less angry about just about everything. And being angry about the world in general does not make for the most sparkling company. We would have to stop work at 4 p.m. every day so that he could go to an AA meeting. That didn't seem to make him any happier. Hurt could talk the hind leg off a donkey, but there wasn't much joy in it. It's funny how you compensate for people like that, and I spent a lot of energy over the filming being positive, cheering him up, trying to lighten the day somehow.

Solveig, on the other hand, liked to drink. She liked just about everything. I liked her too, even though she was a wild thing. She was late for rehearsals on day two, and Bill never forgave her. Bill developed an uncommon loathing for Solveig, which was eventually reciprocated. I wouldn't go so far as to call him a bully, but he certainly acted one with her. The situation became more and more untenable as the film went on. The more he behaved like that towards her, the more cowed she became, and the more she drank. I tried to diplomatically intervene. I would say, 'Bill, you gotta understand, this is her first lead in a big film. She is terrified; we need to be kind.' And I would say to her, 'Look, Solveig, never mind. It's Bill. It's not personal. He's got demons. Just get on with what you have to do. You're gonna be fine.'

Of course, it never worked. Solveig was Wim's girlfriend, but he seemed disinclined to intervene. Wim is a detached, intellectual sort of man, who is never entirely in the same room as everyone else. Rehearsals were chaotic and did not bode well for the months ahead.

There was more fun to be had with others in the cast. Chick Ortega, a stand-up comedian from France I knew from *Delicatessen*, was funny all day long. Rüdiger Vogler, a Wenders regular, was a quiet man and a quietly brilliant actor, with a dry, bent sense of humour. I swear I saw Rüdiger take a big dump by a canal in one of Wim's other films, and I'm fairly sure there was no fakery. That level of the Method puts anything the Actors Studio might advocate to shame. Beyond my capabilities, for sure.

And there was Ernie Dingo, who is always sunny company and funny as hell. We two were Antipodean fish out of water in a Euro art film. Ernie was playing a plain-clothes detective, following Bill Hurt around the world. Oddly, they put him in an Akubra hat and a long Drizabone coat, which didn't look anything out of place in urban Europe. You could spot him from three blocks away.

Nothing daunted, we headed off on our great road trip. Berlin was in a state of chaos, albeit orderly German chaos. You could now travel unhindered from West Berlin to East Berlin; the contrast could not have been more stark. Whatever one thinks about communism, the East was grim and cheerless. The West was vulgar, colourful and prosperous. There were still people from the East, Ossis, wandering into western supermarkets amazed at the sight of well-stocked shelves. The communists had built some grand state buildings, and drab public housing, but much of it seemed as if World War II had only stopped yesterday. Empty bombsites, and bullet holes all over stone buildings. There were demoralised-looking Russian soldiers wandering around, as well as East German ones. The Russians in particular seemed at a loss, and looked as if no one had paid them for quite some time.

They'd sell you their AK-47 if you had a little money. Or even their boots.

There was Portugal and seafood. There was Tokyo and seafood. The Portuguese are the most elegant people—all that Latin style, but without any irritating macho. There were women singing fado in the cafes at night. No idea what they were singing about, but they reduced me to tears anyway. In Tokyo, we filmed in the Ginza, which was all neon and girls and bars, and you'd think we had stepped into some bright dystopic future. We were told to be good and do whatever we were told; we were there, only just, by the grace of the yakuza. One step out of line...Yohji Yamamoto, who is a friend of Wim's, dressed everybody in the cast. I wish I'd kept the suit.

Eventually there was Australia. We went all over the place— the Bungle Bungles, Coober Pedy. In a one-horse town in the middle of nowhere, my character and Bill's come to blows. That fight in the dust of Main Street was perhaps the most frightening moment of my career. Bill was much bigger than me, and he had a mad method-acting thing about him. When he wrestled me to the ground and put me in a choke I thought he was trying to kill me. He seemed out of control, and I was in pain. I never really trusted him again.

The principal base was Alice Springs. I'd been there before, filming *Evil Angels* with Fred Schepisi and Meryl Streep, and we stayed again at the Sheraton. The staff had all changed, but a peacock was still at the door. I'm not sure if it was the exact same peacock that had been the doorman when we were there in 2017 on *Sweet Country*, a very agreeable bird that lived on the grounds and never shat anywhere near the swimming pool. It also had a built-in timing system. He knew exactly when the bus from Darwin was due; he'd be standing at the front door on full display to greet the visitors from the north, every day, on the dot.

Alice Springs. It's at the juncture of so many things, and it's easy to see why it was common ground, a trading place, for tens of thousands of years. It's where you come face to face, like it or not, with contemporary inland Australia. Where you see the distress, the pain of the First Nations people like nowhere else. I was asked to go and listen to a women's collective when I was there in 1987, and I was shocked by the stories I heard of sexual and domestic violence. I wanted to scream. But Alice Springs is also full of success and hope. Filmmakers, activists, artists of all kinds, great music. I am a supporter of the Tangentyere Artists, whom I made contact with when we were doing *Sweet Country*. I love the art that they produce, and the work they do in the community. Find them online, it's worth it.

While we were there on *Until the End of the World*, Sally Dingo organised a fundraiser to buy an eighteen-seater commuter bus for the local youth centre. It was held on a Sunday afternoon at the pub in The Gap. It was an incredible day: all kinds of music legends turned up and played with this big band on stage. Ted Egan, Jimmy Little, Charlie McMahon on didgeridoo, Bart Willoughby, David Gulpilil, slightly the worse for wear, Ernie, of course, and even Bill Hurt at one point. I was mortified to be commanded up on stage by Ernie to play keyboards on the song that we were doing in the film, something by the Kinks. It only needed two chords so it wasn't too much of a stretch. The single complaint we got was from the manager, who ruefully said the music was so good he wasn't selling any beer.

Sally Campbell, the production designer, built a great set up a gorge somewhere. It's where all of the cast come together, expecting the end of the world at the end of the millennium. And here, two heroes of mine turned up. Max von Sydow, stalwart of Swedish cinema, most particularly Bergman. And the completely legendary Jeanne Moreau, who seemed to have been in pretty much all of my favourite French films. Max was a mild, courtly, charming fellow, and I watched with admiration everything he did. I hero-worshipped him, just quietly. He invited me to come and stay on his island near Stockholm; I regret that I never took him up on that kind offer.

Jeanne was perhaps the most compelling woman I'd ever seen in my life. You couldn't keep your eyes off her. She was extremely French, all shrugs, pouts and elegant smoking. Her mother was English. When her parents separated she stayed in France and her sister, Michelle, went to England with their mother. Michelle, with whom she was close, came to visit Jeanne on set. She was quintessentially English. Very tweedy, chipper and brisk, with an accent that could cut glass. The two sisters were like caricatures of each country. I wanted to spend hours with Jeanne to talk about the great directors with whom she'd worked, what the difference was between French acting and everyone else's, to ask about her extremely colourful love life. I wanted to know everything. She was the sort of person who made you want to be French. But...I was too shy, and it wasn't my business, and it wasn't my place.

The greatest privilege of what I do for a living is to work alongside other actors. I love actors. I love their humour, their vulnerability and their generosity. Well, ninety-eight per cent of them anyway. And there's always, always, something to learn. Even at the most difficult times on this film, it would be the other cast members who saw each other through the dark.

We finally finished the film—I think I saw Day 113 on the slate—and we scattered to the winds. Bill and Solveig didn't kill each other, just, but Solveig and Wim had terminated. I never saw Bill again, and for that no regrets. Maybe it's just me, but I think, if you are the lead, you should set the tone, set an example. Try to make it a positive experience for cast and crew, make it fun. Bring some enthusiasm to the set, not your whining and bitching. Bill and the increasingly reckless Solveig made the whole thing jittery and fraught.

I did the narration for the director's cut eventually. It is something like over five hours long. Wim loves it, but I've never seen it. Every time I run into him, he says, I must send it to you. But it's never turned up.

Some films provide experiences that are utterly priceless, and this was certainly one of those. I don't need to see it—I was in it, I was there.

More Stories from the Front

Food Is Everything

IN the unlikely event that an aspiring producer were to ask me for advice about how to be a good producer, I would say make sure you get good catering. After script, director and cast, the most critical thing is this—food. A well-fed crew is a happy crew, and a happy crew will do anything for you. Do not ever save money in the budget on food. Ever.

Rams was filmed at Mount Barker, a very small town south of Perth in Western Australia. I'm of the view that it's a pretty good film, and it should have been fun to make. But it was a kind of miserable time, and I put that down to the awful food. The first caterer was finally fired when one of the make-up people found maggots in the cold chicken. That caterer was then replaced by a nice bloke from the pub who brought up the bain-marie. Oh well.

The great Michael Caton and I would get back to our motel and commiserate over a glass of red. Miranda Richardson ate well, however, since she had days off galore, and was assiduous in seeing all the sights and eating at all the best joints. I bear her no ill will—we've done a few jobs together now, and I am fond of her; she is deeply eccentric and very entertaining.

In fairness, that film and the food were the exception in Australia. One of the reasons I've always been happy to work in Australia is that the food at lunchtime is almost invariably good. It gives you something to look forward to; it sounds simplistic, but it means an awful lot.

Ride Like a Girl, which was filmed around the same time as *Rams,* was constantly fraught at the highest levels with disagreements about all kinds of things, and Rachel Griffiths, our director, was often at odds with the producers. Martin McGrath, who shot the film, was a calm, steady hand who did wonders to keep things on track. I stayed out of all that stuff. I prefer to keep my head down and do my job. But the thing that held it all together was the excellent food. We owe the film to the caterer, I think. The cast and crew were happy, and would have done anything for Rachel. The film works and works well.

If the food is lousy at lunch, make sure you at least eat properly at dinner. On a different occasion, Noriko and I were both working on the same job, and we needed a cook at home. We were doing long days and we had kids to feed. A young woman turned up at the house we were renting with impressive credentials—she had worked in all the best restaurants in town. She spoke well, and seemed pleasant enough, if slightly superior in manner. We gave her a job, even though she looked as if this was all rather beneath her. She was indeed a great cook.

Then Noriko started to miss things, pieces of jewellery, all sorts of things. She told me she thought someone was stealing stuff. Gullible Sam dismissed these fears, trusting as always. But it came to a point when *all* her jewellery had gone. She sat the cook down and told her what had happened. She said she thought maybe someone had been breaking into the house, or maybe she'd just been absent-minded and lost her jewellery somehow. She said, Could you have a look around the house tomorrow, a really good look, and if we don't find them, I'll go to the police. Well, of course everything *did* turn up the next day, and somehow in all the very same places that Noriko had looked herself. Down the back of the sofa, for instance.

Noriko turned to the cook and said, I know it's you, and

before she could say you're fired, the girl stomped out of the house, slamming the door behind her, every inch the injured party. We heard her car furiously backing down the drive, and I thought I heard a squeak. I went outside, and the cook had flattened and killed the very nice cat that came with the house we were renting. I had to make a sorry call to the landlord, and explain why his moggy was now just a stain on the concrete.

I know it was her, because I then went to the trouble of calling a few of the names on her impressive CV. The first thing they'd ask me was, You missing anything?

But back to food on film sets. In 1980, it was a shock to get to Britain and face their film catering. Somehow the whole business of feeding film crews had been monopolised by geezers who thought overcooked meat of an indeterminate origin, plus two over-boiled veggies or chips, was acceptable for a working crew. The crews never seemed to mind, but I did.

It is difficult to describe how badly food was cooked in England back then, but try boiling a cabbage for four hours and you will get the idea.

But then I went to France. I've made quite a few films there, and of course the French do things differently. For a start, French film hours are like no others. For some reason it goes like this— you get up at a leisurely hour, get driven to work, go through hair and make-up, get your frock on…and then you have lunch. Not just any lunch, but lunch at tables that are laid with proper cutlery; there are bottles of wine to be drunk should you feel like it, and the food is superb. The roast beef is rare, the gravy is jus. Well, it is France. After that, you get down to work. Priorities.

In 1984 we started shooting *Plenty* in the UK with the usual British film food. Sigh. But then, to my relief, we went to the Dordogne. Union rules being what they were in those days, pretty much all the British crew came to France as well. After a mere two days of French catering the crew mutinied: 'We are not eating this foreign muck. You need to get our caterers back, or we walk off the job.' This was nothing short of amazing. And, sure enough, the producers did what they were told, and the British caterer drove his horrible catering van all the way to the middle of France, where we were condemned once more to the chippy. The French caterer was obliged to take his brilliance elsewhere, *merci beaucoup*.

My advice to producers still stands. Except when it comes to British crews, who will eat anything. The Dunkirk spirit.

Even Foie Gras

In the Dordogne, working on *Plenty*, Meryl Streep, her hairdresser Roi and I were housed in a relatively modest seventeenth-century chateau. A charming aristocratic family lived there, and that same family had occupied the place for centuries. They did not live in any great luxury; a revolution or two and most certainly the French taxation system had made sure of that. So they were doing what they could to get by.

In this case they were running the chateau as a very small hotel with three or four guests at the most. But they were also producing one of the things that the Dordogne does best—foie gras. Madame was a great cook, so Meryl and I looked forward to getting back there at night to her dinners. After the wretched Brit lunches on set, we deserved it.

While her dinners were nothing short of superb, they were also something of a trial. She cooked everything that was growing on the estate. That meant a preponderance of foie gras. Every night she would cook foie gras in a number of different ways, so a six-course dinner would involve at least three of fresh foie gras cooked in all manner of cunning French *méthodes*. It was exhausting, as she was always somehow there to make sure we cleaned our plates. Bless her, but I swear after a couple of weeks of that, I'd put on a few pounds. Or kilos, given it was France.

On a day off, madame (or was she a comtesse?) asked me if I would like to feed the geese with her. I felt myself blanch, as I was familiar with the supposed cruelty of overfeeding geese or ducks to get a nice fatty liver suitable for foie. But, not wanting to look like some timid Anglo, I gamely volunteered. We took a couple of buckets of corn each out the back, where this huge flock of geese hung out. They were nothing if not free range. The estate was pretty much theirs. A couple of shakes of a bucket and we were completely flash-mobbed by geese. Far from being force-fed, these birds were literally gagging for it. All beaks fully open and directed to us. Feed me, feed me, feed me. My job was to hold the funnel, and madame would go from goose to goose and shovel down heaps of the highly desirable grain. It was never enough. Say what you like about this, and I'm sure you will, there was never a question of any of these creatures being force-fed.

Unlike Meryl and me.

The Art of Kissing

Every profession needs its skills. Plumbers need to know how to fix recalcitrant drainpipes. Pilots need to know how to land planes.

As an actor, you also need some skills. Remember your lines, try not to trip on the furniture, those are the basics, but you should probably have a passing knowledge about some other things as well—how to kiss people, for instance. This may be required multiple times over the course of a long career.

Get it right, for goodness' sake.

I was in Toronto once for some reason, and I saw Meryl Streep was giving a talk, so I turned up and sat about ten rows from the front. I hadn't seen her for years. She spoke brilliantly for about fifty minutes, for the most part about acting. Then she took questions. The questions from the floor were serious, befitting Meryl's status and intellect. And then one question from a woman up the back that took me by surprise.

'Meryl, can I ask, who is the greatest kisser you ever worked with?'

Meryl chuckled, and without hesitation pointed straight at me. She must have spotted me at some point. 'Sam Neill,' she said. 'The greatest kisser of them all.' Much applause, much laughter and much mortification on my part.

Of course, she was being absurd, but it was the kindest fib imaginable.

Incidentally, when we were shooting *Little Fish* I had to kiss my very dear friend, Hugo Weaving. Full on. Kissing a bloke is out of my comfort zone but, if it had to be anyone, it might as well have been Hugo. It gave me a different perspective on a number of things. Not least, how generous lots of women are, how kind, to even contemplate kissing all those bristles. Horrid, frankly.

Another time our family were in New York, and we had a booth at Balthazar. It was getting close to midnight, and we had our nanny with us, very fresh off the boat from New Zealand. The food was excellent, and our nanny was wide-eyed, looking around to spot the odd celebrity.

At one stage I saw her go a little pale. She was gazing over my shoulder. I asked her what the problem was. She said, 'Sam, right behind you there is a man and he is wearing a dress. He has full make-up on.'

I shrugged, grinned and thought no more about it.

Eventually I paid the bill, and we stood up to leave. At the same time the man in the frock behind me also stood up and said loudly, 'Sam!'

I was swept into a grand embrace and kissed full on the lips. It was Eddie Izzard.

I was delighted to see Eddie, whom I heartily embraced in return. I caught a glimpse of the nanny over Eddie's shoulder. The shock, the bemusement…priceless.

Three Sheets

These days, when it comes to bed scenes, and I've done a few, it is the accepted thing that production has someone called an intimacy counsellor on set. This is so that nobody feels uncomfortable.

I'm sure I sound like the dinosaur I am but, after forty years plus of such things, I can put my hand over my heart and say I am confident that none of us, me and whoever else was in bed, has ever been uncomfortable in a bed scene. It's just been a matter of behaving like a civilised human being, making sure that you're friends, and getting through the day as best you can. They are the most awkward things to do but, you never know, they might even be fun; and I've had hilarious times where we're both in stitches, crippled with laughter. I always make sure that the person I'm playing with is okay with the crew around, with what direction we are being given and so on. We collaborate. The whole business is mortifying for everybody, and the more you can take the curse off it with humour the better.

Easily the most difficult bed scene I've ever done was in *Peaky Blinders*. My character, the hideous Major Campbell, rapes Aunt Polly, played by Helen McCrory. It is deeply disturbing, and I was anxious about how we would go. For one thing, this was acting out a situation, a crime, utterly beyond my imagination.

By the time we shot this I knew Helen very well. We found the same things funny, I respected her deeply, and I think she felt the same about me. We spent a whole morning shooting this horrible, horrible scene.

And, as it turned out, we did very well indeed. The more hideous the behaviour, the more hilarity. The worse I was, the more we laughed. The trust was there, which allowed us to go to the extremes. Helen McCrory was one of the greatest people I've ever worked with. A grand actress and a fine person.

Meryl Streep is another of those. When we were shooting *Plenty* we had a bed scene, and of course I was much more terrified than her. I hardly knew her. She was an Oscar winner, she was Meryl Streep. I approached the day with trepidation. But then Meryl suggested something to director Fred Schepisi, which I have to say took me by surprise. She said, I think we should be doing this fully clothed, it's spontaneous and it's also winter. I thought about this, and while I wasn't completely convinced by the rationale, I thought...Well, I'm gonna be much more comfortable, and I'm sure Meryl will be too. So yes, why not. And besides, no one, absolutely no one, says no to Meryl. I still wasn't terribly comfortable, and nor was I very convincing. But we didn't need an intimacy counsellor. We had so many layers and layers of overcoats, jackets, hats, sweaters, trousers and God knows what else between us, it was very far from 'intimate'.

In 2004 I was in a film called *Yes* by Sally Potter. It's an interesting film, at least I found it so. It was also very challenging, because the entire dialogue is in rhyming iambic pentameter. How often do you get to do that? The challenge was in making poetry sound like real dialogue. I did have one completely mortifying scene in it—I was playing a Tony Blair–type British politician, who at one point is at home on his own. He cranks up the music and dances, playing air guitar at the same time. I've done this in private—who hasn't—but to have it seen on film...

I had a bed scene in this movie with Samantha Bond. It sounds an unlikely coincidence given her name, but she had in fact been a 'Bond girl' herself. When we got into bed, she was wrapped in a sheet. She told me this is what they do in Bond films. Three sheets. Two sheets on the bed, and one around her. The actress is wrapped like a mummy, and everybody is comfortable. At least we were. Eminently sensible. The third sheet just looks like part of the mess that happens when there's some action in bed. A good trick—thank you, Mr Bond.

Anyway, nowadays, if I'm in a bed scene, I'm usually to be found in pyjamas, with a pair of glasses and a book. I say, 'Night night, dear,' and turn off the light. No need for counselling at all.

Feminism

I think the first feminist march I took part in would have been about 1972, in Wellington. It was primarily about abortion rights, but as is often the way in such things it covered a lot of topics. Men were in a considerable minority there. I was happy to march with my sisters, in good raucous solidarity. I marched just behind my friend and fellow red-hot lefty, Cathy Isaac. (Cathy later in life turned right, and ran, of all things, the ACT Party in New Zealand for a while. I love her still, for all that.) I did hesitate for a moment, however, as I looked around the crowd, and saw right behind me a large banner that said ALL MEN ARE RAPISTS. I knew from personal experience that this was not true. It was an outrageous lie that offends me still. But there you go, all for the greater good and all that.

In 2021 I went on the March4Justice in Sydney. I took photos of some of the better banners, and the banter had improved immensely. Some of it was very funny. I liked for instance this: 'JUST WANK! You Are Not Entitled To Our Bodies.'

In 1979 I had the opportunity to meet the uber-feminist herself, Germaine Greer. I was at a party, a Christmas party, at Margaret Fink's house. Anything was possible there. I was a neophyte in town, and in awe of the artistic and intellectual gathering around me. I was having a quiet wine when I was seized by Margaret. She shouted at a woman nearby, 'Germaine, darling, you must come, you must meet our *darling* Sam. Isn't he just adorable!'

I was struck dumb in front of one of my heroes. She also said nothing, took a drag on a cigarette, and looked me coolly up and down. Finally, she blew out some smoke and, through half-closed eyes, she looked at Margaret. 'Well, I wouldn't fuck him,' she said, turning on her heel and walking away into the party.

Which brings me to one more yarn. I'm not sure if I want to tell it to you at all. But here goes nothing.

You will recall that I had a terrible time of it in Wellington in my early twenties, desperately in love with Jenny Lindsay and even more desperately celibate. Being full of hormones and craving, I was in mortal agony for a whole year. When the Great Love departed and married another, it was part heartbreak and part relief. I was gutted.

A few weeks later, I fell into conversation with a very nice woman, attractive and slightly older than me, at a party. She must have sensed I needed some looking after, and kindly took me home. It was for me an extraordinary, joyous liberation—I left her bed at about 8 a.m., shredded and happy and completely exhausted. Wellington, as I stepped into a sunny morning, looked a brand-new place altogether.

She married someone I knew, moved to America and I didn't see her for at least another ten years. Finally, I ran into her at another party. I drew her aside for a couple of quiet words. I told her how grateful I was for that night we had, how restored I was, how my confidence in myself as a human being had returned, how wonderful it had been to be back in the realm of the senses again, how kind, how generous she had been, how she had, in a sense, saved my life.

She looked puzzled. 'I'm sorry, Sam. Are you sure? I mean, maybe we did, I just don't remember. No. Don't remember that at all.'

I was crushed. Of course, it happened. I remember most of it still. But for her...it was just...forgettable.

How on earth did that get into a chapter on feminism? I'm definitely losing it.

How to Be a Good Actor

OH, for heaven's sake, why are you asking me? What would I know about that? Ask a *good* actor.

On occasion, I've been asked to go and talk with young actors, mostly at drama schools. I never have any idea what I'm going to talk about until we get there. I mean, I am a completely untutored actor. I never had the opportunity to go to drama school. More than that, it was beyond my imagination that I could become an actor at all. I'm always slightly envious of those who have, and that is the vast majority. They have skills in the toolbox that I simply don't have access to. Not even sure if I've got a toolbox at all. On the other hand, I'm pleased that I didn't have to go through three years of 'trust' exercises. I don't know if things are different now, but back in the day the idea was that students at these places would get dismantled, torn apart—their dignity, their personality, their very selves—and then get put together again in the approved manner of construction by that school. Rather a brutal approach, as far as I can see.

So I am, I think, what is known in the art world as a naive painter. Self-taught. Had to pick things up as best I could along the way. Occasionally I catch glimpses of myself in clips from my old work. I wince, and I think, You've got a lot to learn, mate. But I did learn a bit, and here is some of that. Might be useful for someone else.

There is a part of me that is necessarily quickly suppressed when addressing a class like that. That voice within me wants to say, Look, guys, you've either got it, or you haven't. And there ain't nothing you can do about that. Unless you've got that knack, unless you've got that gift, nothing you can do here will make you an actor. If you have it, this school can make you a better actor.

Of course, I don't say that. I'm surrounded by eager faces, full of optimism and hope. It's touching to see. But it is instructive sometimes to ask other actors when on a job if they've been to drama school. The answer is almost always yes. The next question is—of your class, how many people are still at work as an actor? And bear in mind that these may be people who left drama school as long as forty years ago, or as recently as five. The answer is often: I am the only one. Sometimes there is one other, and once or twice it gets as high as three. But out of a class of twenty or thirty, that's a very high attrition rate. It's a brutal business.

So what is it that ensures that some actors have a sustained career, and others fall by the wayside? Admittedly, in some cases it's all about being in the right place at the right time. A lot of young actors from Australia and New Zealand go straight to Hollywood, learn the accent and dig their heels in, until that something comes along. If you want a career in film, that is definitely the right place. Whether it's the right time, who can tell?

The most important thing is what I've alluded to—do you have it, or do you not? Acting might look easy, but it's actually very hard. In fact, if it looks like it's easy, it means that the actor is doing something very hard very well. If it looks like 'acting', forget it.

Sometimes, if you are learning on the job like me, it's more a matter of what *not* to do. We shot an adaptation of *Ivanhoe* in the early eighties. James Mason was in it, as well as a host of other distinguished British actors: Sir Michael Hordern,

Anthony Andrews, Julian Glover. I played a bad guy, Sir Brian du Bois-Gilbert, alongside John Rhys-Davies and Stuart Wilson. We three had a ball being moustache-twirling villains.

But the centrepiece for me was a scene opposite Olivia Hussey. My character is hopelessly in love with her, and she won't have a bar of it. Things get ugly. Here was my chance, and I would seize it, to do some real acting. I would show all these wonderful actors that I had the chops as well. They may have done years in the Great Tragedies at the Royal Shakespeare Company, and I had done just one or two agitprop things, but I knew, I was certain, I could do what they did. The scene as I remember was full-on, and I pulled out all the organ stops. I was huge. I was SuperActor. We did two takes on my angle. And I gave them a bit more juice than even the rest. When I heard 'Cut!' I felt exhilarated. I'd never been better in my life. And then (this has never happened to me before or since) the crew burst out in spontaneous applause. I was right: I'd been brilliant.

Later in the year, the film came out on television. I eagerly awaited that scene, my golden moment. Alas, I had completely deluded myself. I had made that most elementary of mistakes. I had been acting, and I'd been caught acting. It was grotesquely over the top. I wanted my armchair to swallow me up and ensure I would never be seen again on screen. I was absolutely terrible. It was by far the worst acted scene in the film. Nothing to do with Olivia Hussey, everything to do with me. I might have got away with something so enormous in a two-thousand-seat Palladium. But with a camera you're acting for one. That one person who is watching you on celluloid. It's an intimate relationship, and it doesn't need a fool like me to give it the grunt it never asked for. (For all that, the film has become an unlikely icon— it plays each New Year's Day at 3 p.m. on Swedish television. It's a family tradition to order in pizza and watch the movie.

Warren Oates. The first movie star I ever worked with: so cool, kind and funny as hell.

Clockwise from top left:

Coming to grips with
Judy Davis in *My
Brilliant Career*.

With the remarkable
Isabelle Adjani in
Possession. She won
Best Actress at Cannes
and a César.

The Piano is such a
handsome-looking film.
I am not in this shot,
which helps.

Me as Harry in
My Brilliant Career.
Possibly the only
time I made it onto
a magazine cover.
It was *Gay News*.

Top row: *Sweet Country* with Hamilton Morris; Tim Finn rocks; *In the Wake of Captain Cook*; happily married.

Middle row: Julian Dennison (Ricky Baker) unwisely driving, *Hunt for the Wilderpeople*; Bryan Brown will do anything for sympathy;

Taika Waititi, seriously; with Governor-General Dame Cindy Kiro after being knighted.

Bottom row: every trout I catch returns to fight another day; my beloved sheep; my pig and his beloved mate; wisely, they didn't let Goldblum and me on stage at the Sydney Opera House.

Above: my favourite vineyard: The Last Chance, Alexandra.

Left above: the first house I built: Ian Athfield, architect.

Left below: the last house I built: Richard Naish, architect.

Acting tip—if in doubt, point at something. In this case I am pointing to the future.

Nobody understands why. Many Swedes root for my Sir Brian du Bois-Gilbert, but every year he loses yet again.)

Lesson learnt. Don't be caught acting. Just because everybody else is doing something—being fruity, for instance—doesn't mean that you have to be fruity too.

I sometimes ask people if there's something particular that they bring to every role that would be universal to their career. Meryl Streep had an interesting answer. She claimed that she makes a point of tripping at some stage in a film. I told her that I like to make sure that I do a 360-degree turn somewhere in the flick. I think I've forgotten to do that for a while. I should start again.

I once read something practical and useful that has stood me in good stead. When you go to leave, look at the door before you get up and depart. If you don't do that (and people don't necessarily do that in life), it strangely looks as if you've been more spontaneous than was called for. You might be leaving in a huff, for instance. No, looking at the door first indicates a whole bunch of things—you have another life, you have somewhere to go, you are thinking within the scene. The rule, of course, extrapolates to so many other things; the door is just one example.

We were talking about these little things on the *Jurassic World Dominion* set one day. Chris Pratt sat up and said that every time he leaves by a door he looks back into the room. I must always remember that whenever confronted by a door in the future. Again, it's a simple thing that conveys a tremendous amount. I was very interested to see Chris at work. And here is the big difference between someone like him and me. He's really thought about what it means to be an action hero. It's a real job. I never did that on the *Jurassic* films. On the contrary, I thought I was playing an ordinary guy who finds himself in a heap of trouble and muddles his way to survival. Everyman, not hero. Pratt is absolutely fantastic as a hero.

There is another separate job that acting at a certain level may ask of you. Do you want to be a celebrity? A lot of people are happy to take that on. And with the full knowledge that it is another job. It takes work. You need a publicist. You need to be seen at things. You need to be in all the magazines, possibly with your children if you have any, with whatever partner you have currently. It's a lot of work, and not very agreeable work at that, not for me anyway.

Now, obviously I have friends who are celebrities. And I think, by and large, they enjoy it. Fame, sponsorships, great frocks...there are many benefits that go with being a celebrity. It also pays off in your day job: if you're famous, you get paid more. You are a drawcard for the cinema. So I see what they're up to. I get it. Personally I think they deserve every penny more that they get. I myself have never wanted any of that, were it on offer. The intrusiveness, the complete loss of privacy: at what cost? Having a life that's private is, frankly, priceless. I can walk on pretty much any street in the world without being bothered. These friends of mine, however, need security, a getaway car; there's no end to it.

I am not a celebrity. When I was coming out of my coffee joint the other day, a bloke yelled at me, 'I know you. You're on television. What's your name?'

'I'm Hugo Weaving!' I replied. He seemed satisfied with that and wandered away. I couldn't just leave it at that. I yelled, 'I'm also a shit actor.' A complete falsehood by the way, but it made my morning.

I once asked James Mason how to be a good screen actor. He had only one thing for me. Never eat, drink or smoke in a scene. If you do, you'll be eating, drinking and smoking all day. Good practical advice, but a little superfluous these days. Nobody smokes on the screen any more, and more's the pity. And God forbid you should be seen with a drink in your hand. You never know what the consequences of that might be.

But there is a gift, something beyond your control, you must have to be a screen actor. The audience has to want to watch you, follow you. What is that indefinable thing? Is it looks? Absolutely not. Do they need to fancy you? Who cares? I saw a big movie on my telly last week. It had a young man in it, playing the lead. Clearly a very good actor. But my eyes kept wandering off to the bad guy next to him (Hugo Weaving, as it happened). I couldn't keep my eyes off him.

It's a curious thing—I don't really understand it. And whether I have that gift, I have no idea at all.

I sometimes wonder to what extent screen acting has changed since I began in earnest, which, when I think about it, is forty-five years ago. Probably not a lot; the fundamentals are always the same. Some actors cover the pages with helpful notes. Gregory Peck was famous for his working scripts. Page after page, Peck would write one simple thing at the top. NAR. No Acting Required.

That doesn't mean I don't have a grumble once in a while. Might as well do so now. There's a great deal of mumbling now. I notice this more and more, not least because I'm probably not as sharp in the ear department as I once was. But with actors of a younger generation, it seems common that indistinguishable whispering and mumbling is their modus operandi. This is not realism. I don't know if you've noticed, but in life people speak so that others can understand them. This is no longer the case on a film set. I think the theory is that, because everyone has a throat mike these days, every little grunt and whisper is recordable. So when you turn up the whispering in the mix, the actor in question sounds throaty and sexy. Or something.

Acting with mumblers is a bit of a challenge. If I know that's what they're up to, I just wait until their lips stop moving. And say whatever it is I have to say next. This doesn't make for a very engaged piece of acting between two players. One hasn't a clue about what the other one is saying.

The Twelve had a big cast, and a lovely one too. But, just quietly, there were some shocking mumblers among them. I was playing barrister for the defence, and I struggled quite often to hear what witnesses were saying under cross-examination. From my distance, I'd have to guess when they'd replied to my searching question. The head would stop nodding, or something. Finally it got too much. And one witness copped this preface to my next question. 'Mr X, it would be appreciated if you could make yourself audible to the court. It is important that the jury hear your testimony. Be so good as to speak up for the benefit of us all.' From then on I could hear what he was saying. So there's my next tip: bloody well speak up so that the other actors know what the hell you're on about.

There are actors I know who can articulate well what it is that we do. Bryan Brown is particularly succinct: 'It's simple. Just open your mouth and be real.' If that's helpful, you can use it. I rather like Alan Cumming's definition: 'Pretend to be someone else, but really, really, mean it.' Yes, I agree, conviction is everything. I think that's a pretty good mantra, and worth committing to memory. The mantra always used to be: learn your lines and hit your marks. But marks are now things of the past. Focus pullers and new technology have made them redundant. It remains a good idea to learn your lines.

I'm not sure how much thought I've given it, really, over the years. I probably should've been a bit more diligent. But I must've learnt something along the way, because I think I'm a better actor now than I was thirty years ago. And now that I'm out of action for at least a few months, it throws into sharp relief that deep need I have to act, how much I need to go to work. I love being on a film set; it's always familiar to me. I love being with other actors: how stimulating, how funny, how sad, how vulnerable they can be. They are the best company I know. I love doing what I know how to do. It's a good job. I fit in.

None of this has been helpful at all, has it? So sorry. All right, then, let's leave it here: look and learn. Watch the good ones closely. Not me…the good ones.

Music

ANY fool could have designed a little thing that fits in your pocket and holds twenty thousand of your all-time favourite tracks. Easy. Admit it. But whoever designed the shuffle function was a genius. Shuffle elevated all of that to another level. Add random to pleasure, and that way heaven lies.

And here I am: it's a sunny day on my sofa, while my big fat speaker reverberates around my life all those songs that have meant so much to me over all those years. I don't want to know what's coming up next. That's the fun. Here is Ruby Turner. Here's the Divine Comedy. Fat Freddy's Drop. The Allman Brothers. Ian Dury. The Band. Radiohead. Wilco. Who is this? Oh, of course, it's Lucky Peterson. The Pretenders. John Hiatt. Each one evocative of a period of my life. Life is good.

Life without music, unthinkable.

I haven't sung enough in my life. Singing is good for you. All modesty aside, I think I can sing quite well. Not a career-level voice, you understand, but I can carry a tune. I sometimes sing on Instagram with my uke, but that's more in an attempt to cheer people up in dark times—I massacre songs for the general good. And I can sing harmony with my friends. I can sing harmony right now, and that's Bonnie Raitt singing. We sound good together. Bonnie. After a show once Bonnie looked me in the eye and said, Would you like to come over and make some sweet music with me sometime? I don't think that was actually techni-cally a musical question as such, in fact I'm pretty sure it wasn't.

But I guess I'll never know.

Harmony is everything to me. One thing interests me and it's a real curiosity. Everywhere you go in the Pacific, people are singing. They sing in church, they sing while they work, they sing while they fish. And they sing in harmony, and harmony comes to them as naturally as anyone else breathes. But some people suggest that harmony itself was introduced to the Pacific by, of all people, the bloody missionaries. The choirs that were obligatory in churches required harmony for all those dreary hymns. Well, if that's the one good thing, the only one, that missionaries did, after the destruction they wrought on other cultures, they did us all a favour.

I knew I could sing when I got to Christ's College. I had sung in the choir at Medbury School. All those little boys singing high, some of them singing even higher—descant. Harmony. We were fine. But the first thing that happened at College was that the music master would audition you as a potential choirboy. I knew his game. I knew if I sang well it would mean five years devoted to choir practice three times a week, and putting on a frock for chapel twice every Sunday. I deliberately sang off key and was spared that agony. I kind of regret it now.

The music master's name was Robert Field-Dodgson. A tidy man with an immaculate comb-over. He always wore an academic gown, at least whenever I saw him. The music room was a rather elegant Victorian panelled room, and we commoners would have one music lesson a week. Just the one. He despised all of us. None of us were choirboys, and we were therefore beneath his contempt.

Music was too good for us and, although it was his job, he clearly saw no point in wasting his time trying to teach it to the likes of us. Instead we would get a diatribe about how he saw the world that week. He was very right-wing and, even though I knew nothing of politics, this sounded pretty weird to me. And then, if you were lucky, he might shut up for the last ten minutes of the period and play a record.

One day he played a record that made me sit up straight in my seat. He played Sibelius. I think it was probably *Finlandia*, or perhaps the *Karelia Suite*. But he said this one thing that I've never forgotten. He said, 'Boys, close your eyes and imagine forests and snow.'

I did so. I saw forests, forests under snow. I saw Finland. And my life changed forever. To this day Sibelius for me is the greatest composer that ever there was. And Symphony No. 5 is the greatest thing that any man or woman ever wrote.

Thank you, Mr Field-Dodgson. You did one thing right.

As a sidebar about forests and snow, here's a story from Poland. Some jobs are unforgettable, while others are vivid. It's the winter of 1980–81 and it's Poland. We are shooting *From a Far Country* with Krzysztof Zanussi. After Andrzej Żuławski, he was the second Polish director I had worked with in the space of six months. I don't think anyone saw *From a Far Country*. No matter; for me it was the extraordinary things that happened while we were doing it. A forgettable film, but a vivid experience.

Krzysztof Zanussi took us to meet a very old woman who lived on the top floor of a big palace, in what had been the servants' quarters once upon a time. The palace is in the main square in Krakow. She was in fact a comtessa or something, extremely aristocratic and important. Her pan-European family was apparently older than the Hapsburgs.

The palace was hers by right. But these were communist days, and the secret police had confiscated the building, allowing her a couple of rooms up in the attic. The ceilings were just high enough to accommodate some family portraits along the walls. We climbed the staircase storey after storey until we found her little door. This tiny woman opened her door, smiled kindly, brought us in from the cold, bade us sit down and made us cups of tea.

She had had an extraordinary life, a very rich one, until it was reduced to these miserable circumstances by the communists. But there was nothing bitter about her; she was all graciousness. She entertained us in the most kindly manner. It was very touching. But here's the story about her that Krzysztof swore is true. As a young woman she was in an open cockpit biplane. It was winter, and they were out for a jaunt. The pilot was foolish, did a flip, and she fell out of the plane. She plummeted to earth. But because it was winter, she fell into fir trees covered in snow. She fell through snow-covered branches into a snow drift.

When they found her, there was no sign of life. Cold and blue and not breathing. She was, to all intents and purposes, dead. She was, of course, accorded an important funeral. She was grand aristocracy after all. And then, during her funeral, they heard from inside the coffin…knocking. The corpse was wanting out. They opened the coffin and there she was—alive, and recovered from the coma. Not something I've ever experienced at a funeral.

But back to music. Around 1970, it became possible to have a music system in your house that made a good sound. Prior to that, you played your LPs on a shitty thing that required you to lie on the floor beside its hopeless, tinny speaker to get any idea of what was going on at all. Then one day if you saved up your money you could buy real speakers, stereo speakers, made from wood that had woofers and tweeters and who knows what inside them.

You heard bass for the first time ever. It was transformative.

And it was around about the same time that the people I liked started to make great records. Great records that sounded great on a great system. Rock got ambitious.

The peak of ambition was prog rock. Admittedly, a lot of prog rock was pretentious bullshit. But the best of it was superb. *The Yes Album* is one of the great records of all time. I don't care what you say, it's bloody well true. Get stuffed, Sid Vicious.

The Stones had been part of my life since 1963. But it wasn't until about 1970 that they started to make great records. Up until that point they'd, in effect, been a very good, very cool, cover band. Then came *Let It Bleed*, *Sticky Fingers* and *Exile on Main St*. Just as the Beatles were falling apart, the Stones stepped up and made three or four magnificent albums. Amazingly, all these years later, that band is still going. How on earth is that possible? Without Charlie Watts, I have no idea where they go now. Doesn't matter; those albums are timeless genius. And now I could crank them up to the threshold of pain on my superb speakers that came all the way from America.

One day back then my girlfriend Louise W. brought home an album by, of all people, the Beach Boys. I hadn't listened to them for five or six years. Not since 'Good Vibrations'. The poor Beach Boys had become completely unfashionable. But here was an album with an intriguing cover. There were no surfboards, there were no Californian dudes in evidence. It was called *Holland*, and instead it had a picture of a canal, with a canal boat reflected on the water. I put it on. I couldn't believe my ears. The most amazing record. From 'Sail On Sailor' onwards, everything was wonderful. I don't know how many times I've played it. It never ever disappoints me.

This led me to go back and see what they'd been doing those last few years, when no one had been listening. Again, I was poleaxed. *Surf's Up*, *Carl and the Passions—'So Tough'*. Every one a masterpiece. I couldn't believe I'd ignored them all this time and I couldn't believe I'd had the luck to find them again. They remain a lifelong passion for me. Brian Wilson, we owe you so much. Of course, it is all about the harmonies. Harmony. It makes the world go round. No one, absolutely no one, can sing harmony like the Beach Boys. But it's no use me telling you any of this; no one ever believes me about the Beach Boys. My friend Simon Morris, broadcaster and musician, is the only other Beach Boys tragic I know in the world. We can talk to the point of exhaustion.

Years later, I was lucky enough to make friends with Ricky Fataar. Ricky was a member of the Beach Boys for a while. They'd always felt free to bring in more members, often to fill gaps caused, for instance, by Brian refusing to tour. Ricky and his friend Blondie Chaplin came in for those peak years. Ricky was a friend of friends. And became my friend. He was there back when all that magic happened. He recorded and toured with those guys. He was a Beach Boy. Unbelievable. Unfortunately, Ricky is very discreet and reveals almost nothing about those years. He claims it's rock'n'roll damage and he simply doesn't remember, but who knows. Someone needs to winkle those stories out of him.

As well as being a very sweet guy, Ricky is also one of the greatest drummers alive. Alongside all the other things he's done, he has for years now drummed for Bonnie Raitt. I would go to hear him play, which must account for why Bonnie looked me in the eye that night. I was once at Ricky's house in San Francisco, hanging out. After a few hours the penny dropped and I had to ask him, 'Ricky, you don't have any drums in the house. How do you practise?'

He looked completely baffled, and said, 'Why would I practise? I know how to drum already.'

Fair enough.

Some of the people I love best in the world are musicians. And right now, when times are a bit rough up here, they've been completely splendid. Jimmy Barnes calls me every couple of days to see how things are. What kindness. He is also an incredible musician—that goes without saying. The longevity of that voice defies any law of nature. He can sing at full throttle night after night as if it's still 1976 at the Bombay Rock. He sings soul music as if he was born in Memphis. His own longevity in itself is a miracle. All those things he's battled all these years—it breaks my heart to think about it. All the demons, that childhood, the alcohol, the drugs. Miraculously, he has prevailed. More than that, triumphed. I could not admire anyone more. He also has a generous, kind heart. He's a family man like no one else I know. He's brought up a whole family of great musicians. A great marriage too; Jane is an extraordinary person. He's a lucky man. I don't know anyone who works harder than they do and I feel blessed to know them.

Mark Lizotte, Diesel, lives next door to Jimmy and Jane, with Jane's sister Jeppy. The sweetest people in the world. Like Jane, Jeppy equates good food with love. I benefit from that love, as do a host of others. Diesel is without question the greatest guitarist in Australia. I cannot number the wonderful nights I've had at theirs, with my feet under that welcoming table.

The Finn Brothers, Tim and Neil, have been very important in my life. Their music has been one of the soundtracks that has accompanied me down the years, from *True Colours* on. Tim is a particularly close friend and has been for thirty years, or something ridiculous. He credits me with his happy marriage and it's in part true. We were out one night at dinner and Tim was sitting opposite an attractive girl with a big smile called Marie Azcona. I could tell Tim was captivated, and I could understand why. The next day he was around at our place, and I asked him what he thought of Marie. He brightened. Well, I said, you must ask her out. He blushed and mumbled no, paralysed with shyness. I took charge. Azcona, there can't be many of those in the book. I found it and, sure enough, only two entries. One was M. Things were looking good. Okay, Tim, here is the number, I am dialling and if she answers, I am handing the phone to you, and you are asking her out. He did so, and within a few months they were married, and the rest is history. I got one thing right! I love them both dearly.

Last vignette for now. I was backstage once after a Sting gig. Tom Jones came up, hail fellow well met. We started talking rugby. He's from Wales and I'm from New Zealand. That's what we have in common. Then Herbie Hancock came up to talk to us. Herbie Hancock! The most immaculate man I'd ever seen in my life. Charming too. And then Sting joined us. We all talk, but I'm thinking, What are the odds? You've gotta remember this, son. There are four people talking in a circle here. Tom Jones, Herbie Hancock, Sting and, odd man out, me. Well, I did remember it. And there you go: I just wrote it down.

The Piano

THE Piano. There's a milestone. Jane Campion. Now there's someone to write home about. So why don't I?

Jane comes from a distinguished New Zealand theatre family. Her parents founded the New Zealand Players. Back in the day the New Zealand Players toured the country, taking theatre to the provinces. In 1976 I was in the production of *Juno and the Paycock* at the newly formed Circa Theatre in Wellington. Dick Campion directed it, and Jane's mum, Edith, was also in the cast. I don't remember Jane being around. But years later, in the eighties and nineties, I became aware of this young woman directing and writing groundbreaking stuff at home. I saw *Sweetie* and was dizzy with its strange mixture of humour and infinite sadness. And then *An Angel at My Table* was without question for me the most important film made to that point in New Zealand. Of course, I would work with Jane at the drop of a hat.

I'm always puzzled that it seems necessary to make the point that Jane is a female director. That shouldn't be unusual. I don't understand why there are more men directors than there are women. No one seems to think it's unusual that women act, for instance. I'm gonna stick my neck out and say women are better at acting than men. If women directors had parity with men, I think we'd find that they're better at directing as well. I've always loved working for women, and with women. And, yes, now I say it, there is nothing like being in the scene opposite a great woman who is working with you, against you and alongside you. I always lift my game, I think.

I got the offer from Jane and the script was phenomenal. It's the story of Ada, a mute Scotswoman who is brought to New Zealand to marry a man called Stewart, but ends up loving a local man named Baines. Holly Hunter was to play Ada. I was offered the part of Stewart. To be perfectly honest, I was slightly perplexed, in that I thought I was actually a better fit to play Baines. This peculiar character she wanted me to play was so odd. Deeply troubled and very, very strange. I suppose I also felt I had another romantic hero or two still left in me. The guy who lives happily ever after with her. Not this man.

Nevertheless, I was flattered to be asked. And I was also pleased to be going home for a change to work. I knew this would be a landmark. I couldn't predict just what a landmark. And, the more I thought about it, the more I wanted to play Stewart. I knew it wouldn't be pretty. But there lay the challenge.

I saw *The Power of the Dog* a few weeks ago. And I wrote to Benedict Cumberbatch immediately afterwards. I said, 'My dear Benedict, you played one of Jane's Ugly Men. And you never blinked. I salute you, my friend.' If anyone can say that with assurance, it's most certainly me.

I've never been afraid to play bad people. I think they're fun. And, you know, every bad guy has his reasons. They're damaged. Something happened to them. When I had to play Major Campbell in *Peaky Blinders*, I pictured him growing up as an only child in some grim rectory in Ulster, a small boy without a mother, beaten daily by a brutal man in a dog collar.

Stewart is an archetypal Campion Ugly Man. Patriarchal, uncommonly stupid and incapable of comprehending women or indeed the world he lives in. In particular, colonial New Zealand, where he has settled. His faults are manifest. But, of course, it's the other dimensions you can bring to a character that give them depth and interest and, with luck, some humanity. I felt desperately sorry for Stewart. He so wants to be loved. He is so alone. He is so out of his depth. I thought of an image, a metaphor, that I used throughout the film as a key to the man himself. I felt like, instead of the usual six or seven layers of skin, he only has two. He is raw, tender and vulnerable. And there is pathos to be found in someone like that. That pathetic quality has a comic dimension as well. At least I thought so.

In all of this, Jane was a marvellous collaborator. But it was an uncommonly lonely job for me. Holly and I got along fine. But she was of necessity remote. I understand it. She commits to a role, and any joking around, the everyday currency I'm used to, would've been a distraction for her. Playing our scenes together was disturbing for me. I never knew whether it was Holly looking at Sam, or Ada looking at Stewart. The lines between life and fiction were blurred and it was not in any way comfortable.

Stewart. A complex character indeed.

The famous scene where I drag her out into the mud and sever one of her piano-playing fingers was a big ask. Holly is small, but she is very strong. I realised on the first take that the struggle to get her out there would have to be actual. She wasn't going without a fight. Personally I prefer to fake these things. Acting. Not Holly. And I have to confess I'm still a little hurt that she insisted that my axe be swapped for a rubber replica. I mean, for fuck's sake! Did she really think that I would get carried away and actually cut off her finger? I chuckle as I write this. I'm an actor, not a beast, for heaven's sake. By take three I was absolutely exhausted, and thankfully Jane had what she needed and I didn't have to go through the whole business of fighting Holly out into the mud and the rain machine once more, my friends.

But Holly is incredible in the film. It was an unusual experience, because that extraordinary soundtrack saturated all of the filming. Michael Nyman had already written the theme, and Holly had three or four pieces to perform on camera. So in between takes she would practise what would become that famous score. That music somehow soaked the forest, the beach, the rain. It haunts me to this day.

Holly got an Oscar for this and deserved it. I hope she can say I helped a little bit in my own way. Jane says I did do one thing that helped. We were sitting around waiting for the right weather to shoot the finger chop. No actor could possibly know how they would react to having a finger severed like that. I told a story of David Lean directing Omar Sharif in *Doctor Zhivago*. Omar was dismayed that the entire Saint Petersburg massacre scene would be simply a shot of him reacting to this horror in close-up. Lean apparently gave him this advice: 'Imagine you are having sex, you are close to orgasm, and *you do not want it to finish*!' Try it.

Keitel was another story again. Since we were working in my country, I felt it incumbent on me to be even more than usually hospitable and friendly. It didn't work. Harvey was truculent and hostile for the whole film. Even in rehearsals it was difficult. We rehearsed, one day, a scene where Stewart comes in with a gun. He holds it over Baines and tells them to leave. Weirdly, Harvey would, unbidden, seize the bloody gun out of my hands. Jane would ask him why he was doing that. Harvey would reply, Because I can. Jane would explain, Well, yes, but that's not what's written in the script. It never got better. Thankfully we didn't have many scenes in the film, and I was happy to say goodbye to him.

The fourth character is the remarkable Anna Paquin. She was like nothing I'd ever seen before. That wilful, wild talent. Quicksilver. Her performance in the film must be the greatest ever from a child in a movie. She got an Oscar as well. But Anna was a kid, so I didn't really have any pals.

That is, apart from some of the supporting players. We had a whole bunch of wonderful Māori guys, who play a kind of Greek chorus in the film. Temuera Morrison was the gang leader and we became good friends. There was a huge guy, a lovely sweet guy called Foot, among them. Foot was also a dope dealer back in Auckland and could sort you with the best grass known to man. An abiding memory I have is of him, with full moko (face tattoo), wearing a piupiu skirt, with a military jacket and hat, wading in the creek picking puha (watercress). One hand in the water, the other hand on a huge brick mobile phone doing deals back home.

Genevieve Lemon and Kerry Walker played my aunties, and whenever they turned up they were a breath of fresh air. Funny, irreverent and real. A blessed relief. God, I loved them. But it was a curiously solitary acting experience for me. Happily, Jane is a very caring director for her cast, and was always there to hug me when I was at my lowest.

The great Andrew McAlpine was the designer of the film.

Stewart's cottage was actual, so we could film inside and out. We were buried in dark green bush and mud. It was an immersive experience. Janet Patterson dressed us in drab, atmospheric hues. Stuart Dryburgh's lighting was dark and murky. It felt like we were underwater in the bush. We shot some of it on the west coast beach Karekare. Some parts of New Zealand feel more haunted than others to me. Tim Finn said once that there's often 'too much blood in the soil' in our land. Karekare is like that for me. And indeed I'm told there was a terrible massacre at the south end of the beach in pre-European times. It has always felt stark and grim for me. Darker than just moody.

I first saw the film in North Sydney. Jane invited me to a screening one Thursday morning. I had no idea what to expect. When it was finished, I couldn't leave my seat. I was in tears that Jane had made something so grand. I sat there for a long time thinking about it, and how completely grateful I was to be a part of something so transcendentally beautiful.

We took *The Piano* to Cannes. The audience there doesn't muck around. If they hate it, they let you know. If they love it, they adore you. When the lights came up they rose to their feet and would not stop clapping. It went on and on, cheering and yelling. Yes, they loved it. Eventually, the applause undiminished, we retreated to the foyer before we stepped out into the night and faced the cameras.

It occurred to me to be gracious and have a few words to Harvey. I walked over to him, clapped him on the back, and said, 'Harvey, I think you're fantastic in this. Congratulations, you are amazing.' And I meant it. Every word.

Even if you don't mean it, in common courtesy you would think he'd probably return even a half-arsed compliment. Something like, 'You're not too bad yourself.' Just some ordinary civility.

But no. Not Harvey. He muttered thanks. And turned his back on me. Hmmm.

Jane was unable to be there to accept the Palme d'Or for Best Film, and asked me to go on stage and pick it up on her behalf. I flew back from Spain to do so. I said, as I held the big one in front of that distinguished audience, that it was a long way from New Zealand to the stage upon which I now stood. I was very proud of Jane.

I don't think I can overestimate how important *The Piano* is for me in hindsight. It sits on my funny old CV like a medal on my chest. It wasn't my film. It was Jane's. I wasn't the star of the film. That was Holly. But there is honour to be found in the second fiddle. Or fourth. No one notices you much, you don't get nominated for things. But you served. I was there in an important feminist film. I was there on the front line in an important New Zealand film. Neither of these labels does the film justice. It's a work of art. And look, that tiny little figure in the fabric—see down there on the right—that's me. It's a film that will always have a place in cinema history. And I served in it.

The Odd Couple in Nicaragua

IF you're lucky you have friends. If you're very lucky, you have unlikely friends.

Julian Fellowes is the most unlikely friend I can think of. He's like a parody of an old-school Tory. Blimp in profile. Sporting a club tie. A well-tailored suit determinedly old-fashioned and just worn enough to justify the term shabby chic. His politics are positively archaic. He is the only person I know who actually admits to being a Brexiteer. I'd like to think he might regret this one day, as his beloved Britain slides into increasing isolation and obscurity. Fat chance. Julian is famous for, among other things, writing and producing *Downton Abbey*. It has made him rich, and fair enough. Not only that, he is, of all things, a Conservative peer. Lord Fellowes, the Brexiteer. I'm afraid his dream that Brexit might lead Britain back to something like its former glory is a delusional fantasy. A fantasy as absurd as Downton itself—that seductive dream of an Edwardian age, complete with grateful servants and benign aristocrats.

We met at a dinner party in Los Angeles in 1986. Mine host was my beloved friend Christopher Cazenove. I seem to remember Chris was doing *Dynasty*, one of those prime-time soaps that were all the go at that time. Utter rubbish, but paid well. Chris and I got to know each other in Poland, when we worked together on *From a Far Country*. It was the strangest of times. It was communist Poland and the place was a mess. There was nothing in the shops, just people queueing for whatever might turn up.

We were staying at the Holiday Inn on the outskirts of Kraków. The hotel downstairs had the grandest restaurant in all of the city. The waiters were dressed to the nines in dinner suits and bow ties. Because they basically worked for the state and certainly not for the customer, if they could be bothered at all, they might dawdle over in their own time and present you with a large leather-bound menu. The menu was pages long. So much on offer. The problem was that everything was off. You could run through the whole menu pointing at things, and inevitably they would shake their heads. *Nie.* No. The only thing you could rely on was borscht. An unlimited supply.

You could, however, if you knew who to talk to, buy things on the black market. Chris discovered that you could buy caviar if you asked the taxi drivers. The taxi drivers also worked for the secret police, which I imagine accounted for their easy access to caviar. Corrupt as all hell and ready to dob you in, given half the chance. We could buy pots of caviar for three dollars a pop. I checked at Fortnum & Mason, when I got back to London, to see how much that would cost in the real world. Something like £360. Today I'm told Beluga caviar costs ten thousand dollars a kilo.

Of course, caviar was out of my ken, having never tasted it before, but Chris knew about such things. He was an old Etonian, but a nice one. An army background not unlike my own. We got on like a house on fire from day one. I not only liked him, I admired him. He dressed in an effortlessly elegant manner. He rode a motorbike. Not any motorbike but an extremely stylish Ducati. He drove cars, when he could afford them, like Aston Martins.

One night, driving home into London from the south-west, going too fast and probably a little drunk, he lost control of his sports car at a roundabout. He ploughed straight into a terrace house, right into the sitting room. Demolishing bay windows, bricks and all on the way. It was late at night. Chris was fine, but the house was not. He stumbled out of the car, choking on all the dust, and spotted an outraged house owner stomping down the stairs. The poor man had had half his house destroyed, and there was a wrecked sports car where his sofa used to be. The owner was purple with rage, and Chris went into apology mode, stammering and stuttering—he could not have been more sorry. But then suddenly the anger stopped, and instead a large smile spread over the face of the unfortunate house owner. He looked at Chris and pointed. He said, 'I know you. You're on the telly!' (This prang incidentally mimicked a similar crash in New Zealand about the same time. My idiot friend Nigel Hewat lost control of his Mini, spun off Ferry Road in Christchurch and smashed into an undertaker's chapel. No one hurt, but rather asking for it, you'd have to say.)

So, anyway, a dinner party at Chris's place in the Hollywood Hills was inevitably stylish. Around the table were the beautiful and famous. Joan Collins held court. I sat beside Bianca Jagger. Two exceptions to all this were myself, a plain and awkward Antipodean, and, across from me, a plump, red and slightly sweaty Englishman with a voice like a foghorn and opinions just as loud. Julian Fellowes, at this time of his life, was an actor very seldom in work. In penury. He was also funny and a great conversationalist. Even at his most boorish and pompous, you can forgive Julian just about anything. There was always that little flickering smile; he's very clever and easily smart enough to know how absurd, how ridiculous he often appears, what a complete anachronism. But he also couldn't care less. He's taking the piss. That smile dances somewhere between the smug and the subversive.

Julian wanted to know why I was in Los Angeles. When I told him I was en route to Nicaragua he found it completely hilarious. At the time America was engaged in an unseemly proxy war in Central America. The Reagan administration regarded the Sandinista government in Nicaragua as a threat to Democracy and the Free World. It needed to be eliminated; the CIA and the Pentagon were putting as much force as they could behind the Contras. It was civil war between reactionaries and reformists. As a reflex lefty, my sympathies were with the Sandinistas. They believed in such radical ideas as literacy and health care for all, having dumped the vile Somoza dictatorship. Unpalatable for Washington.

I wanted to go see for myself and had organised a visit through Richard Gere, who had similar views. I was flying down there the next day. Julian thought this was a ridiculous idea, and that the place itself would be ridiculous. I said, Why don't you come and see for yourself, and to my surprise he said he would. And so I found myself for the next ten days in the company of someone I thought might have stepped out of a P. G. Wodehouse novel. Travelling through revolutionary Central America with Colonel Blimp himself.

Of course, I was wrong about Julian. He was much more interesting than that. He turned out to be the most entertaining of companions. He took a somewhat jaundiced view of what the Sandinistas were trying to do, while I tended to see things through rose-tinted glasses. Neither of us was right and neither of us expected what we found. A beautiful mountainous country, with the most charming people. Far from being a monstrous threat to anyone, let alone America, Nicaragua was a place of almost no consequence. Rather than hating America, all anyone in Nicaragua wanted to be was American. They loved baseball to distraction. Managua, the capital, was tiny, with a mere two hotels. One of them had the only elevator in the entire country, and that was bust.

We met several Sandinistas of differing importance. They all seemed like decent people. Out of interest, we dropped by the American embassy, to get another view of things. The ambassador asked us to dinner, to our complete surprise, and we accepted. He and his wife were delighted to see us. He'd apparently said a few mild things in favour of the Sandinistas, and was now persona non grata in Washington. The Sandinistas would have nothing to do with him either. He represented the Beast from the North. So the poor man was isolated from everybody. He was pleased that we were happy to eat his food, and we liked him very much.

We travelled to the front on a bus with a bunch of earnest, drab lefties, mainly women, from the States. All deadly serious. Not a glimmer of humour anywhere. I thought, We're looking at trouble here. Everything they believed in was anathema to Julian, and vice versa. They all had more in common with me than with the plump Tory by my side. However, to my surprise, within a day or so Julian had charmed them all to pieces, and they were helplessly disarmed. All his booming, trenchant right-wing views seemed to cause them no offence at all. They just found him funny. As I did. And he seems to have been amused by me. He tells the story that one night we couldn't get to a hotel and were forced to shelter in a public lavatory beside 'a very ancient and smelly urinal', along with one of the activists, who made it clear that he was not happy about our improvised sleeping quarters. Apparently, fed up, I snapped at our grumbling companion, 'It is obvious to me that you have never spent any time at an English public school.'

Perhaps this was why the activists ignored me. I was no fun at all.

We saw no action at the front, nor did we want to. The most sober moment of the trip was when we were introduced to the Mothers of the Revolution, women who had lost sons or daughters in combat with the Contras. Their quiet, dignified grief was moving beyond measure.

We both left Nicaragua with our views on things completely unchanged. It was one of those vivid times in your life when you've witnessed some history. We both learnt, if we didn't know it already, that you can be friends with people who have completely contrary views to your own. Unlikely friends.

Subsequently, the Sandinistas declined into corruption and bad governance. All that idealism has long evaporated. Their leader, Daniel Ortega, is back and effectively a dictator now, not completely unlike the Somoza he was instrumental in deposing. Ironies abound. Julian's suspicions were justified. I am disappointed.

And now it's Lord Fellowes. You can see pictures on the net of Julian wearing his ermine or mink kit and a hat that beggars belief, walking into the chamber to be invested. To me he looks ridiculous, but the great thing about Julian is—he couldn't give a stuff. I happen to think that, if one has to have an upper house in parliament, the House of Lords is an absurdity. It is utterly undemocratic and, despite reform, full of privilege and entitlement. It embodies the class system, still the worst thing about Britain.

Julian has been extraordinarily successful. The dilatory appearance is deceptive; he works very hard. He directs, writes novels, musicals (the book for *Mary Poppins*, for instance), and a string of vastly popular series and films about posh people, and it's done him very well. I'm happy for him.

From Sean's Shubmarine to the Sistine Chapel

IN 1990 I found myself in Los Angeles working alongside Sean Connery, for John McTiernan. The film was *The Hunt for Red October*, and it was enormously successful. If there's one truism in Hollywood it's this: submarine movies always make money.

Sean was an old hero of mine, and I'd grown up on his movies. In particular the Bond films in which he was so definitive. There was a moment in the 1980s when I myself was in the running to play Bond. I was made to do an abortive audition at Pinewood Studios by my agent. I hated every moment of it, and knew with utter certainty I did not want the gig. I had no desire to be the one Bond that no one liked. It didn't come my way, so no decision was necessary anyway. Years later, at La Colombe d'Or, Roger Moore popped over to our table. 'You should have been Bond,' he said. I was a little lost for words. I couldn't really tell him I'd hate to be Bond, since that might have been obliquely insulting to him. Nice man.

I played Sean's 2IC in *Red October*; it was a good part among a very large cast, full of excellent actors. Courtney B. Vance, Scott Glenn, James Earl Jones, Alec Baldwin, Tim Curry…a long list. Much of the action takes place in two submarines, and for that reason is necessarily claustrophobic.

I was very happy to be working alongside Sean for a few weeks, and there was much to learn. One thing I didn't need to take on board was his diligence in tax avoidance. We would finish early on a Friday so he could fly up to Canada for the weekend, returning on Monday morning. Admittedly up there he was able to indulge in golf, the only thing that he unreservedly loved in all the world, but mainly it was to ensure that he wouldn't spend any more time than necessary in the US. God forbid he should have to pay tax to Uncle Sam. Or anyone else for that matter. Many years earlier my accountant in Britain had persuaded me that I needed to go to the Bahamas on my week off and look at buying a house. He foresaw a career for me in which tax would be absolutely out of the question. I had a look at the Bahamas, and the hapless existence of those tax exiles, condemned forever to a damned golf course in the company of other exiles. To me, this was not only wrong, but utterly miserable. I never went back.

Before we started shooting, the US Navy was kind enough to invite us out for a weekend on a nuclear sub, the USS *Houston*. Tim Curry, Courtney B. Vance, Peter Firth and me. Post September 11 this would be unthinkable; most of us weren't even American. The navy were very hospitable, and we had a great weekend. It's very quiet down there; it's not called the Silent Service for nothing. You don't even get the sensation that the submarine is moving. I was handed the controls for a minute or so. I didn't cause an emergency. However, a VIP guest, the mayor of a major midwestern city, was given the wheel after me and he plunged the sub into a nosedive for some reason. Panic, perhaps. He froze and had to be wrestled out of the chair; an ordinary seaman pulled us out of our nosedive and a spectacular nuclear death at the bottom of the ocean.

We were given a tour of the entire submarine. There was, however, a point towards the bow where heavily armed marines ensured we could go no further. Up there were nuclear torpedoes. On the same tour I got to listen to the ocean through sonic headphones. You could hear dolphins whistling and clicking, whales singing their strange, haunting songs, all kinds of creatures communicating with each other across great distances. But not us. We were quiet as mice, eavesdropping.

The first time you see us in the film, Sean and I are in the conning tower of an enormous Russian submarine. In fact it was a set built on top of two barges, towed by a tug. It's here that we somehow stop speaking Russian and speak English instead. It's the movies. We were told to use our own voices, and not assume a fake Russian accent. I tended to ignore that instruction; the idea of a Russian officer from Leningrad with a New Zealand accent was frankly absurd. I put just a hint of Russian in there, or tried to. Sean, of course, spoke as only Sean speaks. I was told that the barges that carried our sub set flipped upside down a few weeks later, when they were shooting wide shots without cast. Had Sean and I had been there, we would've drowned. I imagined Sean shouting something like 'Sham! Shave your shelf!'

All of our interiors were shot on a stage at Paramount, beautifully detailed, and mounted on a kind of gimbal. This meant that we could tip forwards, backwards, sideways, at will. It was pretty cool, and we had a lot of guests come by to have a look. I was pleased and relieved to see them; it's the only film I've ever done that had an entirely male cast and an entirely male crew. It was like being in a sweaty rugby locker room for a couple of months.

David Crosby came by once; he was a fan of submarine films. He never climbed the stairs to look at the set, but instead spent the time grazing at the snack table. More craft service, less sea craft. Grace Jones came by, seemingly wired; she didn't eat anything. The oddest visit was by Eddie Murphy. He was shooting something else on the lot. You'd see him drive past sometimes on a golf buggy customised with a Rolls-Royce grille. One day we were told Eddie would be coming by to see Sean. Mid-afternoon we heard a lot of stomping across the studio floor. Eddie was on approach, with a large entourage in attendance. They stomped up the stairs looking for Sean. I was in the set corridor as they drew near. A huge guy in front of Eddie put out a massive hand and flattened me against the wall, so that Eddie could walk by unimpeded. Once Eddie had passed, I was released. As they circled the set looking for Sean, who wasn't there, I thought, Did that really just happen? Satisfied that Connery was absent, they departed, having ignored everyone else. And, sure enough, the same guy, on the way out, flattened me against the wall once more. Good to know where you come in the order of things.

John McTiernan was a very good director. It seems a shame to me that he hasn't made more films—he's a real talent. Courtney Vance was my best pal on the film, a very cool guy and a great actor. I only got to work with Alec Baldwin for a day or two. I admire Baldwin, and his work. But we were on different sides in a Cold War film, and ne'er the twain shall meet. Pity.

*

The Cold War was over by the time *The Hunt for Red October* was in the cinemas. But it was still in full swing when we were shooting *From a Far Country* in Poland with Krzysztof Zanussi. This was the time of *Solidarność*, and we were expecting the Russians to roll in with tanks at any time, like Hungary in 1956. Or indeed Ukraine in 2022. Poland was still oppressively Soviet, but the Poles we were working with were all subversive in one way or another. The unity of being anti-government gave everyone in the arts there a sense of purpose. It's no accident, I think, that many of the best movies in countries like Poland and Czechoslovakia were made under Soviet rule *in spite of* the government. The same is true of China; the great era of Chinese films is the 1990s.

Brilliant films that had something to say, the subtext often being a subtle critique of their regimes.

This was an Italian–Polish co-production, and the contrast between the Italians and the Poles was marked. I remember Krzysztof saying to me how sorry he felt that, in the middle of the snow and the mud, the Polish crew were all wearing their best clothes. I looked around and saw nothing particularly remarkable. He said, 'Look at their jeans.' You couldn't get jeans in communist Poland except on the black market, where they were extremely desirable and expensive. The Poles were embarrassed to be wearing their shitty communist clothes in front of the heedless Italians, all dressed, of course, in Milan, carelessly, casually fashionable. So the poor Polish crew were wearing their best dress-up clothes so as not to look entirely foolish beside all the Gucci.

I was playing a priest, based on a real person, who ended up in Auschwitz but somehow survived. I visited the site to check things out the day before I was due to shoot there. Auschwitz is enormous, a place where even the soil is soaked with misery and blood. I wandered about in the snow trying to find the crew. Finally I turned a corner around another dreary grey building, and that's where I had a vivid experience I will never forget. It was as if I had time-travelled to 1942. In front of me were sleek German guards strolling up and down, with snarling alsatians on leashes. And lined up against the grey building were rows and rows of inmates, in striped pyjamas and hats, shivering in the cold. They all looked starved and frightened. It was, of course, our set, but it looked more than real to me. There was no sign of the camera crew, just the starkest scene from the dark past. It physically shocked me.

(I have just been to the Jewish Museum opposite the hospital for a quick look at the Sidney Nolan Auschwitz exhibition.

Instead of ten minutes, it took me another fifteen in there to stop
heaving with tears. Plan ahead, my advice.)

The extras—the inmates—had all been recruited from desti-
tute men's old-age homes and juvenile detention centres. I
suspect they were all, in fact, half starved. And bloody miserable.
Later we filmed in a prison, a real prison, and my character had
to be tortured by the Gestapo. This involved a lot of screaming
and carrying on by me in a large, dank concrete cell. The prison
authorities rushed down the corridor to demand that we quieten
it down. They thought we might start a riot among the prisoners.
This rather put a dampener on proceedings. But they came back
a short time later and told us to carry on as before. It seemed that
since I was being tortured in English, and the whole prison could
hear my screams, this might be a salutary lesson to the inmates. If
the prisoners imagined they were actually torturing *tourists* now,

Filming *From a Far Country* in Auschwitz.

that might give these tough nuts some pause for thought.

Later, another vivid moment, but magical. We were staying with Sławomir Idziak, our cinematographer, in the Tatra Mountains, midwinter. We were taken for a long night-time sleigh ride through the mountain forests, freezing cold with moonlight reflecting off snow in the trees. We were wrapped snug under big fur rugs; the only sounds were the soft, rhythmic jingling of bells and muffled hooves trotting on snow-covered paths. Our breaths were orange clouds lit by the flambeaus beside the driver. We got home exuberant, beating the freeze out of ourselves, and drank convivial vodka.

Later we moved to Italy and filmed in the Vatican, and there, more vividness. A very rare privilege, but then the film was about the origins of Pope John Paul II. I was the one cast member to make it to Rome. We met the Pope himself, and I kissed the holy ring. We were given a tour of the Pope's private treasury. There was one curiosity there, among all the gilded, jewel-encrusted robes and so on, that I've never forgotten. It was a solid silver hammer. It seems that, when a pope dies, it is used for confirmation of same. They hit him on the head three times with the hammer, and say his name three times. Bong. John Paul. Bong. John Paul. Bong. John Paul. If there's no response, he's dead for sure.

But the vivid moment was this. We were night shooting, and I wasn't needed for a couple of hours. I wandered down a few corridors and found the Sistine Chapel. There was one Swiss Guard on duty. He was pleased to see me and invited me in. I had the whole place to myself. I lay on the floor for a couple of hours and gazed at the ceiling, communing with Michelangelo and the celestial heavens until I was saturated. That was a vivid moment indeed.

Another reason to be grateful for that film is that I became friends with Warren Clarke and Chris Cazenove. Both extremely

English but completely different. Warren, working class, from Manchester, with a face like a bulldog. Chris, verging on upper class, dapper, charming and handsome. I loved them both, and they're both now long gone. They were enthusiastic smokers, which a lot of people were back then, and that may have had something to do with both of them dying too soon. Great shame.

They were vivid friends, made during a vivid time.

The Self and Others

THIS evening I started to think.

To be specific, I started to think about myself. The self. Not in a selfish way, particularly, but about who I am. That takes some thinking.

When I was asked in the past whether I think about things, I would always say reflexively, 'No, I'm not much of a thinker. I'm as shallow as a puddle.' It's amusing to say that. At least, it amuses me. It's also, I suspect, partly true. Admittedly, it's slightly defensive. I'm always likely to be overawed by intelligence in someone who properly thinks.

By contrast, I've always been a rather more instinctive person. I don't give things a lot of thought. And until tonight it's probably true that I haven't thought much about myself. I don't have a great deal of self-regard. I don't have tickets on myself. I think I can honestly say I don't have a big ego. I am, after all, a New Zealander; we don't do ego much. On the other hand, it's probably true that I could've done with a little more introspection from time to time. Perhaps there would've been fewer mistakes.

It's been useful to me, digging back into my memory these past few months. But remembering is not the same thing as thinking. For a change, this evening I am thinking about who I am and where I am. Now.

It's good to remember the past. It's good to remember all the things you've been grateful for. It's good to remember all those people and animals and things that you've loved over all those years. But it is the past.

The useful thing at this moment is to think about the present. Thinking about the future is of no great consequence to me right now, or at least it shouldn't be.

Now, just because you know something to be true doesn't mean you always subscribe to it. For instance, I know with certainty that this is true—you should live by the motto Be Here Now. It's so easy to forget that. Thinking about the future can often be self-defeating. Especially right now, right in *this* now, when I find myself in this particular present.

Thinking into the future is a very human thing. It allows us to plan, to make a blueprint. Most achievements are owed to people who can project into the future with a map. But it also can be counterproductive to be in the future. For one thing, it can spoil the pleasure of the present. It can also fill us with fear. What is the worst thing that can happen? Fear is of no use to me now, none. I know there's something inside me that's trying to kill me. It's not even worth giving a name to it. I don't care for it. So I won't call it anything.

Let's talk about that for a moment. I'm not afraid of dying at all. If they give me four weeks to live, that's four weeks of living, and thanks for that. The dying part I couldn't care less about.

Before I went to bed tonight, I looked at myself in the mirror. Properly. I've never been much of a mirror man. But these past few weeks I've been actively avoiding looking at my reflection at all. I haven't recognised myself. There's a bald, wizened old man there. By any objective standard it's an unattractive sight. Completely hairless and creased like an old sheet.

I raised both arms towards the sky. There is no gesture you can make that says you are alive, on a planet, more than that, with your face turned upwards to the sky. There I was, all old bone and sinew and ribs.

And then I looked again. I looked properly at my true self. Without any judgment. And I saw me. I told myself this one thing. You are unique. There is only one you. And that is you there, right here, for better or worse. Except that there is no better, and there is no worse. It's just you.

And I am alive. Right now in this moment I am truly alive. This me.

Most of what I've written has been about other people. And the truth is that I find other people more interesting than I find myself. Well, they just are. The lives of others.

So many of the stories in this book are about people who enriched my life immeasurably. Or, occasionally, not. If I've made a film that turns out to be good, that's a good result. If I've made a film that's good and made a couple of friends, that's a great result. If I've made a film that's no good, but I made a friend, that's still another great result.

It's at a time like now that the importance of other people is thrown into even sharper relief. You realise who your friends are. You know where the love is. My children are extraordinary, and I now have eight grandchildren. I am immensely proud of them all. My girls were just here, with family. So affectionate and support-ive. So easy to be with, so funny. I love the ease that comes when you're all adults, the shorthand you have, the gentle teasing that we all do that makes us comfortable and really known. They are sunbeams. My son Tim calls me every day from New Zealand. That concern for me, that worry about my wellbeing, touches me more than I can say. His endless, anarchic good humour buoys me.

I don't talk much about my children; they don't feature in *Who* or the *Women's Weekly*. But being a parent has been one of the great privileges of my life. It's a lot of work, and I worked hard not just with them, but outside, on their behalf. I might be making excuses there for not being around enough when they were growing up, but I'm sticking with it anyway.

And I would be remiss if I did not mention how important, how completely vital, how central some women have been to me. First of all as friends. As companions. And also as lovers. But remiss I am going to be, I'm afraid. This is decidedly not *Woman's Day* or *People*, so I'm going to pass on this subject altogether. We do not need anything that would embarrass them or me. Particularly as I am so completely and humbly grateful that anyone ever bothered with me at all.

Yesterday was another time when the importance of friends was at the fore. The day started glum, but I dragged myself out. Sass and Craig, actor pals, were over from New Zealand and no one had seen them for about three years. It's a long absence. There was a gathering of their mates, most of whom are my mates as well. A long afternoon of chat, good food, laughing and some singing with the old familiars. There's Paul, who can talk about anything and does if you give him a chance. Michael and Anthony squirming with delight at things. Jeppy, who can make the room warm without lighting the heater. Elise, who looks you in the eye with the companionship that only someone on the same journey as you can have. Mark, who is delightful to follow down some obscure topic and wring it by the neck. Yesterday it was fish oil and liquefied Weet-Bix, for goodness' sake. Scott, who is often on some other planet, but it's always a nice one. Jenny, who just gets me. Erika, who has been needlessly kind to me for decades.

And then, when I got home, a video call with Rob Sitch and Jane Kennedy from Melbourne. An hour and a half; it flew by, everything to talk about and still not enough time, and more than anything weeping with laughter. I don't think there's any tonic in the world, any medicine, any chemotherapy, that is better than laughter. Most particularly with old friends who know you better than you know yourself.

As an aside, there's a mild form of this therapy that I developed during the isolation that was COVID lockdown. It's simple. If I'm feeling glum, I make myself smile. For no good reason, just smile. You can feel something happening physically to you, as well as mentally. Endorphins kicking in. Just those muscles on your dial trigger good emotions. I have no idea why they don't teach this in venerable institutions. I should copyright it.

But, then again, don't take this too seriously. I am, after all, shallow as a puddle.

Ralph Hotere

FOR some reason New Zealand has always been blessed with great visual artists, in particular painters.

This is a puzzle to me. Is it because we're not articulate people? We see things and see them well, but don't have the wherewithal to express our perceptions in words? But then I think of all the great poets we've produced: Glover, Baxter, O'Sullivan, Manhire, Bornholdt, McQueen, Curnow, Tūwhare, Turner and so on.

But great painters—we are awash with them.

In 1972 I saw a major retrospective of Colin McCahon's work in the old Dunedin City Art Gallery in Logan Park, starting with those wonderful views of the Otago peninsula that I knew only too well. The privilege of wandering through a man's imagination, his own personal take on my country, his progress, his ambition, his courage against the critics and the naysayers, his journey into pop art (cartoon speech bubbles) long before pop art, the limpid simplicity of a North Otago landscape, the refusal to flinch from the darkness I also saw in our land, the use of words, the sheer audacity to go your own way in a stitched-up country as it was then.

I'm pretty sure it was this exhibition of McCahon's that led me to fall in love with painting in general, and in particular New Zealand painters. Rita Angus, Toss Woollaston, Bill Hammond, Gordon Walters, Shane Cotton, Dick Frizzell, Don Binney, John Pule, Robin White, among many others, have meant more to me than I can possibly express. They fill me with wonder and gratitude. I'm lucky enough to own one or two things of theirs.

Some even became friends. Grahame Sydney, the regionalist, as I disparagingly call him, lives down the road from me in the Maniototo. We have a splendidly affectionate, competitive and rude relationship. Our emails are loud with abuse of the worst kind. We are the sort of friends who can be inordinately cruel to each other and none of it hurts. That's rare. It's underpinned with mutual admiration, which is never ever stated. That would be a betrayal of our unique shared savagery. I own a couple of Grahame Sydney paintings which I dearly love, but I would never, of course, tell him that. He's iconic.

A few years ago we went together to the funeral of Ralph Hotere. Ralph is arguably, after McCahon, the most important New Zealand painter of the twentieth century. Grahame and I sat there aghast in St Joseph's Cathedral in Dunedin. Our friend Ralph was in a box up by the altar, guarded touchingly by whanau, including his adored daughter, Andrea. The pomp and ceremony was above and around him. The main addresses were mostly by people who hardly knew Ralph. One of them was the minister for the arts, whose name I've forgotten. I'm sure he's a perfectly nice man, but he was unforgivably from the National Party. Ralph was a socialist through and through, politically astute and angry with it, and I could sense Ralph rolling in his coffin at the idea that a right-winger would be asked to talk on this of all days.

Ralph and I were friends for many, many years. I first got to know him soon after he'd moved to Dunedin permanently, after he won a Frances Hodgkins Fellowship. He was about the coolest guy in Dunedin, dark, good-looking, quiet and charismatic. You could see why women adored him and he adored them—some of Ralph's best work are sketches of nudes. He had a flat near the university where, if you were lucky, you might end up on a Saturday night. Or, luckier still, earlier in the day, for a cup of coffee and a chat.

Later he moved to Port Chalmers and began some of his greatest work in the space a dedicated studio allowed: a shed really, perched on the hill above the port. Soon after I joined the National Film Unit, Sam Pillsbury made a half-hour film there about Ralph. Ralph, as was his wont, was happy enough to participate, but refused to talk about his work. Other people talk about Ralph instead. Obdurate silence about his art only deepened the mystery. You have to work out for yourself what his painting meant. Some of the political stuff later on was explicit enough anyway, and no commentary from Ralph was necessary. Ralph appears all the way through the film at work, and remains doubly enigmatic behind a gas mask, as he spray-paints some of his highly lacquered surfaces.

But one of the things about Ralph was that you didn't need conversation. Sometimes we'd sit, smoke a cigarette, drink a glass of wine and say nothing. We were perfectly content. Years later he'd come and stay with me in Sydney. Sometimes he'd turn up with a woman I hadn't met before, sometimes it was just Ralph. On one trip he travelled to Lake Mungo—somewhere archaeologists were finding ancient human remains, and proof of the oldest living culture in the world. His work in response was very beautiful.

One day we decided to go to Bondi Beach. We smoked a joint on the way. We sat on the beach with hardly a word, but I do remember saying, 'Wow, Ralph, everything is so blue.'

'Sam,' he said, 'you're right, it's very blue.'

I thought that was deep, but those were the times. Later at home he got out some paper and did a drawing for me. It's signed, and it's titled *Sam on the Blue 2*. I asked him why 2, and he said that years ago he'd done another work called *Sam on the Blue*.

Ralph Hotere in his studio. Photograph by Marti Friedlander.

I loved going to Ralph's studio when I was back in New Zealand in the eighties and nineties, just to hang out. Sometimes we'd meet for fish and chips, the best in the country, at The Best Cafe near the station. Later I could be with him for a while in the studio. Ralph hardly ever had people around when he worked, but seemed okay with this, perhaps because I was so seldom in New Zealand. I liked the feeling that I was more or less keeping up with where Ralph was at with his work. Around a couple of bays was Ralph's house, an old villa up the hill, with a classic Jag in the garage, a cabbage tree by the gate and a warm kitchen. When he was with the poet Cilla McQueen you were always welcome, and the chat was grand. She was great fun.

Ralph had a splendid collection of New Zealand art; like many of his contemporaries he would often swap his work for others'. I remember one day I was looking at a small *Muriwai: Necessary Protection* drawing by McCahon. Ralph was pointing at it and spluttering, 'Framer. Bastard. Look what he did! All the little gulls and birds that were there. Bloody framer took a rubber and fuckin' rubbed 'em out! Thought they were just smudges. Bastard.'

Ralph would come up to the house at Queenstown to stay with me sometimes. He liked to play golf up there, a game I loathe. He would always bring a drawing or two, so much so I had to forbid it. It was great to be in Ralph's company of an evening; that was enough for me. Ralph was forever giving things away—there were many blokes with boats in Port Chalmers with good Hoteres, quid pro quo for some freshly caught salmon. And many women under whose beds a grateful Ralph would leave a drawing.

I was always mindful I was humbly in the presence of great-ness.

In the early 2000s Ralph remarried. For some reason, I no

longer found it the warm welcoming place it used to be. I rather felt I was mistrusted somehow, perhaps a reminder of Ralph's previous life, who knows. Ralph also became very ill, after a severe stroke. He was pretty much confined to a wheelchair, and speech became difficult for him. His work became near impossible. This was unutterably sad. I found it very difficult to visit. I wanted to sit with Ralph, just the two of us, like the old days. It didn't matter about his speech, because the thing about Ralph was he never really said much anyway. But it seemed like you were always supervised there. It's possible I've got all this wrong; perhaps they were concerned he might have a seizure. I don't know. But it was very upsetting for me.

In 1984 I happened to be in Dunedin, at my parents', and Ralph was having a big exhibition at Patricia Bosshard's gallery. There were some eight large stretched canvases, all about two metres square. They were predominantly red and black, with some words from his friend the poet Bill Manhire, and often the numbers one to fourteen. They were all simply wonderful. I got there at opening time and I was immediately drawn to one particular painting. It was the greatest Hotere I had ever seen, and I still think that is true. I noted with alarm it already had a red sticker beside it. Ralph sidled up with a cigarette and a glass of red wine. I told him that I had completely fallen in love with that painting, *Empty of Shadows and Making a Shadow*, but it had a red sticker on it. How come?

Ralph said something like 'What the fuck?' And rushed off. He came back in five minutes, muttering, 'Fucking Bosshard. That's her bloody sticker. Fuck that. That's your fucking painting, Sam. Don't worry.'

I felt elated. I felt sorry for his dealer, but not that sorry. She did well on the commission. I lost that painting in my divorce. But I'm fine with that. It is still loved, and that's fine by me.

Ralph's work is now carefully guarded by a trust of some kind. I don't quite understand what they do. Their job, it seems to me, should be to make Ralph's work as familiar, as available, to every New Zealander, every New Zealand kid, as, say, the work of Andy Warhol is to Americans. That doesn't quite appear to be happening, somehow, at least from where I stand. It seems very sad that there are no paintings whatsoever featured in Vincent O'Sullivan's brilliant and definitive biography of Ralph, written at the request of Ralph himself. Who knows why? I hope the next edition will include images of his art. Coffee-table sized, please!

Thinking about Ralph's trust reminded me of when, some twenty-five years ago, I played the artist Norman Lindsay in *Sirens*. My memory is that his estate allowed us to use, from his vast output of riotous, joyful, licentious works, no more than a handful of lithographs. What could have been a celebration of his art was reduced to something considerably less. Well, probably doesn't matter now. Bacchanalia is so last century.

But back to Ralph. A couple of years ago there was a considerable Hotere retrospective mounted at the Dunedin Public Art Gallery. There was no illustrated catalogue. In my view Ralph's work should be everywhere. If we can't see it, I fear he will become increasingly obscure. And provincial. My friend deserves better.

I got there early to see that show in Dunedin. I pretty much had it to myself. It was like being in Ralph's presence all the way round; silent and enigmatic. The work was, like Ralph, deeply profound and complex. It is always instructive to see an artist's work laid out like their life, lived through the long years. Then I walked into the room with *Black Phoenix* dominating the space— immensely powerful. I had helped on that work in 1984, sanding back the charred wood under Ralph's instructions. One of those days was hot, and Ralph wandered off to the pub for a drink. He didn't come back—I think he forgot about us. The bugger. But here, standing in front of this great monument behind the yellow line, I started to weep. I couldn't stop, and the woman keeping an eye on things tactfully wandered away. I wept for Ralph.

Black Phoenix, 1984–88, Port Chalmers, by Ralph Hotere.

The Blockbuster
and the Bomb

IN 1992, I found myself the lead in an enormous blockbuster featuring dinosaurs, directed by no less than Steven Spielberg. Of the main twists and turns in an unlikely career, this seemed the most unlikely of all.

How on earth did that happen? *Jurassic Park* was for quite some time the most successful film ever, and today the franchise, six strong, is the most successful franchise ever. And there I was, the lead, along with Laura Dern, Jeff Goldblum and Richard Attenborough. Let's not forget Samuel L. Jackson, Bob Peck, Wayne Knight and BD Wong.

I was racked by the usual insecurities. Why me? I'm certainly not an action hero. The idea of me going hand to hand with Sylvester Stallone or Arnold Schwarzenegger is simply absurd. I'm more of the ordinary guy on screen. If indeed I was supposed to be that sort of action guy, I was already, I think, forty-five years old, and as always had left things about ten or fifteen years too late. The impostor syndrome would be enhanced later on when we were out and about promoting the movie; the more or less official line from Universal Pictures was that, with *Jurassic Park*, they had set out to prove that they, with Spielberg, could make huge blockbusters without 'movie stars'. This was true enough, but I think it slightly irked us, the actors, to be reminded from time to time we were not real 'stars'. It also rather overlooked the well-established and highly respected careers of Laura, Jeff and

Dicky. As it turned out, we know now that Harrison Ford turned down the part, so the 'no movie star' plan may be not entirely true. I emphasise the word 'slightly', because more than anything we were all delighted to be working with Steven. And to be working on something that would be absolutely groundbreaking, as it turned out.

That delight was justified. I was fascinated by Steven, and I asked someone beforehand, who knew him, for some insight. She said, 'You have to understand—he is part wonder-filled child and part ruthless Hollywood mogul.' Interesting mix. The child-like, enthusiastic part is what people warm to in his best films. I loved his wild enthusiasm, as well as his absolute certainty about what was needed and what he wanted. Good fun.

We almost died in the first few weeks where we were filming on Kauai in the Hawaiian archipelago. One morning we were told to stay back at the hotel and expect a hurricane later in the day. I was down on the beach with Laura Dern, who asked me: 'Sam, do you think we might die today?' As these massive black clouds approached over the Pacific I found I had to tell her that in all honesty the answer was yes, I thought we might. It turned out we came very close. They herded us into a ballroom, all the cast and crew, a few hours before Hurricane Iniki hit us. Iniki was a Category 4 hurricane and it absolutely wrecked the islands, including all our sets. Six people died, and it caused more than three billion dollars' worth of damage.

Iniki was extremely destructive, but it also moved very fast. I think that within three or four hours it had moved on, leaving us surrounded by the wreckage of our huge resort hotel. I'm pretty sure that is why we were spared a large tidal surge through our ballroom, which was just a couple of metres above sea level, a surge that would have probably drowned us all. After a couple of days, we were flown back to Los Angeles. Our producer, Kathleen

Kennedy, worked a miracle there, and filming continued at the studio. Later we did some more scenes on the Big Island, including the run from the Gallimimus. The log that the kids and I hide behind in all that chaos is still much visited by tourists, I'm told. Some years later, a man behind a car rental desk in Honolulu asked me if I would like to take the tour to visit the valley, and that log. I politely declined. I thought it might be churlish to say I'd been there, and done it.

We did break new ground with this film. There was a perfect collision of coming-of-age computer-generated imagery (Steve Williams) with state-of-the-art puppetry (Stan Winston). Some describe the rise of CGI as a contributor to the death of cinema—CGI took the world subsequently by storm, and movies often became spectacles robbed of content. You could destroy cities on your laptop, and not have a reason to care. But *Jurassic* still had both. Audiences loved it, all around the world.

My son Tim was ten at the time, the primo audience, age-wise, for the film. Sadly he wasn't able to visit the set, but he came with us to the premiere in London, in the presence of royalty. He hates me telling the story, but I will do so anyway. I was sitting with Princess Di on my left and Tim and my wife Noriko on my right. About the time the T. Rex first stomps into view, Tim started to drop the most appalling farts. They had to be from him—he was carried away by the action and was oblivious to any social niceties. The draft at the Empire Cinema was wafting this toxic gas across me and straight to Her Royal Highness. Forty-five minutes of gassing—it was like the Somme in there. I was aghast—she can only have thought it was me. I broke out in a cold sweat. After the lights went up, she was very sweet to Tim and pretty much ignored me, which only served to confirm my suspicions.

Jeff, Laura and I became lifelong friends. Jeff went on to lead *The Lost World: Jurassic Park*, and I did so in *Jurassic Park III*, and we all joined forces with Chris Pratt and Bryce Dallas Howard in *Jurassic World Dominion.* In the thirty years since the first *Jurassic,* Alan Grant has become a rather beloved character. Not a super-hero—no magic powers. A man who faints at his first sight of a brachiosaurus is just a man. An ordinary bloke, doing the best he can under extreme circumstances. A man who can't stand kids, but somehow always ends up taking care of them under extreme danger. Running from dinosaurs.

Colin Trevorrow, the director of *Jurassic World Dominion,* a very nice man, dropped me a line recently. He is working on a longer cut, for the fans. I thought it was quite long already, with a lot of characters and even more dinosaurs, but there we go. Colin is of the view that I will enjoy this cut, because there are at least a couple more minutes of Alan Grant in there. Well, who can't get enough of Sam Neill, right? Please read that last sentence in a wry, ironic tone.

Thirty years later and the gang is back.

This *Jurassic* is considerably different from the other two I've been in. Given that it's almost thirty years since the first one, that's not surprising. It's much more of an action film, for one thing, and the action is breathtakingly good. Spielberg had plenty of action, but it's only in the second half that things heat up. Colin likes lots of dinosaurs, as do the *Jurassic World* fans, but I often think it's the dinosaurs you *don't* see that are the scary ones. It's the unknown that can be terrifying. And that, my friends, is true of life and death.

We shot *Jurassic World Dominion* in 2020, peak COVID time. We lived in a little hotel about five minutes' drive from my old stomping ground, Pinewood Studios. The hotel is surrounded by a park, very English and bucolic, and we were allowed, at least, to do our daily walks there if we weren't shooting. Making the film was rather like being the canary in the mine—at one point we were the only film production shooting in the entire world—and our rigorous set of protocols was to prove to the film community worldwide that you could shoot a film and keep everybody relatively safe. This was before any vaccine had made an appearance. It meant five months with the cast all together and I enjoyed it a lot. If you have to hunker down in the midst of a pandemic, in the unknown, you couldn't ask for better companions than a bunch of actors.

I was very pleased to be working again with Goldblum and Dern after so long. We'd had a great time on the first *Jurassic*, and we fell back comfortably into each other's company. Jeff and I would jam sometimes on a day off, with me plunking stolidly away on my ukulele and Jeff playing his superb jazz piano. Jeff is a musical wunderkind, and I am not. That was half the fun. I would have liked to rehearse a couple of times when we filmed these things on our phones. But Jeff was adamant—it's once and once only. This approach does wonders for the spontaneity, but sadly nothing for my small skills. It says a lot for Jeff's generosity that he would play at all with a musical dud like me.

Laura is the sweetest and most delightful person I know. Can't sing for nuts, but no one is perfect. And then there were Chris Pratt, Bryce Dallas Howard, BD Wong, Mamoudou Athie, DeWanda Wise, Dichen Lachman. Great bunch. Omar Sy turned up for a couple of weeks. I am in awe of him—what an actor. He contacts me every week or so right now, checking on my health. Campbell Scott, who plays the only real bad guy in the film (aside from Dichen, who was a real good bad gal), became a close friend.

After all these years, some children still call me the Dinosaur Man. It's a compliment, and beats being a mere dinosaur. Which of course I am. It was great to be in such a success, and I owe so much to Spielberg and everyone involved, but I don't think the *Jurassic* series made any seismic shift in my career. I didn't become Mr Action Hero or anything, though there is a weird action-man figurine from 1992 in which a muscular version of me wears peculiar underpants. Between *Jurassic Park* and *Jurassic World Dominion*, I went back to making films that interested me here and there, of varying quality: Mark Peploe's *Victory* by Joseph Conrad (I play Mr Jones, one of the most degenerate characters imaginable) with the marvellous Willem Dafoe as Axel Heyst (we've made three movies together now), as well as Rufus Sewell and Irène Jacob; *Wimbledon* with Kirsten Dunst; *Little Fish* with Cate Blanchett; John Carpenter's *In the Mouth of Madness*; *Sirens* with Hugh Grant and Elle Macpherson; Rob Sitch's *The Dish*; and *Event Horizon* with Laurence Fishburne.

Speaking of seismic shifts, I had dinner in London with Hugh Grant soon after *Sirens*. I asked him what he'd been up to. 'Oh,' he said, 'a piece of complete crap called *Four Weddings and a Funeral*. Mike Newell wouldn't know comedy if he tripped over it. Disaster. Absolute and utter rubbish.' Well, that rubbish helped to make him exactly the kind of star I guess Universal meant back then.

*

I have to confess that I have made the odd rubbish film too. People talk about actors' 'choices'. The raw truth is that very few actors, maybe half-a-dozen in the world, get to choose whatever they want, whenever they want. The rest of us have careers that are simply about an offer for something, and you happen to be free. There are many reasons to go to work, but perhaps the most compelling, certainly in my case, is that you have mouths to feed. It's a job. And for every job you are grateful. Sometimes it's a good idea to remind the mouths you fed that you did it for them. At the end of the day you are a jobbing actor. Nothing special.

One of those movies best avoided was called, egregiously, *United Passions*. Possibly the worst title ever of a film. And I'm reliably told (I haven't seen it) that it is rated as one of the worst films ever made, if not *the* worst. Frankly, I couldn't give a damn.

United Passions was the official film for FIFA prior to the World Cup in 2014. It was financed by FIFA itself, a vanity project if ever there was one. The offer came, and it came with a lot of money. Ridiculous. In addition two actors I admire were already signed up—Gérard Depardieu and Tim Roth. It would mean three weeks in Switzerland, three weeks in Paris and three weeks in Rio. What is not to love about that? Not having any real comprehension that FIFA, which controls the game globally, was regarded with considerable contempt and loathing for its evident corruption, I thought, Why not? Soccer means naught to me. Sounds like fun. And you know what? It was indeed a lot of fun.

We started in Switzerland, in Zurich. FIFA had built

themselves some sparkling new headquarters down the road, but we got to shoot in their old HQ. The president of FIFA, Sepp Blatter, visited the set a couple of times: Tim Roth was playing Sepp. The script, I'd have to say, was flattering for Sepp, and I was interested to meet him when he popped out of a limousine, to our complete surprise. Blatter was one of the most charming people you could imagine: short, rotund, engaging and very amusing. I was vaguely aware that he was under a cloud, and that cloud certainly gave him a good soaking subsequently. But he was fascinating. One of those people you can't keep your eyes off once they enter a room. Charisma personified.

I was playing Sepp's predecessor João Havelange. He was, I think, one of the longest-serving FIFA presidents, and during his tenure FIFA achieved a lot: it built the World Cup into the biggest sporting event on the planet. It also introduced the women's World Cup. The script was less than flattering to him, but did not, however, make mention of the millions he allegedly took in bribes. If I cared at all about soccer, and many people do, I would be outraged. But it is a ridiculous game. So many matches are scoreless, and all too often it comes down to a shootout. After ninety minutes of play, that is patently absurd. The beautiful game? Bah!

But a corrupt powerful guy like Havelange to play? What fun.

Since I was playing a real person, I thought I should do as much research on him as I could. I couldn't find much footage of him, however. I asked Sepp what sort of person he was. He looked at me carefully, the twinkle left his eye, and he said, 'When João enters the room, the temperature falls by ten degrees.'

I could not have been more grateful for such an insight. That kind of thing is gold for an actor.

We went on to shoot the film in France and Brazil as well, and I had a great time. When it was released it was universally damned.

Having not clapped eyes on it, I couldn't possibly comment. It got a rating of zero per cent on Rotten Tomatoes. That is not good. Not good at all. Am I bothered? Nup.

This one thing saddened me. The director was a very nice man called Frédéric Auburtin. We spoke by phone—he was devastated by its reception. It felt like a career-stopper to him. I tried some words of comfort, 'Don't worry, we move on,' and the like, but I don't think it worked. Poor Fred.

During the filming, Tim Roth and I were having a drink in this rather nice courtyard in this rather nice Paris hotel that the producers of *United Passions* had put us in. I thought the question needed to be asked.

I put down my drink and turned to him. I asked, slightly ruefully, 'Tim, tell me honestly, do you think we should be doing this film?'

He put down his drink too. 'Sam,' he said, 'listen to me. This movie will put my kids through college.'

Fair point. But, with everything that we now know about FIFA, would I get involved in another project like this one? In all honesty, no. Even I would have to pass.

Stephen Fry and Whoreson Comedy

FRY has been writing me encouraging, laugh-out-loud letters through all of this. He has been, as is well known, on his own 'journey', like this one. 'Journey' being a word we both particularly abhor in this context.

He has a way with words, but you know that. He called my cancer a 'whoreson pisser' this morning. I think that's rather terrific, and something of a contrast to the more prosaic swearing I get around these parts. As a matter of fact, I think it rather elevates the beast; it sounds like a villain in a Jacobean tragedy. More than it deserves.

I've been reading Stephen's memoirs at the same time. They fill me with an immense pleasure, as well as an uncommon despair. He remembers everything, absolutely everything, which is infuriating, and he also writes like some literary angel. My God, he is good.

Another memoir I recommend highly is Gabriel Byrne's *Walking with Ghosts*. It is a truly wonderful book, up there with any of the greatest Irish literature, and that is saying a lot. Don't try telling me actors are only good for one thing. A lot of people have tried to tell me that—if I speak out on something I am sure to hear 'Why don't you stick to acting. You are *just an actor.*' Christ on a bike, really.

I met Gabriel in Toronto once. I was doing a job there and Gabriel came in, I think, for a film festival. He called me at the hotel and said he was mortified with embarrassment, but could I do him a favour. I said, Of course. He confessed that he was there with his son Jack, aged about eight at a guess, and he'd told Jack that Dr Alan Grant was in the hotel. Jack was apparently overexcited and said he'd love to meet him. Gabriel said, Look, I found a dinosaur claw; I'll send it up to your room and when we come and visit said he'd love be kind enough to just take it out of your pocket and give it to Jack, as Alan Grant?

I did so. I hope Jack kept the claw, because I did a good twenty minutes of Alan Grant for his benefit. He didn't, in all honesty, look terribly impressed, and I can hardly blame him.

When I first started living in London in the early 1980s, England was still pretty dreary. Strikes everywhere, Thatcher, the Falklands War, the Yorkshire Ripper, the dying of British industry as well as a poisonous atmosphere. The IRA were bombing Britain; you never quite knew when a parked car might demolish you along with the rest of the street. No wonder the royal wedding, absurd as it was, perked up a monochrome nation for a day or two. For all that, I found it exciting and I was happy to be there.

I was there in the 1980s, but I missed them. I was in London, but I didn't belong there. I've never been part of that fabric, nor did I mind. I wasn't fashionable, nor interested in fashion. I knew that Sloane Square and the King's Road were braying with Sloane Rangers, but they were risible. *Brideshead Revisited* had made class acceptable once again among young people with little chin and less brain. Everywhere else there was boofy hair and shoulder pads, and music was in sharp decline. Aside from Annie Lennox and Talking Heads. Discos I found repellent.

I'm not exactly old-fashioned, but close to it. I wore a jacket and tie to fly abroad, decades after everyone else had changed into tracksuits. The 1980s really didn't look good on me. I always had a soft spot for a good tweed jacket, ever since my favourite was lost off the back of a motorbike somewhere between Timaru and Temuka in 1966. One year in London, I thought I would have one made for me in Savile Row. It was superb as well as very expensive. I wore it with pride to the Ivy with a tie for lunch. We were placed right beside Trevor Nunn and Ian McKellen, that overly snappy dresser. Ian looked me up and down dubiously, and pinged me with the best put-down of my life. 'Darling! What *have* you come as?'

An enduring weakness for tweed.

Early in the 1980s, new comedy burst onto the scene. Suddenly one was aware of the likes of Adrian Edmondson, Rik Mayall, Robbie Coltrane, Nigel Planer, Dawn French, Jennifer Saunders, Alexi Sayle, Ben Elton and so on. I used to go and see them in little joints around Soho at its seedy zenith. One venue was normally the Raymond Revuebar, but apparently strippers got the night off on Sundays. There is, after all, evensong and mass to attend on that day of the week. On Sundays it was instead the Comic Strip.

I feel a bit nostalgic for the Soho of those days. Every great city needs a Soho. A place where low life meets high life. In Soho at that time you could drink in a bar or club alongside the likes of Francis Bacon or Jeffrey Bernard. You might find an erudite bookshop next to a brothel: 'French model third floor'. The film industry had its offices on Wardour Street. A producer who wanted you for a job might take you for a nice Italian around the corner; food was still pretty ordinary in London otherwise, back then. There were tailors and shoemakers, as well as costumiers for film and television. It was vivid, lively, slightly dangerous and right next door to the pomposity of Mayfair and Park Lane.

It's all been cleaned up now and sanitised. The place is full of high-end brands and high-end hotels. The low life, such as they are, are mostly young wankers who do too much cocaine in members-only clubs.

Something similar happened more recently in Kings Cross in Sydney. When I first got to Australia it was magnificent— again, full of low life, but also everyone you knew. There was a club called Arthur's, run by Claudia Karvan's parents. Every actor you knew or wanted to know would be there. They had bouncers on the door who would recognise me and usher me in, shame- lessly, in front of a long queue; once in a while it feels good to be a little bit known. Great nights there, and a lot of bad behaviour. Sometimes we'd kick on to three or four in the morning. I remember one packed night at the Manzil Room: a red-hot Chrissy Amphlett was fronting Divinyls at their roaring best. Bryan Brown and I had separated somehow in the melee, but I spotted him across the room. He was taller than those around, and he had passed out; he was unconscious on his feet. But the crowd was so tight that they unwittingly held him upright for at least three songs. I dragged him out of there eventually and shoved him in a cab.

Kings Cross was also full of brothels and strip clubs, as well as the odd office attached to the film industry. A little later came a more informal office very much to do with the film industry and entertainment—the Brasserie. The food was excellent, and if you turned up at lunch you'd find at least four or five other tables of people you liked. Next door to the Brasserie was a brothel that advertised the Biggest Bed in the World.

The Cross is just a shadow of its former self now. The Baird state government—right-wing, of course—'cleaned it up', introduced ridiculous curfews and killed the nightlife. The place withered and died. This was nothing to do with safety or anything else, just real estate. Greed.

Back to comedy in the UK. This young bunch, about ten years younger than me, were a breath of fresh air in a rather stale London. I didn't know them, but I did run into a whole lot of them backstage when I was being interviewed by Terry Wogan. Did I tell you how excruciatingly bad I am on talk shows? Another time, perhaps. I was pretty shy and dumbstruck to be in their company. They were a cheerful, friendly bunch, with the honourable exception of Jennifer Saunders. I don't think I've ever been more terrified by anybody. If looks could kill, I would still be tiny and shrivelled down on that draughty studio floor.

They seemed to often work in pairs—Mayall and Edmondson, French and Saunders, and so on. Another pair I became aware of was Fry and Laurie. I heard them before I saw them, on BBC Radio. Back then I used to drive around London; hard to believe now, but you could often find somewhere to park. On my Blaupunkt radio came this very strange, very funny couple. I'd never heard anything like it. Entirely different from the rest of the bunch, brand-new and yet somehow comfortingly old-fashioned. I parked my car outside my flat, which was near Paddington station, turned off the engine and sat in there until they were done. Didn't want to miss a thing. I became a lifelong convert to Fry and Laurie, both.

Just as they were wrapping up, the passenger door opened and to my complete surprise a woman got in, sat down beside me and closed the door. I was startled, to say the least, but could only manage a tentative 'Hello?'

She said hello back. There was silence for a little while. 'Can I ask,' I said, 'what are you doing in my car?'

'Don't you want to do business, darling?'

'Um. Business? No. I live here. That is my flat up there. This is where I park.'

'Oh well,' she said, 'another time,' and left.

You live and learn.

My Wine Life

RATHER like acting, my other career as a vigneron came about somewhat accidentally. In the highly unlikely event that you've never heard of Two Paddocks, the world's greatest producer of premium organic pinot noir, you need to know that I am The Proprietor of this illustrious company.

I probably should've taken more interest in wine when I was growing up. One of the core parts of the family firm, Neill and Co., a private company that later became Wilson Neill, a public company, was wines and spirits. The emphasis there was on spirits—wine, certainly fine wine, being almost completely unknown in the New Zealand I grew up in. We'd heard of it, but we never got to drink it. We drank beer, mostly, and not very good beer at that. My parents' generation drank gin and tonic, and whisky. My grandmother drank sherry, albeit good sherry. Neill and Co., incidentally, had the highest selling brandy in New Zealand—Beehive Brandy. My father always maintained it sold well because New Zealanders could pronounce Beehive. French in a bottle shop would just embarrass everyone. If only more people had drunk brandy back then, we might have been rich. You notice you don't need a degree in French to say Two Paddocks.

In the 1970s Louise W. knew some people of Dalmatian origin who produced wine; they lived in Henderson near her parents. The staple for the wine industry then was a very rough and ready port, which would be sold in gallon flagons. Or alternatively sherry—always sickeningly sweet. Alcoholics loved it, of course. But these friends of Louise's were trying something pretty radical—table wine. We would get cases of it cheap and drink it at dinner, and it was...well, all right. Sweet, of course. Drinking wine at the table reminded us of travelling around Europe in a Kombi van and buying perfectly drinkable wine, for a few francs, that came in a litre bottle with a cap for which you needed a bottle opener. We couldn't afford wine with a cork.

Ironically, this cap that needs a bottle opener, the crown seal, while cheap, is in fact the best possible closure for any wine. Unfortunately, it looks cheap, and as such we cannot use it at Two Paddocks. We are a premium brand. But crown seals beat corks by a country mile. Unless you have one of the very best corks in the world, and you probably need to be a Rothschild for that, corks are downright unreliable. Our 1999 vintage was completely ruined by dud corks, and I have sworn never to use them again. I'm pleased to say that most of New Zealand and Australia and even some of the old world are in agreement. When you have a completely corked wine it is easily identified. Call the waiter. But it is that arguable bottle, the one that doesn't taste quite right, the one the waiter will say there's nothing wrong with, the one that's disappointingly not fresh, the one that puts you off that brand forever—those are the corks that do the damage. Since 2001, we have only used Stelvin screw caps. *Je ne regrette rien*, as they say in Burgundy.

The first time I remember tasting a dry table wine in New Zealand was my father bringing home some bottles of McWilliam's Bakano. Dad was the sort of chap who would put a positive spin on most things. He'd drink it with relish. If he felt jolly, perhaps with one glass too many of the Bakano, you could persuade Dad to crack a walnut with his forehead. This was a spectacular business. He would put the walnut on the dining room table, lower his head so that it was touching the walnut, lift his fist in the air, and bang himself hard on the back of the head. Bang! Smash! Nut cracked! I winced every time. The nuts always smashed and somehow not Dad's head, thank God. No lasting injury. Do *not* try this at home.

The fact was, Bakano was rough as guts; it was a mashup of pinotage and who knows what else, as long as it was red. But at least it was a table wine. It would take another ten or twenty years before New Zealand started to produce really good table wine. When I was living in London in the eighties, I began to notice New Zealand wine sitting on shelves alongside good wine from Australia and elsewhere in the new world.

My love affair with wine began before that. After his unexpected phone call, James Mason and his wife, Clarissa, picked me up from the airport in Geneva in early January 1980. They lived in a comfortable but not particularly flash house in Menton with views over Lake Geneva. But then James wasn't a flash person; he eschewed the vulgar business of celebrity, and enjoyed a quiet life in the mountains. During the day we would get out and about, walking mostly, but also cross-country skiing. This was the first time I'd done that, and even though I was forty years younger than James, he was match fit and I was not. He was good. I sweated profusely as we glided silently through the snow under fir trees.

In the evening they liked to go out and eat well. No opposition from me. At a particular restaurant in Lausanne, the third course was a whole truffle. I'd never heard of a truffle, let alone eaten a whole one. It sounds kind of appalling when I say it but, like everything I ate with them, it was superb.

On another night, we went to an old auberge, which James said had been Charlie Chaplin's favourite restaurant. And, in fact, right beside my seat, there in the old wood panelling, was Charlie

Chaplin's name. He had carved it into the wall. James suggested that I should carve my name right under that of the great man. Of course, I could not do that. That would've been a monstrous presumption. But that evening they poured a red wine that made me sit up straight. It was another experience altogether. I had never drunk anything like it in my life. Now, I have no idea what *exactly* that wine was, except for this. I asked James what it was. He said, 'This is Burgundy, my boy. And don't forget it.' I never have. On reflection, James was perhaps pointing to a signpost—a direction my life would follow.

James was inordinately kind to me. It's always been a puzzle, why he tracked me down to say to me, someone he knew not at all, Come and stay with us in Switzerland. I think you are good. I want you to go to London. And I think you should audition for the new *Omen* film.

But that is what happened, and I still blink to think of this random kindness. I often wonder if I showed my gratitude sufficiently; in interviews I didn't want to lean further on this kindness more than would embarrass him or me. In addition, if people saw me in his mould or some such, those were enormous shoes to fill. If he saw in me something of his inimitable self on film, I could not be more flattered. He was a master.

We finally worked together on *Ivanhoe* in 1981. I was overjoyed to be on set with him, but we had no scenes together, sadly. I miss James, and I thank him always.

After that, I settled in London, in a flat just off the Edgware Road. I found and frequented a good wine merchant up the road. I would wander in and say, 'Burgundy!' in my best James Mason voice. They were very obliging in that store, and I began to explore all the intriguing subregions of that great region. It was white that hooked me initially: Meursault, Volnay; in those days twelve quid would get you a top Puligny-Montrachet Premier Cru.

But then I gradually shifted to red. Red Burgundy. I remembered James's direction. It's a frustration for me to this day, but I am still not sure what exactly that bottle was in Switzerland that was so transformative. Was it a Gevrey-Chambertin? A Vosne-Romanée? Chambolle-Musigny? I will never know. I'd like to know, because it, as well as James, changed my life.

But not right away. First of all, I needed to know what grape this was. Pinot noir. That noble wine that has its origin right there in Burgundy. I continued my love affair with Burgundy for the next twelve years or so. I discovered that pinot was grown elsewhere in the world—I drank some from Oregon when I was in the States, and they were very good.

And then one summer, back in New Zealand, I popped over the hill to see another old friend and mentor: Rolfe Mills. Rolfe and his wife, Lois, had devoted the last fifteen or twenty years of their lives to growing wine at Rippon near Wanaka. They'd planted just about every grape you can imagine, to see what would work. Absolutely no one knew; they were true pioneers. Most varieties were dismal failures, but suddenly a grape stood up and said, I like it here. I love it here. And that grape was pinot noir. Rudi Bauer, from Austria, was making wine at Rippon at that time, and when I was visiting Rolfe and Lois for lunch they poured me their 1991 and 1992 Rippon noirs. It was another sit-up-straight moment—not only could you grow wine well in Central Otago, but you could grow pinot noir, and very well. The wine was outstanding.

The idea that you could grow and produce my favourite wine in the world right where I lived, in my favourite place on the planet, Central Otago, was simply intoxicating. Very soon after that I ran into Greg Hay in a car park. Greg was, along with his brother Rob, the founder of Chard Farm wines. I knew them a little and they had a pretty good fledgling wine operation in a very unlikely spot—right in the Kawarau Gorge. Greg and I caught up quickly, and then he moved on to a different subject altogether. He said that he and a couple of mates were buying a hundred hectares further down the road in the Gibbston Valley. The idea was that they would plant out six different vineyards in pinot noir and sell them off. They needed capital, and he wanted to know if I was interested in being an investor, and indeed an owner of one of those little vineyards. This went off like a light bulb in my head. It was exactly the sort of thing I'd been thinking about since my lunch with Rolfe. I pondered deeply on this for at least five seconds, and said yes. We shook hands and it was all on. My one condition was this: I wanted the pick of the sites. Greg readily agreed. I said I would take his advice on this as he knew more about viticulture than I could possibly imagine.

Thus it was that within a year I was the owner of a vineyard right in the middle of the Gibbston Valley. My first. It was something of a gamble. No one knew how those initial two hectares of pinot would fare in what is quite an extreme climate. We were one of the very first at Gibbston. It is the highest region in Central, surrounded by alps. It gets very cold there in the winter, and heat in the summer is not by any means assured. Early or late frosts are always a menace. I put the care of the vineyard into the capable hands of Mike Wolter. Mike had also been my gardener for quite some time in Queenstown, so we knew each other well. Mike was a man of very few words and a great deal of capability, like many New Zealand men of the land. Not long after this Mike decided in addition that he wanted to set up a winemaking business, which struck me as a very good idea. Bear in mind this was very early in the days of winegrowing in Central, and there was virtually nowhere to go to have your grapes made into wine. Mike wanted a partner, and I gladly went in as one. I am still, as of today, the third partner in the Central

Otago Wine Company Limited (COWCO). Mike made the first two vintages of Two Paddocks Pinot Noir. But soon after that he died, tragically young, in an industrial accident at work. He is still very much missed in Central and at Two Paddocks.

I had no expectations or ambitions for Two Paddocks. I now had a mere two hectares of pinot, and that was fine for me. I simply thought I'd be making something passable, that I could share with friends and family, whether they liked it or not. Cheerful and drinkable, that's about all I demanded.

The name Two Paddocks baffles a lot of people, but the origins of it are this. The next vineyard to me is owned by my friend Roger Donaldson, whom I had worked with all those years before on *Sleeping Dogs*. We decided that we would join forces, and make wine from our combined vineyards. We needed a brand and, bearing in mind the lesson I'd learnt from Dad about giving booze unpretentious names, I suggested Two Paddocks. Sam's paddock and Roger's paddock. We trademarked it, and expected our first vintage in 1997. Roger's site is ever so slightly colder than mine. (Is this why Greg pointed me towards what is now my vineyard, which is frankly far less pretty than Roger's?) Both 1997 and 1998 were cool years, and Roger failed to produce a crop both times. Next door we managed two, admittedly small, crops, and went ahead and made wine without Roger. I was therefore stuck with the name, for better or ill, and all these years later it's Two Paddocks still.

I remember very clearly the night in Queenstown when a case, a dozen of my first vintage of Two Paddocks Pinot Noir, 1997, turned up. My wife Noriko and I opened the bottle with some trepidation. I didn't expect grand cru, just something I enjoyed. Not much to ask. I poured two glasses. It looked good, but I was still nervous. What if it was rubbish? This was a major investment I had made, and I didn't want it to be wasted. I applied my nose to the glass, and again it looked good. And then I took a sip. What was this? I took another sip and let it roll around my mouth for a while. Oh boy. Oh boy. This wine far exceeded any modest expectations I might have had. It wasn't just drinkable. It wasn't just good. It was very good indeed.

That was one of the greatest single moments of my life. Another of those moments that change everything.

An early vintage, 1999. Pleasing too.

Let's Dance

LAST week was difficult. I am in the middle of the fourth cycle of chemo, and things have got a bit bumpy on the road. No great surprise for anyone, but disappointing.

It's clearly impossible for me to film anything at the moment, but I thought, in order to keep myself off the streets, I should at least do some voice-over work. This was all very well, but on Monday I started recording a major series, ten hourly parts, and my voice simply ran out on episode two. This was something of a psychological blow. I've never not finished a day's work before, never. Rightly or wrongly, it made me feel enfeebled.

I went to my GP because I'd had this roaring sore throat for some days. He had a look at things and, sure enough, the damn throat was ulcerated. So much for a ten-part series. My oncologist asked my GP to do some blood tests, and the phone went almost immediately with a slightly urgent tone to it. My T-cell count, whatever that is, had bottomed out. Oh dear. So I've been having these injections daily of who knows what, and, as a result, pretty unpleasant nights, where I drench the bed in unearned sweat. Disgusting.

But apart from the odd dark moment, I am still optimistic, and this optimism is maximised when I do a bit of a dance around the place. To the right music, of course.

In my day (another handy, old-fart phrase) only girls danced. Young blokes like me danced under extreme sufferance. We felt awkward, we looked awkward; we were just plain awkward. It was not a pretty sight. Mind you, you would give it a go if you had to. It might have even meant a bit of a pash when they turned the lights down low towards the end of a dance. That could pretty much make up for everything.

In our second year at College, aged fourteen or fifteen, we had dancing lessons once a fortnight. These were held in a church hall and were grim affairs. The upside was that there were an equal number of girls from St Margaret's present, about the same age as us and just as spotty. The downside was they were as petrified of us as we were of them. No eye contact was ever made, nor was any conversation to be had. The dancing teacher was a tiny terrifying woman called Miss Thomas, of quite advanced years. She tried to teach us to foxtrot and waltz. Neither of which would be a blind bit of use later on in life, except possibly for me—I have had to waltz in more than one movie. If you were particularly incompetent, like me, you would be seized by the minuscule Miss Thomas, and she would throw you around to demonstrate how it was done. This was exactly the sort of thing that would put an adolescent boy into a cold sweat. It meant, for one thing, putting your arm around the iron-clad waist of Miss Thomas—I swear she wore a corset made from good British steel. Not quite the same thing as the intriguing waist of a girl your age.

I still don't dance well; that was never going to happen. I am a dancing fool on the floor, but at least I enjoy it now. And I'm finding it here, in my flat, very therapeutic. I put on the 'Eagle Rock', and I'm away. Or Cold Chisel. Split Enz. Pub rock in my kitchen. The years slip away and I make a fool of myself, gladly. There's no one here to witness this silly-arse business, and just as well. But I feel alive. That's the thing; never take being alive for granted.

I was once in New York City with Tim Finn, now that I think of Split Enz. We went to Madison Square Garden to see a salsa/mambo show, an incredible day and night with Tito Puente headlining, along with Marc Anthony and a bunch of huge Latin stars. Twenty thousand people at least on their feet, every one of them dancing nonstop. Tim and I were undoubtedly the only Anglos there, and you could tell. We just didn't have the moves. We looked like white dancing dorks.

We were drinking volumes of beer out of giant American buckets. I needed to pee, so I rushed out and found a big lavatory down a long corridor. I was unzipped and about to let go when something stopped me. I became aware that about twenty guys, big guys, had followed me in, and were standing behind me in ominous silence. Awkward, and not a little scary. I thought, This is bad, very bad, I am about to be beaten to a pulp in, of all places, a urinal. In the silence, as they waited, I slowly zipped up, and turned to meet my fate.

And then something unexpected happened. The suspicious looks changed. The guys were suddenly all wreathed in smiles. I was greeted like an old friend. The cheers went up. Joorassic Park! Doctor Grant! Much joy and clapping backs and signing autographs. The relief for me, I cannot tell you. But not for my bladder. As soon as I could, I rushed off, waving to the cheering gang behind me, to find another lavatory where I could pee unobserved.

I must learn some salsa, I really must.

I once flew from Prague to Amsterdam on a Saturday night to see Tim and Neil Finn play. They were superb, and even I was on my feet making awkward, dancy moves. Tim does something similar on stage, but to his advantage. It was always a Split Enz thing.

They left Amsterdam very early Sunday morning, and my plane was not until mid-afternoon. I wandered alone around the empty city, a bit hungover. A low sun was reflecting off the quiet canals. I love that city. Nothing was open yet, not even a coffee shop, except for one shop with no signage. While not clear what it was, I stumbled in anyway. It was a sex shop. I was about to leave, not my scene at all, when I became, despite myself, horrifyingly fascinated. Good God, exactly what do you do with that? No, please…you do *what*? I mean, large is one thing, but the size of a small SUV? Are you kidding?

The shop was quiet, just a half-dozen people or so, studiously not looking at each other. Then I became aware of a loud, authoritative, Dutch-accented voice at the counter. 'I know you!' Oh my God, there must be a sex offender or someone in here, time to leave. 'I know you!' I looked around. He was pointing at me. He most certainly did *not* know me, so I smiled mildly, shrugged and started to leave, knowing everyone was staring at me now. As I neared the exit he yelled again, 'I know you! *Jurassic Park*!' All eyes were on me. This time I did not stay for autographs, and made a quick-smart exit, mortified.

Never again.

But back to dancing. Bryan Brown and I have hosted three major parties, which might just as well have been dances. We've had a fiftieth, a sixtieth and, of course, a seventieth. Every ten years a big bash. Bryan says we should have a seventy-fifth, as he's not sure we'll make it to our eightieth, nor a lot of our friends. I suspect he might be pointing the bone here. I'm looking away and insisting on nothing less than an eightieth, ninetieth and, of course, a century.

I call them dances because there was a lot of dancing, every time. We've always had at least three hundred people. We get people dancing because we always have brilliant music. Between us we have a lot of musician friends, and we are shameless about asking them to perform. That national treasure Jenny Morris always organises a great core band, with backup singers. Then we ask our friends to sing with them; just two songs each, songs by someone else. I made this rule, just so the poor buggers don't have to get up and sing their two greatest hits, which would be cringeworthy all round. And any more than two would be even more of an imposition. No one ever says no, miraculously, unless they are on tour or something.

We make a list of some of our favourite songs ever, and say, Would you mind singing these two? Somehow these requests are always met with enthusiasm. Jimmy Barnes sang for us at our first big birthday bash. Rachel insisted that he sing 'Working Class Man' for Bryan. Working-class man indeed, but also a bloody gent. (Jimmy that is, not Bryan.) Bryan and I even sang once, as a tribute to our friend Billy Thorpe, who had not long died. The song, one of Billy's, was 'Hot Potato'. Even Bryan could remember the words. There are only two, and they are repeated all the way through the song. 'Hot potato, hot potato, hot potato, hot potato…'

Here's a list of people who have performed for us. I'm fairly sure it's not definitive, so at the risk of offending someone who has been left off, here goes: Tim Finn, Neil Finn, James Reyne, Joel Tobeck, Rick Bryant, Glenn Shorrock, Justine Clarke, Genevieve Lemon, Simon Morris, Bic Runga, Diesel, Brendan Gallagher, my daughter Maiko, Mahalia Barnes, EJ Barnes, Ceci Herbert, Lime Cordiale, Tex Perkins, Jenny Morris, Peter Garrett, Jimmy Barnes. Royalty from both sides of the Tasman. It makes me dizzy just looking at that list. What luck. What generosity, all those sweet people. Some of the above have sung at every one of those parties.

For a partygoer it has to be confusing. You really want to dance, but you're also close-up to maybe the best rock concert you've ever been to in your life. What to do? Well, get your arms in the air, for one thing. Dancing, even at seventy, if not dignified, is at the very least good for you.

My beloved random feature on all my favourite music comes into play with this. It also makes me ricochet into good times in the past. I was getting in the shower just now and a song came on that took me straight to John Clarke. John once emailed me just to tell me this—you must listen to Joni Mitchell's 'A Case of You'. I did so, and indeed it is one of the greatest love songs ever written. My personal preference is for k. d. lang singing it. And now I recommend it to you.

The following track took me straight to New Zealand, and Toa Fraser. I absolutely adored Toa's film *No. 2*, which came out in 2006. It was *No. 2* that in large part persuaded me to play my most difficult role ever—the title role in *Dean Spanley*, which Toa directed a couple of years later in England, with Peter O'Toole, Jeremy Northam, Bryan Brown and Judy Parfitt. *No. 2* ends with the most inspirational song imaginable: 'Bathe in the River', written by Don McGlashan and sung by Hollie Smith plus choir.

Now I recommend this to you. And if you're going through a bit of an ordeal like this one, I recommend it twice. 'Bathe in the River'. There is absolution to be had, oh yes.

Dancing: that's the other way, absolution and life!

I Play a Dog and Robin Plays a Robot

WHICH brings me neatly to…It amazes me how often people tell me that *Dean Spanley* is not just their favourite film of mine, but their favourite movie, period.

Not many people have seen it, which makes that reaction all the more surprising. If you haven't—stop reading now. I'd like you to see it, but inevitably what I'm about to say will entail spoilers. I myself am very fond of it.

It scared the life out of me before we started—this was a very complicated role altogether. I said no a couple of times, but they kept coming back, and eventually I buckled. I'm glad I did. It's a comedic role, but full of pathos as well. Two masks of drama right there.

I'm not a comedian, and I don't know how to be funny. That takes a very special skill, and I'm jealous of those who have it. You are either funny, or you're not. When we were doing *Hunt for the Wilderpeople*, I kept telling our (hilarious) director, Taika Waititi, 'I'm not funny. If you want funny, show me.' He never did, so I guess he didn't need funny.

The funniest person I ever worked with, or indeed ever met, was Robin Williams. We were cast together in *Bicentennial Man*. Robin played a robot. He was irresistibly, outrageously, irrepressibly, gigantically funny. He was also, I think, the saddest person I ever met. I suspect this might be true of many comedians; they're not happy at all unless they're being funny. Robin didn't just need to be funny; he needed to be funny with an audience. Sometimes I would visit him in his trailer. We would talk about this and that, sometimes even about the work we were about to do. We had great chats. But at the same time, part of me was observing him closely. He seemed inconsolably solitary, and deeply depressed. If you were unkind, you might say it was my company. But I know it wasn't that. When you were with Robin you could sense the dark space inside. It was palpable. Ostensibly, he had everything. He had fame, he was rich, people loved him, great kids—the world was his oyster. And yet I felt more sorry for him than I can express. He was the loneliest man on a lonely planet.

That is, until he stepped out of the trailer. Outside were runners, assistant directors, personal assistants, make-up artists… a motley gaggle. As soon as he flung open the door, he was on. He might as well have been playing Madison Square Garden. He was not just on, he was full-on, and he was incredibly funny. And it was all spontaneous, all made up on the spot. He would riff off the name, for instance, of the person standing next to him. It was impossible that this was old material. He had this—I do not use the word lightly—genius. Funny stuff just poured out of him. And everybody was in stitches, and when everybody was in stitches you could see Robin was happy.

Eventually they could persuade him to walk onto the sound-stage, where the crew would be waiting. Perfect. An even bigger audience. And off he would go. Sometimes for twenty minutes; he was inexhaustible. Reluctantly, the first assistant director would finally say, Robin, I think we should perhaps make a start. And reluctantly we all would. We knew we were listening to something priceless, something that would never be repeated, something unique.

They would screw the robot head onto him and perforce he would shut up. Apparently it was hell in there, and it was better for Robin to get it over and done with. This was a bit of a relief for us as well, as there are only so many hours in the day. Only so many times you can roar with laughter in a day. We did, after all, have work to do.

I might as well drop another name here. The honourable exception I know to the sad-clown cliché to which I refer is Martin Short. We made *Merlin* together at the end of the 1990s, and I loved every day he was around. He is always at ease, always comfortable in his own skin. And, like Robin, ungovernably funny. But happy at the same time. Lucky man.

While we are on the topic of science fiction, I was pleased to be offered a film called *Event Horizon* in the late 1990s, to be directed by Paul W. S. Anderson. I would be playing with the great Laurence Fishburne, for one thing, and the story was wild and crazy. Sci-fi combined with horror; almost always a good idea. Sounded like fun, and indeed it was, with a great gang—Sean Pertwee, Joely Richardson, Jason Isaacs et al. A wild bunch.

The movie is set in 2047, half a century after it was being made. A missing spaceship turns up orbiting around Neptune, and a rescue vessel is launched to find out what's going on. I play Dr Billy Weir, a kind of nerdy science guy who goes bad, very bad, at the end when things turn to horror. They suggested I play the role as if I was from Australia and, as every character wore a uniform bearing a flag that denoted their country of origin, I had to decide what the Australian flag might look like in 2047. It seemed to me self-evident that there would no longer be a Union Jack in the top left-hand corner, denoting loyalty to a long-extinct empire, so we replaced it with the three-coloured Aboriginal flag. This detail has been much remarked upon. In the unlikely event that I'm still around in 2047, we can see whether I was right.

By way of contrast, for the duration of the shoot, my family were renting a place in Chelsea that had once been the home of A. A. Milne, he of Christopher Robin fame. So it was Winnie the Pooh at night and deep, dark space trauma by day. I found it rather soothing to read *The House at Pooh Corner* to my kids at bedtime, after all the craziness at Pinewood Studios.

Make-up was the true trauma for me here. Dr Weir morphs into something completely hideous towards the end of the film: naked, fully scarified, ripped-out genitals and so on. Not a pretty sight at all. More seriously, it took a minimum of eight hours to apply the SFX make-up, most of which involved me standing still. In a word—agony. I found the best way to get through this was to watch videotapes of comedies. *Father Ted* worked the best, and I now know pretty much every line by heart. Wonderful show, and a great way to get your mind off things. I found, during COVID lockdowns, a similar relief in watching *Seinfeld*, my ultimate comfort television.

As an aside: during those tedious and somewhat anxious-making COVID months, I attempted a number of mildly entertaining things on Instagram, to which a lot of people responded warmly. I committed to making a fool of myself if it made people feel a little better. I played the ukulele and sang. (Really, the ukulele should only be played between consenting adults, and my somewhat amateur strumming, with even worse singing, is something that I prefer to keep in the privacy of my own place.) I had conversations with a rather dodgy-looking garden gnome called Sir Gerald. I read poetry, stuff I love. I made a crappy cooking show. I gave dubious advice on sex. And some friends and I made a bunch of little films. I called them Cinema Quarantino. I would write a script and send it to a pal, usually locked down in another country, and get them to shoot their stuff on their phone. Continuity be damned. Hugh Morris-Clarke was kind enough to cut these together and make them into little two-minute films. I would give them bad art-house titles, in cod-German. Like *Otto und Hans in Gangland*. Or *Das Fone Hell*. Well, at least it gave me something to do. Find them on the Two Paddocks website or YouTube, if you must—starring Helena Bonham Carter, Stephen Fry, Hugo Weaving, David Wenham, Timothy Spall, Heather Mitchell, Oscar Kightley, Rachel Ward, Bryan Brown, Steven Weber, Geoff Stults, Cohen Holloway and more. All damn good sports.

But we were talking about *Event Horizon*. After eight hours of make-up, I would be gingerly transported to the 007 Stage, where we had a massive set that was a space engine of some kind. This was midwinter and the immense 007 stage was icy. Naked as I was, they could not put anything around me to keep me warm, so I was condemned to a two-bar heater. Anything else would have buggered up those eight hours of make-up. I could warm myself, almost, one side at a time, which also tended to dry up all the blood and slime, so I was resprayed on a regular basis with this uncommonly cold mixture. I tried to muffle my screams. The script insisted that I was crazy at this point, but no acting was required. I was already there.

Event Horizon has a lot of fans. I like it, although the editing process was compromised because the studio wanted the movie out in a hurry. I am sure Paul Anderson would have liked the movie to breathe a bit more. It's cut too fast—I always like horror when you're not entirely sure what is out there in the dark, so you need to hold your breath in the silence. Paul is often quoted as wanting another cut, but apparently all the footage that was taken out is now lost. A shame.

Back to *Dean Spanley*. I play a pompous senior Anglican cleric. Like quite a few C of E ministers I have known, Dean Spanley is a dull man, capable of sermons that could send the worst insomniac off to a good week's sleep. He is also, at another level, a dog.

He has enjoyed a canine world in a previous incarnation, and his inner dog is never very far from the surface. All it takes is for a very fine glass of Tokay and he's away, barking. We often talk about the inner life of the characters we play, but this was next level. Of course, this is absurdity, but there was more than that. The film is about grief and loss and forgiveness. It's ridiculous and profound at the same time. The dean himself is oblivious to it all.

This is an actors' film if ever there was one; we had a fantastic cast. Jeremy Northam plays the lead. Jeremy is a good friend, and I'm surprised he doesn't work more; there are very few good leading men like him in the world. He's choosy in what he does and maybe too much so. He can be a bit of a grumbler, and on day two Bryan Brown said to him, 'Mate, don't wanna hear it. We're gonna have a good time on this, and that's that.' And indeed that *was* that, and we enjoyed the whole thing. Weekends

Dean Spanley. Mad as a hatter.

we'd hang out, all three of us, head for the coast, lunch in pubs, all that English stuff. It's a fine, understated performance that he gives in this film, exquisitely English.

Bryan was playing a bit of a chancer—rather like life, when you think about it. We were mostly staying in a tiny hotel in the middle of nowhere, in Norfolk. I'm still scarred from popping by his room one night and seeing his underwear drying on the wall heaters. Bryan is too mean to use the hotel laundry and does his own in the sink. All of these appalling threadbare underpants dated at least from the 1960s. 'Mate. Bloke's gotta save a quid.' Some things you just can't unsee.

And then there was the amazing Peter O'Toole. I had done two jobs with Peter, but we were never there at the same time. I once did a job in the middle of China—Peter had left already, but he was kind enough to leave me a note. He said, There's only one place to eat, and one place to have a massage. I recommend them both. I tried the restaurant and he was right.

And then I tried the massage. It was a foot-massage place. This was a new idea to me, and I wasn't at all sure whether getting your feet rubbed was worth wasting an hour for, but Peter had been insistent. My translator and I climbed the stairs to an unpromising, neon-lit windowless room. We sat on these awful leatherette Chinese La-Z-Boys for a while, watching impenetrable state television, bored to death. And then two women came in with towels and basins, and set to work. Hand over my heart, probably the best hour ever. Just as well I had my translator with me. This woman could tell by handling my feet exactly what had happened to me in terms of health since my birth, and exactly what age I was when whatever happened. It was astounding. We left the place, and I felt completely rejuvenated. All this from…feet.

This time, years later in Norfolk, much of my work would be with Peter. Now, bear in mind, I had held Peter in the highest regard ever since *Lawrence of Arabia* in 1962, and it's always a little daunting to go to work with your heroes. There is a scene towards the end of the film where the dean starts talking and will not stop. I kid you not, it was something like twelve pages long. To my horror, there on the schedule, Days 1–4, we would be shooting that very scene over the next three or four days. The most difficult scene of my life and that's where we would begin. The very first shot was a wide, with Peter, Jeremy, Bryan and me around the table. Two pages of verbiage from me. We shot three takes and Toa said, 'Okay, move on.' I turned to Peter and said quietly, 'I am *so* sorry Peter, you have days and days of listening to all this.' He looked me straight in the eye, clamped my hand firmly to the table and said, 'Dear boy. I was enchanted. *Enchanted.*' You cannot imagine the relief, and now I suddenly felt I could actually pull this off.

Peter's own performance is immaculate. Such dexterity. I love the way he relished every word. It makes you think—all that bollocks about throwaway lines. It would be unthinkable for Peter O'Toole to throw away a line. Every line is a gift, every word should be given its appropriate weight. It's language. It's the English language. It is rich, it is powerful, it is yours. All you mumble-bums who throw away lines—you've worked to the point where people are giving you lines, and now you want to throw them away? Take up plumbing, or mow lawns. Please.

As an aside, when I was on a previous job with Peter in Canada, he was asked by a couple of the cast about people he knew and had worked with. The legends. When asked what Elizabeth Taylor was like, he replied succinctly, 'Elizabeth Taylor...is a cunt.'

Anyway, there it is—*Dean Spanley*. You be the judge. I thank Toa Fraser for it, and I think I speak for the others that we would all hang our hats there if we could.

Dad Makes an Exit
and I Confess

I'VE had cancer twice now.

Who knows why? I can take a few guesses, but in truth it's always a number of factors. Not least because, if you live long enough, something will inevitably bite you in the bum one day. There could always be a genetic answer, but who knows?

My dad died of cancer in 1991.

After he and Mum moved to their farm, Dad started to breed sheep, black-faced Suffolks, and I carry on this tradition on my small farm to this day. For a while, he had a majestic ram, of whom he was very fond, called Ramikin. Rashly, he decided to enter the ram in the Mosgiel agricultural show. Ramikin was the only one in his class. The judges, miserable bastards, nevertheless awarded poor Ramikin second place! Dad was incensed, and so am I.

Mum started breeding kākārikis, a native parakeet that, like so many of our birds, is under threat. How exactly she got started I have no idea, but when the Department of Conservation got wind of this, she was expressly told to stop. She ignored them. She must have released at least fifty pairs over the years, and sometimes, if I stop on the Three Mile Hill on the way to Dunedin, I can hear them chattering away in the distance, and I know they are the descendants of Mum's beloved birds. Some even turned up at her funeral, talking twenty to the dozen.

Mum was central to the Welsh Pony Society, and bred

those ponies too. She was a useful judge at agricultural shows; her knowledge of horses was profound. Dad, on the other hand, got increasingly interested in dressage, built himself a covered dressage ring, and every day he would saddle up and swan about, riding to music from an enormous boombox in his splendid stadium. The deafer he got, the louder the music, and, if the wind was right, you could hear it in Mosgiel, about five miles away. The first horse he tried to train was an ex-racehorse, and a halfwit. Life and dressage became a lot easier when he imported a magnificent Lusitano gelding from Portugal. Every year he would go to Europe and spend a couple of weeks learning with the maestro, Nuno Oliveira, near Lisbon. He got pretty good, and enjoyed all of it.

Dear old boy. Dad. He died superbly. All the family were home, and he was gaunt and enfeebled in his now single bed, but still handsome and charismatic. For some reason Mum and Dad were in twin beds those last few years, in their bedroom down the end of the hall. He was, as always, slightly distant. A dreamer. A soldier, who was always partly absent, his mind perhaps drifted off to some place where he'd served. The friends who'd been killed there. When I was a kid, I'd round the corner to the vegetable garden to find Dad stock-still, leaning on his spade with a faraway look. He wouldn't even know you were there. My brother and I agree he must have had PTSD of some kind. I mean, who didn't, coming back from that or any other war?

Like so many of his peers, he never spoke about the war. But he did get round to telling us two stories not long before he died. I like them both.

Before the war, he'd been sent to Germany twice to learn German. He spent a few months there. Sensible idea, given that conflict between the European democracies and the Nazis seemed inevitable. He was billeted with an old German general of some kind and his family. Dad later served in Italy for over two years as the British and the Americans fought the ferociously dogged Germans all the way up the Italian peninsula. I heard him say once or twice that, while he loathed the Nazis, he always had enormous respect for the German fighting man. They were great soldiers.

One day in the Apennines, Dad was leading a patrol along a tortuous mountain road. To their complete surprise, they turned a corner and ran slap into a German force of a similar size. Both sides froze; the Germans were just as surprised as Dad's lot.

Dad said he had no idea how it came to him so quickly. But in perfect German, he yelled, 'Put your weapons down, and your hands in the air!' The Germans did exactly as they were told. If there's one thing about Germans, they are good at taking orders. And they must have been astonished to hear such a command in perfect Deutsch. A reflex, if you like. Dad was just as astonished. He was able to reflect later in life, with some satisfaction, that his learning of German saved a lot of lives that day.

The other story concerned an action at night. Dad and his men had to overrun a German position on a small hill across a river. They made the approach stealthily in the dark, and then suddenly, at the top, there was bedlam. The attack was a success, and the Germans retreated. Unfortunately for Dad, in the dark and at the height of the battle, he fell into a German latrine. 'I was up to my neck in German shit!' If that wasn't bad enough, they had to hunker down for the day, and hold the position until the following night. Dad spent a whole day covered in shit, in the intense sun of a long midsummer Italian day. 'I stank like a badger!'

Dad detested sentimentality of any kind. But you could tell there was a soft heart in there, below the slightly stiff army exterior. He was a gentle man. He only raised his hand to me once; he didn't beat children or anyone else. I must have done something awful, I have no idea what, and Mum insisted he discipline me. Dad reluctantly directed me to the bathroom. I was told to bend over, and he smacked me twice lightly on the bum. Stupidly I laughed when I stood up. Dad briefly got angry at that, and made me bend over again. Harder this time, but it still didn't hurt. I was smart enough to pretend it did. We left the bathroom, Dad looking more relieved than I did that it was all over.

But back to his last. My niece Anna tells this story. She and Juliet were sitting in vigil, in the early hours. Dad had not just been sleeping, but had been truly unconscious for a day or two, drifting away from us in an opioid cloud. Juliet was crooning comforting new-age mottoes to him like, 'Look for the light, Dad. You're going to a better place, Dad. Look to the golden light.'

To their astonishment, his blue eyes snapped open, and he barked, 'Oh, for Christ's sake, Juliet! As if it's not bad enough I'm dying, but I have to listen to this crap!' Oh my God, brilliant.

Juliet tells a different story. Dad was unconscious, and she was there alone holding his hand. He suddenly yelled in pain and woke.

'It's all right, Dad,' Juliet said. 'You won't have to put up with this much longer.'

Dad replied sharply, 'You really didn't need to remind me of *that*.'

Something even odder happened the next morning. Dad, although unconscious, seemed in pain despite the morphine drip. We called the GP, who was soon there and decided to give him a shot of something that would help.

Suddenly, and we all recoiled in surprise, Dad woke up. Big blue eyes. He looked around. First of all he spotted the doctor, squirting an enormous syringe. Then he spotted us, solemn and gathered all around the bed. He can only have thought he was being given the big one, and he had about a minute to live. He hadn't sat up for days, but now he sat bolt upright, and looked around at us all.

This is what he said: 'I am not afraid. I have never been afraid of anything or anyone in my life. And I'm not afraid now. And that's how I want *you* to be.'

We were speechless.

Then he did something really out of character.

'Let us all hold hands. And sing. "Auld Lang Syne".'

Again, no words from anyone. We all joined hands. You should know we are not a touchy-feely sort of family, nor a sing-y sort, come to that. I don't remember anyone actually singing. Perhaps Dad did, because he was nodding his head along to something or other. 'Auld Lang Syne', I guess.

He opened his eyes again and said, with some finality, 'Well. Enough of these theatricals.'

Then he lay down and closed his eyes. They were his last words. Superb.

During that last, long, dark night, Mum came into the room. She had been sleeping somewhere else in the house so as not to disturb Dad. I think she'd been in a kind of denial, the last few days, pottering about doing her things. Now, being the sort of people they were, the most affection they ever showed would be a brisk peck on the cheek. But now Mum ignored us all, got into Dad's bed and held him tight, her arms wrapped around him. The penny had dropped. Her Dermot was dying and she was there to comfort him. It made me cry.

He had lived just long enough that I was able to tell him quietly, when I was on my own with him, that I was being made an OBE. I think it meant more to him than to me and gave him some small pleasure in his last days. He raised a hand from the bed and I took it; he looked me in the eye, and said, 'Well done, old boy.'

Mum and Dad. Better days.

*

Perhaps I should confess all now. I smoked quite a bit when I was a young fella. We all did. I don't think I was ever a heavy smoker as such, but certainly a social smoker. I can't think why; it's not even something you really enjoy. Maybe it felt grown up, or naughty.

It was against the rules. That is what mattered.

My friend John Hay and I, plus a few others, would sometimes climb the school walls to the forbidden botanic gardens in Christchurch, risking heavy punishment, to have a few filthy Stuyvesants ('the International Passport to Smoking Pleasure') behind some rhododendrons. We had three favoured spots that offered the best cover. 'See you at Number Two at 700.' Later, any photo of me out and about and I've always got a fag between fingers one and two. Dances, balls, the races, with girls—always a smoke. I've never been able to completely disassociate cigarettes and good times.

The thing was, smoking was just way too fucking *cool*. It was always all over the movies. Cigarettes seemed like foreplay; a good smoker could get laid, that was clear. Films aren't the same without them. Seduction means nothing on celluloid without some cigarette smoke curling languorously from some smiling, delicious, lipsticked mouth.

School was duller than that, of course, but John was committed, and a heavy smoker all his life. Of course, ultimately he died of cancer. He was as close a friend as you could wish for. Funny that; we had almost nothing in common you could put your finger on. We led completely different lives. He started life as a farmer and ended as an auctioneer in Nelson. I don't think he ever saw a play in his life and hardly read a book. But that dry wit. That wicked laugh. The bandy walk. The one drink too many, and the inelegant pissed lurch into the shrubbery. He came to my fiftieth birthday in Sydney and didn't go to bed before the morning plane back. He startled people in the queue by crashing into and toppling several security barriers at Departures. Pip Hall had to pick him up off the floor. I loved him. We just got on, from the moment we met at school.

The one good thing about cancer is you know you're on the way out. You get to say goodbye. So as soon as I could, once I heard his news, I got myself to Nelson, twice, in the time he took to die. The first time we had fun, and John was John, smoking outside again, with the attitude that 'it wasn't going to make any fucking difference now'. The second time he was a shrunken version of John, bedridden, but still sharp and funny. His adored wife, Di, was tactful enough to leave us alone for a while before I had to leave. I'm so grateful for that. Because we got to say some things we would *never* have dreamt of saying normally. Like how very, very much his loyal friendship had meant to me over so many years.

Other than the smoking (and honestly, doctor, at its worst, it was never more than four or five a day) one other thing has always been a sharp clue for me. One summer my friend Gordon Strang and I got a job with an agricultural contractor in Southland. I'd always liked farm work and this sounded like a breeze compared to carting hay in Mid Canterbury (three summers in total of that). It was filthy work. We lavishly sprayed a chemical called Tordon over gorse and a fair chunk of the province in the process. We didn't think much of it at the time, and were assured it was safe. It wasn't. Turned out it was effectively Agent Orange, a chemical horror that the Americans were hellishly visiting upon the unfortunate Vietnamese at exactly that time. We'd cop it ourselves when the wind was against us.

We also had a strange mobile sheep-dip affair that we'd cart around to some pretty remote farms. When I say dip, it was more like a circular sheep shower. Our job was to hurry fifty or so sheep up a ramp into said shower. Then they'd get a thorough drenching with a mix of freezing cold water, all the shit left by the last lot and God knows what hideous chemicals they used in those days to kill the various creatures that beleaguer sheep. The theory was that, once the shower was off and you opened the gate, they'd bolt for freedom down the exit ramp. All well and good, except many times the poor critters were so traumatised by the sudden wet and cold, they'd just stand there shivering and refusing to move. Then it was our job to get in there and get the buggers out, with the contractor effing and blinding at our clear reluctance to do so. There are few more humiliating experiences you can have than to be cheek by jowl, on your knees, jostling with freezing wet Merinos, crawling under a still dripping shower. We'd go home to a shed, wet and cold ourselves, and stinking of animal shit and piss and lethal chemicals unknown.

I used to joke, it's a wonder I didn't get cancer. And then, one day, I did.

In the early days of cultivating pinot noir grapes at Gibbston, I had viticultural contractors do the work there, and they did it well. I didn't take a lot of interest in what they did; it was conventional and everybody was doing it. Conventional means using, you guessed it, a lot of chemicals. In particular Roundup, a herbicide for weeds. Now Roundup was already subject to rumour—was it damaging to health?

Same propaganda, of course. 'Don't be a wuss. You can drink it. Do you good. Go on, mate.'

I eventually did some research and decided I didn't want it anywhere near me, my family, anyone who worked for me or indeed my wine. As far as I'm concerned, it's not a lot better than Tordon—killing every living thing around your vines, and in the soil as well. Without healthy soil we are doomed, my friends.

So then began the slow, arduous and expensive business of converting what would become four vineyards to organics. It's a lot more work—weeds grow aplenty in the verdant summers of Central Otago. But I am very proud to say that for years now my vineyards have been healthy living places again. There were only a handful of us winegrowers interested in this in the beginning, including our friends the Mills, at Rippon. We called ourselves the Filthy Five for a while. You can always tell an organic vineyard—they always look a trifle wild. Conventional vineyards on the other hand look like the OCD Department of Neatness has been running the joint.

My hope is that, after I'm gone, all four vineyards will continue to be organic, for everyone's sake. A small legacy, if you like.

As a sidebar, if you are interested in 'natural wines', and these days many people are, you might want to ask how 'natural' the wine you are drinking actually is. Is it organically grown, as well as being a low-sulphur wine? The answer is almost never. The winemaker has simply bought up some (sprayed) grapes, and made the wine (badly), with little or no added sulphur. We also make a 'natural' wine, and a very good one, and, like all our wines, it is organic.

But back to Dad. He passed away peacefully the next morning about 8 a.m. I missed it; we hadn't got back to the house yet. Morphine eased his passage in those last few days, as well as the presence of those who loved him. He wasn't afraid, and that was a comfort for us as well.

It rained at his funeral. Ralph Hotere said that happens when a chief dies. We scattered his ashes under the kauri trees down the hill. I would walk his dog every day past the spot, and for days his ashes stayed where they lay. And then about a week later—there was nothing. No trace.

I keep his medals and his officer's sword. Above my desk here is a photo of Dad holding that sword as he escorts the Queen while inspecting the troops. Just as I remember him: tall, handsome and every inch a soldier.

Architecture, Te Papa and Crime by Committee

LAST time I was back at the farm, I found my original boots from the first *Jurassic Park*. I kicked at least three dinosaurs with those very boots. I remembered that my friend John Clarke had donated his Fred Dagg gumboots to New Zealand's national museum, Te Papa. I thought that Te Papa might like my *Jurassic* boots. If not, I could sell them for charity. Laura Dern sold hers for a motza. So we made the offer to Te Papa and my PA, Lauren, got this reply.

> Kia ora Lauren,
>
> I tabled Sir Sam's boots at our History Acquisitions meeting this morning, and the team agreed that we would like to consider them for Te Papa's permanent collection.
>
> Our acquisition process takes a couple of months to go through—firstly I need to write an acquisition proposal justifying collecting the boots, which is then assessed by my colleagues, including a conservator. Our Collection Development Committee would then make the final decision. If approved, we would send a Deed of Gift for Sam's signature.
>
> If that process sounds ok, could I please ask a few questions to help me write the proposal?
> - Who made the boots, and where? Any manufacturing details would be helpful.
> - What are the boots made from? Are they leather with a rubber

sole? Is there any damage or deterioration?

- Their measurements? Height x width x length.
- Has Sam worn them since the first film?
- Did he have any say in what boots his character wore?
- Did they help him get into the character?
- Would Sam be happy to write a statement about their signif-
  icance? What do they mean to him? Such a statement would
  be part of our interpretation.
- What would be an appropriate credit line, e.g. 'Gift of Sir
  Sam Neill'?
- Are the boots here in New Zealand? What is their address?

If you could please send me more photographs of the boots,
that would be very helpful for our conservator who will want to
see details of their materials and condition.

Thank you very much!

It looks as if the bar is set high, and I await the momentous
decision about whether my humble boots pass the committee
test.

In the meantime, let's discuss Te Papa for a moment. Te Papa
is up there as one of our great national tragedies.

It is an eminently important institution. It is superbly situated right on Wellington Harbour—one of the most beautiful
harbours in the world. On that site they have placed a sodden
lump of a building. It's dull and prosaic. It doesn't even function
well. We spent a fortune building something second-rate. It is a
monument to mediocrity.

It was the winner of a competition, believe it or not. You
would think everything else in that competition would be even
worse. Well, no. In fact, Frank Gehry, the world's greatest living
architect, made a joint submission with New Zealand's greatest
architect, Ian Athfield. Gehry, in the unlikely event you are not

aware of him, designed the Guggenheim Museum in Bilbao, probably the finest building of the twentieth century. One that paid for itself in a few years, became a world-famous attraction, and in the process transformed and enriched Bilbao. Have a look online at the initial concept that Athfield and Gehry produced for Te Papa. It is exhilarating. We could have had something to rival even the Sydney Opera House. We could have had something unique. We could have had architecture. Instead we got a lumpy, understeamed pudding.

And here's the thing. The committee judging the competition didn't even put the Gehry-Athfield proposal in the five finalists. You could weep.

Just on cost alone, you'd think they might have paused for thought. The Gehry-Athfield building would have been *cheaper*...

The second crime by committee was this—it was decided that Te Papa would absorb our national gallery. What benighted collection of idiots decided that? Te Papa is many things to many people, but it is not, never can be, a national gallery. Granted, they have the odd good show. The Gordon Walters was incredible. But, at the end of the day, our national collection has been relegated to the basement, or the attic. This is a disgrace. We need a national gallery, for reasons of self-respect, for our dignity as a nation: no other comparable country I know of is without one.

A museum is *different* from a gallery. Simple example—if you've been to London, you have probably been to the British Museum and the National Gallery. They are both brilliant, but they do *different* things. Try to imagine the National Gallery jammed awkwardly into spare parts of the museum. That's right, you can't, nor should you have to.

And remember this—the visual arts are what we do best, and we do them no honour by relegating them to the spare rooms upstairs.

As it happens, a golden opportunity presents itself to rectify this egregious situation as we speak.

A new convention centre is being built right across the road from Te Papa. Now, no one needs another damn convention centre, particularly in Wellington, where the Miles Warren–designed town hall (the Michael Fowler Centre) has served that purpose admirably for years. Convention centres are common as muck; national galleries are rare as pink diamonds.

It looks to me ideal; with not a great amount of outlay, this convention centre could be adapted to be a proper national gallery. Our pride would be restored. The visitors it would attract to Wellington would far outstrip those coming to a common-or-garden convention centre. Win-win.

Those in charge of art at Te Papa—which must be the most frustrating job on earth, given that most of what they look after is stored down in the stacks—would need only walk across the road.

I pray the government might step in and make this possible. I dream.

Back to architecture. I first started getting interested in architecture, in modern architecture, back in the 1960s, when I was at school. At that time there were a bunch of very interesting architects in Christchurch, doing very interesting work. I'm thinking here of Paul Pascoe, Humphrey Hall (father of my friend Pip), Peter Beaven and, in particular, Miles Warren. Miles because he built a couple of buildings at my school, and gave us a talk at the same time. That's the kind of thing that you take on for life. He also designed College House, where I spent my first two years at the University of Canterbury. I went there recently and I was impressed at how well this collection of buildings has aged. Happily it was one of the few Miles Warren buildings that was not demolished as a result of the massive earthquakes a decade or so ago.

I might have been an architect myself, but that could never be. I didn't have the maths, sir. But I did at least make two films about architecture at the National Film Unit. I'd always dreamt that I might build a house of my own with a really good architect. Eventually I got to do that, a few times.

In 1985 I was sufficiently cashed up to commission Ian Athfield to design me a house. I had a beautiful four hectares of bare rural land near Queenstown, right under the skifield of Coronet Peak, the scene of so many of my adventures. I wanted to build something splendid there. And Ath was the man. It could arguably be said that, after two years of us bickering with each other, he produced and we built the best house of his career. It's built from honey-coloured Oamaru limestone and that idiosyncratically New Zealand roofing material, corrugated iron. It makes gestures to my Irish roots and my Dunedin background, and yet it is decidedly a contemporary building. It's one of the best things I've done in my life. I think it was also extremely influential, and you see echoes of that house all around Queenstown.

I selfishly forbade publication at the time in New Zealand and forbade Ath from entering it into anything competitive, for reasons of privacy. Nevertheless, it turns up in the history of New Zealand architecture, and in *Architectural Digest*.

The house was, in fact, deliberately built for privacy, and you can't see it from the road. There is a certain amount of helicopter traffic, but reasonably distant. I was fairly sure that it would be overlooked and unremarked. I took my mother-in-law up once on a sightseeing trip, the standard go-round, with commentary from the pilot himself. I could see our house down on the left, and then, to my amazement, the chopper pilot said: 'On the left, there is the house of Hollywood actor, Sam Neill. You might remember him from *Jurassic Park*.' I looked over in horror. He looked horrified too. The poor bugger had learnt his script by heart and was stuck with it. He was powerless to stop. 'Sam lives here when he isn't away working in Hollywood, and he produces pinot noir wine' and so on.

Over the ditch in Sydney a few years later, I had the brilliant Furio Valich enlarge our tiny house, which had been built around 1900. I insisted we retain the street half of the house, so it remains untouched and in keeping with the Federation cottage neighbourhood. We exploded the rear, and built two storeys of Australian-Japanese contemporary: all steel, wood and glass. It really worked.

In the early 2000s, I got New Zealand's most underrated architect, Max Wild, to design a house for the manager on my farm. It's somewhere between a New Zealand cowshed and an ideal Los Angeles modernist home. It is exceptionally successful, albeit understated. We had a lot of fun, Max and I, going back and forth about the design.

And about four years ago, I talked Richard Naish into designing a good house for me, on my farm. Prior to that, I'd been living in a converted seed shed at the back. Life is like that sometimes, but at least it had a woodburner. The new house is very austere, modest in size but bold in concept. We completed it in 2020, during COVID. Again, I think it is a masterpiece.

I've built a bunch of other things as well—farm buildings, offices and so on. I love building, even though I myself can't hammer a nail in straight. When you make a film you know it will evaporate, be forgotten. When you build architecture you leave something beautiful and tangible behind.

Update, some months later: not a word from Te Papa. I guess my poor boots failed the test. Ah, well.

Apple Pie

I love America. Who doesn't? The whole world is secretly in love with America, whether they admit it or not.

I don't myself love America entirely unconditionally. In fact, there are many things that deeply trouble me about America, things that I hate. Here is a short list: semiautomatic weapons, crap foreign policy (see Vietnam, Iraq and Afghanistan), awful fast food, Donald Trump, the reversal of Roe v. Wade, Disneyland, the far right, Richard Nixon, malls and—worst of all—cinnamon. I have an incurable sweet tooth, which is invariably thwarted in America; cinnamon is simply disgusting, and they throw it liberally over anything and everything that is sweet. American pie, the apple version, could be good, but it isn't, because they drench it with this inedible crap.

To linger for a moment on the subject of America and guns—I recently read that the US now averages two mass shootings a day. Two per day! Good God, the National Rifle Association must be proud of themselves. I worked on John Carpenter's *In the Mouth of Madness* with Charlton Heston, once head of that illustrious organisation. For a dangerous man, he was surprisingly dull. Also, you had to pretend, if you worked in the hair department, that his rather bad hairpiece was in fact his own hair. Embarrassing.

In 2017 we were in Alaska, filming *The Pacific: In the Wake of Captain Cook*, when it occurred to me to ask any locals I met how many guns they owned. The record was held by a very nice chap I went fishing with. He had fifty-one. Nothing out of the ordinary, as he told it. By contrast, I struck up a conversation with another mild man whose job was to look after the parking meters. He had a mere twenty guns. He did, however, tell me a story both horrific and hilarious at the same time.

He pointed to a building over the road that had eight or ten storeys. A man had recently attempted to murder his estranged wife there. His plan was to pilot a small plane directly into the building, September 11–style, killing not only his wife but her colleagues too. Sadly for him, he really dicked things up.

First of all, he flew into the building at 8.45 a.m., a good quarter of an hour before she got to work. Happily, no one else was there either. Second, he got the wrong bloody building, hitting with pinpoint accuracy the office building next door, also equally empty. The only death was of the good pilot himself.

While there is a great deal of sadness in the tale, you'd have to concede that not much, especially in America, can beat a mass murder that, through sheer incompetence, goes horribly wrong.

Still, America has given us many things we can be grateful for, including the following random list: cars with fins, Diane Arbus, bebop jazz, Toni Morrison, blue jeans, the Golden Gate Bridge, Frances McDormand, rock'n'roll, Andy Warhol, Jack Nicholson, the Staten Island Ferry, freeways, Motown, Westerns, skyscrapers, the blues, Broadway, pedal steel guitars, Kurt Vonnegut, diners, the Beach Boys, Bill Burr, Airstream trailers, Elvis, *The Big Lebowski*, drive-in cinemas, *Seinfeld*, Ella Fitzgerald, gospel choirs, *Breaking Bad*, Miles Davis, hot dogs, Martin Scorsese and, best of all, NASA. They took mankind to the moon, and we all watched it.

That list tells you this—we all love American culture, to some degree or other. That is as much to do with the movies as anything. The power of Hollywood soft propaganda you cannot overestimate—we saw it on the big screen and we all wanted some of that pie. The Russians, the Iranians, the Taliban are powerless there. What do you want from Russia when you watch a Russian film? Just a little hope that that butcher Putin doesn't send missiles your way. Seeing astronauts from NASA blast off on completely different rockets, on the other hand, was worth five thousand ICBMs as far as the world was concerned. Different missions altogether. It was inspirational; it was about the future and hope.

In about 2000, we made a film about NASA and the moon landings, *The Dish*. It's based on fact: how the telescope at Parkes, New South Wales, was critical in the first landing on the moon in 1969. People often cite it to me as among their favourite films, so do see it if you haven't. Like *The Castle*, from the same team, it holds a warm place in many Australians' hearts.

Critically, it was directed by Rob Sitch. Rob and Working

Cricket on *The Dish*. With Kevin Harrington and Tom Long.

Dog were and remain central to Australian comedy and television. Rob had directed *The Castle*. He was keen for me to do *The Dish* and flew up to Sydney to persuade me. I answered the door, we shook hands, and I told him I'd read the script and I wanted to do the film. For some reason that didn't stop him giving me the pitch, and two hours later he was still at it. I had to say more than once, Rob, I am doing the film, okay? Finally the penny dropped, and within a few weeks we were shooting under this enormous dish telescope at Parkes, out in western New South Wales, under a clear, star-filled southern night sky.

I'm fond of the film. It stands up. It's full of warmth and compassion and humour. In the context of what I'm talking about—it is an Australian film about a crucially American achievement and, in its humble, self-deprecating way, Australia's contribution to that. The movie itself is an Australian achievement. Modestly.

I had a fine time in Parkes, along with Fire, my little staffy. I made lifelong close friends in Rob Sitch and Jane Kennedy. The cast were perfect. Tom Long was outstanding as my nerdy scientist offsider. We all loved Tom, and the innocence you see in the film came from a true sweet spot inside him. RIP. Roy Billing, someone I often describe as the most handsome man in New Zealand, was hilarious as the small-town mayor. Patrick Warburton, as the guy from NASA, was immaculate. Sweetheart of a man. There's a cricket game played on the dish itself by the staff—that part at least was made up, and to good effect.

Parkes is a long way from anywhere much, and is quite an odd little town. Near the motel where we stayed, there's a park that contains the Elvis Wall of Fame, which paradoxically honours Australian rock legends. This is supposedly a scaled-down version of Elvis's gates at Graceland—the walls are tall enough to come up to your waist. I think it had a total of four names when we were there, including Johnny O'Keefe, Little Pattie and Brian Henderson (who I thought was a newsreader anyway). There wasn't much to do on a day off apart from visit The Wall—it's a quiet town. But Parkes is famous now and, when it's not Elvis Fest (once a year), most visitors come because of *The Dish*.

You can't really describe *The Dish* as a comedy, for all the laughs. That's in some small part to do with my character, the leader at the telescope: a mild, cerebral man in an extraordinary situation. It becomes apparent that he is full of grief and regret, his wife having passed away some time ago.

There are parallels in *Hunt for the Wilderpeople*, another film that a lot of people put in their favourites. Taika Waititi, the writer-director, like Rob, comes out of comedy, and the film has plenty of big laughs. There is also a seam of sadness that runs through the whole narrative. I played a very different character here, a bushman who probably hardly went to school at all. He's done time in prison. The archetypal New Zealand 'Man Alone'. But Uncle Hec is also consumed by a deep grief, a grief he is unable to articulate. The film is about friendship and loss and love, and it is profoundly of its place—New Zealand/Aotearoa. They always say write about what you know—the same is often true about cinema.

In partnership with Judy Rymer, I made a documentary film about New Zealand cinema in 1995; it's called *Cinema of Unease*. It was made as part of a series to commemorate a hundred years of cinema, commissioned by the British Film Institute. I just watched it, and I'm pleased to say I reckon it stands up very well after all these years. I like the ironic tone of the presenter—*moi*. I think that cynical voice has pretty much left me in the intervening thirty years or so. Age, not wisdom. But it's a good analysis of what was going on in New Zealand, and contains quite a lot of autobiographical material, if that's of any interest at all. You can see it online, free, what is more. I mention it here because Taika makes tribute in *Wilderpeople* to so many of the films contained therein, particularly *Smash Palace*. The scene where the authorities finally run down Hec and the kid we shot in the *Smash Palace* car yard itself. As *Unease* makes clear, the authorities never look good in New Zealand film. Never mind that it's actually Ricky that shoots Hec in the bum.

Julian Dennison plays the kid, Ricky Baker, in the film. Abandoned and troubled, he is found by Hec's wife and finds love and care for the first time in his life. She is torn away from him as well, and Uncle and child are reluctantly stuck together, both in grief. Ultimately they save each other. The film is comedic, but is shadowed with pain. I think this makes the work great; Taika's best work is full of heartache and poignancy. For all the immense success he has enjoyed subsequently with blockbusters, for me *Wilderpeople* and *Boy* are still his best. *What We Do in the Shadows* is also wonderful, but of an altogether different genre.

Boy I rewatched recently. It is hilarious, but is more than anything immensely sad. I suspect there is a lot of autobiographical material there, but you'd need to ask Taika about that. The boy himself (James Rolleston)—what a heartbreak. And I cannot say enough good things about Taika as the mood-swinging derelict dad. The boy desperately wants to be cool—like Michael Jackson. Toe curling, but touching. Julian's Ricky also wants to be cool, but hip-hop cool. Annoying, but great.

Both these films of Taika's are absolutely of our place. They speak of New Zealand, of Aotearoa. Of course, they have the resonance of historical New Zealand cinema, but those earlier films were much influenced in turn by film from overseas, like road movies, B movies from Hollywood, buddy movies, which often contained big helpings of that apple pie. But these are our films. Ours. Film lineage always leads back to America, but until you make your own films, tell your own stories, you are a culture, a canoe, without a paddle.

As a footnote: we were supposed to sing 'Happy Birthday' to Ricky Baker early in the film but, just before the camera rolled, the producer ran in and said, Stop, we don't have copyright and we can't use it. Instead, mostly driven by the wonderful Rima Te Wiata, we made up 'The Ricky Baker Song' on the spot in about ten minutes. It's *much* better. See what I mean? You start with something American, discard the pie and make something that is uniquely yours.

Further Stories from the Front

Reilly the Spy and the Per Diem Man

WHEN I first started working in films I was surprised to receive every week a small bonus, in a brown envelope, as a matter of course. If you were away on location, production would give you some extra cash, say fifty dollars a day, to cover the additional expense of being away from home. These payments were called per diems. They were intended to cover meals, toll calls, taxis, the extreme inconvenience of not having to do school runs with your children, the washing-up and the laundry at home, and so on. I couldn't believe my luck—per diems *and* I was being paid. These days they're taxed and no one has cash any more so I don't know why they bother. It's a formality, but it really mattered back then.

In the early 1980s I played the title role in a series in the UK, twelve hours long, called *Reilly, Ace of Spies*. It was quite a big deal. Every year in England there would be one major production on the BBC or ITV, and in 1983 it was *Reilly*. At least half of it was good: in particular those episodes directed by Martin Campbell. Martin went on to do a couple of James Bond films and has had a huge career in feature films.

I was hyperventilating as to whether I was good enough to be the lead over twelve hours in a major historical series. Not the least of my anxieties was that, things being rather quiet on film there at the time, they were able to cast an extraordinary line-up around me. I was a new kid in town, and these were exactly the sort of actors whom I had admired from afar, actors who had cut their teeth on Shakespeare at Stratford or the National. I was a nobody, and yet here I was—at the front and centre of it all. Would I be up to snuff? I was racked with self-doubt. If ever I had impostor syndrome, this was it. Just writing down some of their names all these years later, and I'm terrified all over again.

Listen—Tom Bell, Norman Rodway, Leo McKern, Hugh Fraser, Michael Bryant, Ken Cranham, Peter Egan, Clive Merrison, Ian Charleson, Anthony Higgins, Bill Nighy, Fred Molina, David Suchet, John Rhys-Davies, Sebastian Shaw and more. Not to mention—oh, all right I will, because Reilly was something of a ladies' man—a string of extraordinary women—Lindsay Duncan, Jeananne Crowley, Laura Davenport, Frances Barber, Joanne Whalley, Joanne Pearce.

First up was the redoubtable Leo McKern. Leo was one of the greatest of all Australian actors, but most of his work had been in England. It was a wide and varied career, but he was, of course, best known for playing John Mortimer's Rumpole of the Bailey. He told me he'd spent a good year at least learning to be British before he got decent work there. One of his first jobs was touring with one of the great actor-managers, who told him, 'It is only five pounds a week, but the food in Act Three is actual.'

Another Australian expat actor I worked with later was Ed Devereaux. Ed had first got the idea to work in the UK when Laurence Olivier and Vivien Leigh were touring Australia; the Oliviers would cast locals in theatre productions on tour. Ed said he met them for a coffee up at the Cross somewhere. He said, 'I sat down beside Vivien Leigh, and she had her hand on me old fella in a coupla minutes. Yeah. Vivian Leigh. Under the table.'

Leo McKern was all of five foot seven but he completely commanded the space. An immensely impressive actor. He lived up near Oxford somewhere, but would drive into London like a maniac every day, in a Porsche, and was always right on time.

This with only one eye, the other one being glass. If he wasn't so personable and friendly I would've been even more daunted.

Reilly, Ace of Spies was like a litmus test for me. I came away knowing that I was all right in this august company. They were no better than I was. I was certainly no better than they were, and we worked fine together. I cut the mustard, more or less. It was enormously beneficial for my confidence.

With one caveat, and that is the reason I will not go back now and review any of *Reilly*. By the time we got to about episode six, halfway, I got one little note, a passing comment, from Martin Campbell, the director. I wish he'd given it earlier because I could've responded to it, I could've made it better. Reilly is an inscrutable character, the hardest man to read in the room. This, in part, makes him a great spy. The problem with being a leading man is that you never get much overall direction; the director assumes you know what you're doing.

Reilly with his poker face.

Martin's note said, 'It's a bit pompous, darling.'

Oh, Christ, was that what I'd been doing for six episodes? Was my version of enigmatic simply dull and pretentious? Devastating.

It took about another twenty years before I worked with Leo again. This was on *Molokai*, which would sadly prove to be his last film. Derek Jacobi and Leo were playing bishops, and I played a prime minister in a colonial room somewhere in Hawaii. Leo was pretty much stone deaf by this point and sported an enormous hearing aid, which didn't suit 1860s Hawaii. He would have to remove it for the shot. Quite a long scene, quite a lot of dialogue, and dear old Leo had the first line. We ran through it a few times until we were happy to film. An assistant took away the hearing aid, and the command came: 'Turnover. And action!'

Derek and I turned towards the great man, and waited for the first line to roll from that familiar, rich, booming voice. The archbishop was in deep thought; there were heavy decisions to be made. It took a long time, the pause was more than pregnant, but eventually a line did come. With unmistakable thundering McKern resonance.

'Have you had your per diems yet?'

My Colourful Agent, Ed Limato

I could write a book just on Ed Limato, but you've got a train to catch.

Ed was my agent in Los Angeles for, I dunno, twenty-five years. Ed was a famous, old-school agent. Bellicose, temperamental, tough and extremely good. He had a lot of clients much bigger than me—Mel, Denzel, Michelle Pfeiffer, Steve Martin, a long list of big-time actors. Ed wore Armani every day, top to toe, immaculate in his prestigious corner office at William Morris. At home he preferred loud Versace shirts and bare feet.

He was gay. And very naughty. He lived in a splendid house, a mini chateau if you like, that had originally been built by the sort of old screen actors he adored—Joan Blondell and Dick Powell. He lived life there as he wanted it, in decadent but tasteful splendour. The house overlooked a swimming pool, in which he never swam, and a tennis court he never stepped foot on. Indoors were often good-looking young men, cocktails and a cinema he'd built to prevent, God forbid, his ever having to see a movie with the great unwashed; some things he was fastidious about.

One night we watched *Charlie's Angels* after dinner. There was a joint on the little table beside me, so I smoked some. It did the trick; I thought *Charlie's Angels* the funniest movie ever made, a masterpiece in its own right.

Sometimes, if you timed it well, you might get asked for pasta on a Sunday night. Ed's tiny, ancient Brooklyn Italian parents would stay in a wing of the house, and his mother would cook on Sundays. They were marvellously out of step with showbiz. All the stars that came through the house meant nothing to them. Apparently, one Sunday dinner, in a conversation lull, Ed's dad turned to Richard Gere and pronounced loudly, 'Hey, Richard. That last movie you made. We watched it. It stank out the house.'

No one had better parties than Ed. You would always slip away before midnight, when things got decadent. There were invariably interesting people to meet and chat to. The funniest introduction I ever heard was from Matthew Modine, who stopped me walking past to the bar. Matthew was talking to someone I knew slightly, an accountant from the Antipodes called Trevor. Trevor (not his real name) was a nice enough bloke, but not terribly big in the humour department.

Matthew clapped Trevor cheerily on the back and said, 'Hey, Sam. Have you met Trevor? Yeah. Trevor has just had a penis transplant. *Big* success!'

I am not sure if flummox is a noun, but Trevor personified it.

Ed was famous for his extravagant pre-Oscar parties. Everyone would be there. Big crowd around the swimming pool in which no one was swimming, an even bigger crowd in and around the house.

Once, at the pool, someone handed me a joint and, against my better judgment, I had a couple of puffs. The social anxiety vanished and I decided to brave the louder party up at the house.

The immaculate Ed Limato, flanked by his assistants.

I was pretty stoned when I got there, and I was surprised when the front door was opened for me by a grin. A huge grin.

The Grin said, 'Hi, Saaam!'

I realised I had turned into a Big Grin myself. 'Hi, Jaaack!'

It was Jack Nicholson. I didn't know him. The Grins just stared at each other for a few beats, and then realised that was all they needed to say. I nodded and moved on.

All the bathrooms were full downstairs, of course, so I tried to find one upstairs. I opened a door, and inside a bedroom I saw someone I recognised as Farrah Fawcett-Majors. She looked pretty damned wasted. Around her were five or six young men, also in no fit state, but very attentive. This worried me.

I went straight down and found Ed in this year's Versace shirt. I told him that Farrah was upstairs with all these guys and I was very concerned.

Ed smiled. 'Sam. With those boys, she is *perfectly* safe.'

Oh, I see. Read the room, Sam.

Ed died about ten years ago. I went with my other agent, Philip Grenz, to view his body at a chapel a few days later. There was Ed in an open coffin, wearing the perfect suit and the perfect watch. But it didn't look like Ed at all. The body smiled a little, and looked calm and serene. In life Ed was far from either, and he hardly ever smiled. He was too dry and grumpy for that.

Everyone wanted to work for Ed; to be his assistant was as brutal and good a training in agency as you could wish for. But there was a high rate of attrition, so Ed could never be sure of their names. He would just yell, 'Get in here, Number One!' He had numbers one, two and three to scream at. They ran.

Ed devoted his life to his clients. Our welfare was his main concern. On the big piano in the drawing room Ed had all our pictures in silver frames. I was very happy to sit on that piano all those years. I miss Ed.

The Laundry Man

My agent Philip called one morning recently and I called him back. 'Sorry I didn't pick up the first time,' I said, 'I was hanging out my laundry.'

He was horrified. 'You do your own laundry? Oh...my... God!'

The two of us had lunch once at the Beverly Wilshire Hotel, and left at the same time. He pulled up beside me at the lights in his large Mercedes-Benz.

I was driving a rental VW Golf. He caught my eye and wound down his window, as did I. He was aghast.

'Sam!' he yelled. 'I never ever want to see you driving a Golf in this town again. Jesus! You hear me? You're *Sam fucking Neill*, for Chrissakes!'

I was with another agent in Los Angeles for a while. I dropped into her place one morning. The dog walker turned up to take her pooch for its walk, and off they went, dog plus walker for a good hour's exercise.

Meanwhile my agent, the dog owner, was doing *her* morning exercise on her walking machine.

It's a different planet, Los Angeles.

Ancestral Homes and Another Faux Pas

I love making new buildings, but I have a soft spot for old buildings too. In 1975 I hitchhiked around Ireland. In County Sligo, I was to stay with some old relatives, cousins of Mum's, the Coopers. It was dusk already when my ride dropped me in the village, near where they lived. I had no idea how to find their house, which was called Markree, but eventually a kind local policeman offered to take me in his Austin 1100. It was much further than I had imagined, and we made our way up a long, winding driveway, which eventually ended at an enormous crumbling castle. I thanked him, and he drove away.

I was at a bit of a loss. The place was seemingly deserted. I started to walk around the perimeter of the castle, knocking in vain at a number of huge doors. It was getting dark, and the only living things seemed to be a murder of crows that were circling in a rather threatening manner overhead. It all felt eerie and haunted. Eventually, at the smallest of all these doors, I heard dogs barking from high above. They were on approach, winding down what turned out to be a staircase. The door opened and there was an ageing cousin, Francis Cooper. He and his wife, Elizabeth, brought me in and poured me a gin and tonic, and we made awkward conversation. The Coopers are an old and distinguished family, and Francis's father was the last Irish member of parliament to sit both in Dublin and at Westminster.

I stayed with them for two or three nights. Whole wings of the castle were out of bounds—there was dry rot in the floors, and the fear was you might plummet straight through, storey after storey, to an untimely death. The Coopers were delightful and sweet, but as far as I could see they hardly ate anything, and pretty much survived on gin. In spite of the vast castle they lived in, they seemed to have retreated to three small rooms that they could just about keep warm. I think their main source of income was that they had fishing rights to a great length of the best salmon-fishing river in Ireland. I loved the atmosphere of the place, how the evenings lingered gold to rose in those neglected gardens. Years later I dropped in, and it's now a hotel and much restored. They hold weddings there. I'm sorry to say I preferred that wonderful, crumbling, corroded castle.

Twenty years later, Noriko got a job on Jane Campion's *Portrait of a Lady*, which would be shot in Tuscany. I kept the summer free, and rented a fine old villa situated among old vines in the hills above Lucca, where the movie would be shot for a couple of months. It was owned by a family that had its origins in the 1200s. That's rather a long time to be aristocracy.

It was a perfect summer, and we had a lot of friends come and stay, including Dennis Hearfield and Gerry Nucifora. We'd have lunches on the weekend, and Jane, Tom Cruise, Nicole Kidman and various others would have a long Sunday with us, with good food, lots of good wine and good weather. They made their own wine on the estate, and the wine cellar was under our villa. When we left, the bill included something like 295 bottles of the red. At about three bucks a bottle, I could afford this excess. I was curious as to what grapes produced this very drinkable wine. The family had no idea. It was just these old vines that they'd grown on their hills for centuries.

Lucca is perhaps the most overlooked Italian city, and it was wonderful to discover and explore. We rode bikes atop the walls of the city. The food was brilliant, especially from a local woman who cooked for us most nights. Gerry and I would get increasingly anxious on nights when it looked like she might be late, or forget altogether. She never did.

A couple of hundred metres away, across vines and gardens, was another lovely old villa. The owners of our villa lived there: a sweet young couple with small children. The wife was from a very distinguished old Sicilian family. They would rent out their spare villa to paying guests like us. They asked us over for a drink one night, telling us that they would be leaving soon, and they wanted to say goodbye. They were very excited, as it was their first trip outside Italy since they'd been married. They had two weeks away.

I asked what their holiday plans were. Their first week would be in New York, and neither had been to the States before. I was excited for them.

I then asked what the second week would be. She said they

were going to Belgium. I couldn't help but chuckle. Really? Belgium?

I said, 'You're having one week in New York and the second week you're going to be in Belgium? For the love of God, why?'

She said, 'My sister is married to a Belgian man.'

I think I chuckled again. That still didn't seem quite a good enough reason to spend half of your so longed-for holiday in Belgium, for goodness' sake.

'A Belgian man,' I said. 'I see. And…um…what does he do? This Belgian man. Who's married to your sister?'

'Well,' she said quietly, 'he's the king.'

The Blue City

While we're on the subject of fine accommodation, we shot *The Jungle Book* in the early 1990s, starring Jason Scott Lee, with Lena Headey, Jason Flemyng and John Cleese, directed by Steve Sommers.

Most of the production was shot in India and we were in large part based in Jodhpur, the Blue City, in Rajasthan. When I say accommodation, it was actually a palace. Half of the maharajah's splendid 1920s palace is devoted to a hotel, and very fine it is too. He and his family live elsewhere in this vast building, but it is so capacious you could be there for weeks and never see them. I did so only once, at a party the royals threw for us in the incredible gardens that surround the palace. I had one too many cups of bhang lassi, and had to be helped off to bed. Never again.

It was in part a Disney production, and of course these days *The Jungle Book* is more associated with 'The Bare Necessities' than with the author Rudyard Kipling. But this *was* Kipling, and, as we were living like nabobs up on the hill, the whole thing had echoes of the British Raj, particularly for me, as so many of my family (on my mother's side) served in India. I can go back to a great-great-great-grandfather there. Army, of course.

My grandfather Bob Ingham was a junior officer on the ill-fated Younghusband expedition into Tibet. I have a painting, by my Gaggie, of his polo pony, The Oont (Hindi for 'camel'; he was rather a plain horse, in all truth). The poor thing became lame in Lhasa. Bob was very fond of The Oont, and led him on foot for three hundred miles back into India, where he recovered and played on. My great-grandfather Brigadier General Charles Triscott C. B., C. M. G., D. S. O. served most of his life there, and took part in the relief of Kandahar, as well as the third British conquest of Burma in 1885. In Burma he commanded the expedition to Lake Endawgyi (now Indawgyi) and the Jade Mines—which is about as Boys' Own Adventure–sounding as it gets.

I know this about Charles Triscott, passed down the family—I have a picture here on my desk of the old boy in uniform with all his medals and his huge moustache. His family were Quakers. (I'm pleased that there is a little pacifist blood in my veins along with all the military.) When he told his family that he was

My great-grandfather, Brigadier General Charles Triscott. Me in *The Jungle Book* a century later.

joining the army, my great-great-grandfather had this to say: 'Charles. Thou art a Man of Blood!' And here I was, a century or more later, playing a colonel in the Indian Army. Looking, I might say, remarkably like my father in uniform, the moustache almost identical to his. Or even my grandfather times three, who knows.

In the evening, minus uniform, our favourite thing was to have a gin and tonic on the terrace of the palace, and watch the sun go down over the Rajasthani desert. They always had a little three-piece band playing raga music, and my daughter Elena, only three, took it upon herself to dance every night for the benefit of the two dozen or so other guests. She loved the applause. John Cleese was great company, full of anecdotes, all the better after the second G & T. Jason Flemyng fell helplessly in love with Lena, and why wouldn't you? We'd watch monkeys clamber down the dizzy heights of palace walls and disappear into the formal gardens. It could have been 1864 or 1994, who knew?

If you stood up and looked right, you could see the ancient blue city itself. Once you walked in there, after the hectic streets almost big enough for vehicles, again it was as if time stood still. Steve wanted to shoot a sequence with Mowgli being chased helter-skelter through the alleyways. Having scouted the area carefully, they'd worked out exactly where they wanted to shoot.

On arrival in the morning, to Steve's consternation, in the middle of his shot was a television aerial. Clearly not of the period. Someone was sent to find the owner of that aerial. A gentleman came out of this little house, and someone from production remonstrated with him. 'Why do you have a television aerial on your roof? It wasn't there yesterday! I mean, goodness gracious, what is it doing there? Because you don't even have a television set? Do you?'

The gentleman smiled serenely. He nodded in that counter-intuitive Indian manner, put out his hands and replied, 'Well, I do now!'

Half an hour later, and on receipt of a box containing a new television set, the aerial was duly taken down by said owner, and shooting commenced.

Which is known as a win-win situation.

Heroes

A few years ago I made a film in New Orleans with Arnold Schwarzenegger and Sylvester Stallone. *Escape Plan*. Bad title. It kind of gives away the story.

It wasn't a very big part, so I had a lot of days off, and a great driver called Norman. Norman was African-American and an ex-cop. I was in safe hands. Norman took me everywhere, including a lot of the neighbourhoods he knew well, which had suffered disproportionately in the floods. These were predominantly African-American. He was insightful about many things and I learnt a lot. He showed me a site where his forebears had been auctioned as slaves. He also introduced me to grilled oysters—the gift of a lifetime. In one of these neighbourhoods lived Fats Domino. A humble house, if slightly bigger than its tiny neighbours. Shotgun houses. I asked Norman if we could just sit outside for a while in the car, so I could breathe the same air as my hero Fats.

Norman took me to his church one day. He said the women there wanted to meet me, and we all had a good chat. The minister also. When it came time to leave, three of them came out to say goodbye and enveloped me in a massive group squeeze. Well. The things they said to me. I can't write them all here for fear of blushing, but it started with things like 'Mmm mmm. My white sugar right here. Well, come on, honey...' I draw a veil over the rest; we were, after all, on church grounds. I escaped into Norman's SUV more or less intact.

I had no scenes with Schwarzenegger, but we talked a couple of times. I was surprised to find myself taller than him, but clearly not quite as well defined in the muscle department. He was the most charming man and delightful to meet.

Most of my scenes were with Stallone. We got on fine, although he was very preoccupied a lot of the time. I would sit mildly beside him in an unmuscular way, while he pumped his considerable musculature all day with a couple of the sort of clamps that grips use around a set. As a result he was fully pumped, veins a-popping, all day.

There was one exchange I will never forget. I said, 'Sly, you get beaten up a lot in this movie. They just beat the shit out of you. All the time.'

He said, 'Well, that's a hero, Sam.'

'What do you mean?' I said.

'All these new guys, Statham…all the rest. All these new guys. They walk into a room and there's ten bad guys. Then they beat up all those ten bad guys. That's not me. I get knocked down. I stand up. I get knocked down. I stand up. I get knocked down and knocked down and knocked down. And finally I stand up. That's a hero.'

I've thought about that a lot. It's more than just a story point. It's a lesson in life. I'm remembering it now. Now that I've been knocked down.

I will stand up.

One more thing about heroes, on film. It's a special skill. Some have it and some never will. I am not that hero guy, not really. But Liam Neeson has it. I watched him for a whole hour once, doing just one thing. It was a scene where a plane has crashed in the snow; the survivors huddle around a fire in the night. They hear the howl of wolves. Liam stands with a blazing torch to see into the dark. Fearful, the others gather behind him. And here's the thing—I would too. He stood like a hero. Liam made that simple act convey so much. I was fascinated.

My Wine Life (Continued)

I'VE been to quite a number of wine shows, but I have only once been asked to judge at such an event. This was in Hong Kong in 2007 at their annual Wines of the Pacific Rim Festival. John Avery (from Averys of Bristol, and highly respected in the wine business) had invited me and he was the main judge. It sounded like the ultimate jaunt—four days of tasting wonderful wines, in a place I like very much, and staying at the Mandarin Oriental.

I had severely underestimated how much work these things entail. The days were endless, and you would swill literally hundreds of wines a day. Every night I would get back to my room and feel like all the enamel had been stripped from my teeth. I was very much the newbie there, but luckily Peter Lehmann, who was also a judge, took me under his wing. I was in awe of Peter, the Baron of Barossa. The man who had done so much to save one of the greatest wine regions in the world. Peter was my wise guide in what was an intense few days; what you should be looking for, pacing yourself and—not least—how not to get drunk. He was looking, for instance, for hints of kerosene in riesling. I thought those disagreeable then, but I have come round completely on that one.

Peter was also incredibly good company, naughty and irreverent, and a willing foil to his equally sharp and funny wife, Margaret. They were both dedicated smokers, and I would often join them outside, because I wanted to join the banter. And listen to Peter, all his jokes.

The chairman of the organisation that ran the show was the very distinguished Sir Noel Power, who had been chief justice of the Supreme Court of Hong Kong. His elegant wife, Lady Irma Power, served as the gracious hostess at more formal events. On the Saturday night there was a grand black-tie dinner at the Mandarin. I was sitting beside the Lehmanns, and it was quite a night. I think I made a speech at one point, but I couldn't swear to it, and I certainly have no idea of what I might have said.

I do, however, remember Lady Power doing the rounds of the tables, in the most enchanting way imaginable. Eventually she found her way to our table and charmed us all one by one. She was standing on the other side of Peter, talking to his neighbour and bending over to hear what was said in all the hubbub. I saw Peter take a glance at her behind, and he then said, reasonably loudly, 'Hey, Irma. Bet you were good in a knee-trembler back in the day.' I feel almost certain she heard what the old ratbag had just said.

She turned around and looked at Peter. 'I'm sorry, Peter. What did you just say to me?'

'I said, you are a very attractive woman, Lady Power.'

She smiled graciously. 'Why, thank you, Peter.'

I hope you will forgive me if I have a little whinge after remembering that wine show. One of the cruel side effects of my current chemo treatment is this—for three or four days at a time I cannot taste or smell a thing. A lot of long COVID sufferers know of what I speak.

I live for food. And wine. And my life has taken me to some of the greatest food in the world. I don't like fancy restaurants at all—I detest them. I loathe waiters who are up themselves. I've seen a few, let me tell you. But great food is another thing altogether. St. JOHN in London is an example of my dream restaurant—marvellous food in a plain joint with plain paper on the table. The opposite of pretentious. As were Paris brasseries thirty years ago. They are crap now; another story.

Here is what has shocked me about losing my taste—I've learnt that the appetite for food is pretty much the same thing as the appetite for life. When I have an appetite, I can't wait to get up and have breakfast and get into life. When I don't want to eat, I can hardly be bothered to get out of bed. I almost feel I've lost my will to live.

And along with food there is wine, my other great love. Nowadays, for me, a dinner without wine is like a car without petrol. Food, wine, friends, laughter—that is living.

When it comes to wine, I may have mentioned that my obsession became pinot noir. Why that wine, that grape? Today, my tastebuds are at work, so I'm happy to help with a few words. My iron-hard discipline means I will keep this mercifully short.

I tend to think of pinot as feminine. Very pretty, subtle, deeply complex and fine, and often elusive. The opposite of masculine shiraz, for instance—massive, obvious, muscular, even aggressive.

I often see people progress as wine drinkers. They start as savvy slurpers, often of the easily downed sauvignon blanc (sometimes known in the wine business as 'bitch diesel'), progress to chardonnay, mature to cabernet sauvignon and then, when they are proper grown-ups, they become pinot converts. Don't worry if you're not there yet—you will be.

The next land I acquired for wine (see, I told you this was boring) was a north-facing ten-hectare block about five kilometres out of Alexandra. We planted pinot there, in what is my favourite vineyard. Overlooking the vines are extraordinary cliffs, sculpted into the strangest shapes by millions of years of wind. It's called the Last Chance; I took its name from the watercourse that runs through the property and provides the life-giving water that makes viticulture possible on this extraordinary site. From atop the hill, you can see most of the Alexandra Basin and beyond to the alps. The Last Chance watercourse was dug by hand by gold miners in the 1860s; the water comes from far-off mountains. I love the idea of the unthinkably hard, back-breaking work that went into the creation of this little canal that winds all that distance to our little vineyard. The gold was mined long ago, but the beautiful pinot that comes from this site justifies all that sweat and blood 150 years later, by my reckoning. We have 2.15 hectares of pinot there, and part of that is a tiny plot over the ridge (0.27 hectares) named for my mother, Priscilla's Paddock. I like to say it is the southernmost vineyard in the world, although it is possible that someone else on our Ridgeline is a metre or three past us. Either way, you just cannot grow grapes successfully any closer to Antarctica. To attempt it where we are takes courage, and that is in part what makes The Last Chance my favourite vineyard.

Three years later, in 2000, about a dozen or so kilometres across the other side of the valley, I bought my farm—Redbank. It is now about fifty hectares, a portion of which we planted in vineyards—four hectares of pinot, two hectares of riesling. It is also where I now live, and I consider it my little corner of the world. My refuge, my hobby, my love. All my animals are there, my pets. We don't just grow wine, we grow lavender and we make, I think, the greatest lavender oil in the world. It had been a government agricultural research station in a previous life, so the lavender was already there, thirty-eight different varieties of it. The lavender still was also there. They also grew saffron, wormwood, licorice and other strange crops, some of which we maintain. We have orchards as well: apricots, pears, nectarines, walnuts, persimmons, cherries…all sorts.

Redbank is my home now. I am planted there. I am of that

land. I nurture the land and it nurtures me. It is my sanctuary and shelter. My happy place.

Apart from all the native trees and shrubs we've planted, I've devoted a hectare to oak trees. This is to salve my conscience about how much oak is used in producing wine. In two hundred years' time those trees will themselves be barrels, before Two Paddocks uses the next ones planted. You will also notice a great number of cypress trees around the place, simply because they are one of my favourite things about Italy. They look great at home here: verticals, exclamation marks.

And finally in 2014—a fourth vineyard. It's the only vineyard we have that we didn't develop ourselves. It was planted in 2000, and called Desert Heart, until I bought it and changed its name to The Fusilier. At 5.7 hectares of pinot it's our largest vineyard. It is named obliquely for my father, he of the Royal Irish Fusiliers. We converted it to organics posthaste, which took three years. It's a beautiful vineyard and produces great wine. Just this week The Fusilier Pinot Noir 2019 garnered 97 points from Cameron Douglas, New Zealand's sole Master Sommelier.

But here a confession—I partly bought it out of some small sense of chagrin. There's always been a kind of unstated sense in Central Otago (for all that we who grow wine in Central are united in everything) that Bannockburn, and in particular Felton Road, are slightly a cut above everybody else. At least, they think themselves as that. For outliers like Two Paddocks this was a tad irritating, particularly as we knew we were producing wine as good if not better. I was a little tired of not being taken seriously.

Eventually, the annoyance got to me, and when Desert Heart came up for sale, I thought, Stuff it, I will buy it. And there it is, right next to the famous Felton Road vineyards themselves, in what's known as the dress circle. Unarguably one of the best sites in our region. And you know what—they *do* take us seriously now. The critics, the neighbours, the punters…It feels good. It's almost ten years now of feeling good. More than that, we always sell out early. Not a bad problem to have.

I'm away a lot and it's essential that Two Paddocks is in the best hands, and it is. Mike Wing, viticulturist, has been with me for nearly twenty years. He's a legend, and he's done all the heavy lifting when it comes to the conversion to organics. He's a good boss, and always has a top crew with him as a result. It's a shame he's retired from rugby, because he was a valued enforcer at number eight for Clyde. It was fun to see him sin-binned for giving someone the knuckle; Mike is otherwise the gentlest of men. Clyde F. C. has never been quite the same without him.

Jacqui Murphy is the general manager and manages everything. She understands business, which is just as well, as I do not. She understands wine and the wine market. I know a little about that, but she knows more. She also always has a good team with her, a credit to her. I really value her commitment, and her company as well. She's good!

Dean Shaw at COWCO has made Two Paddocks wine since 1979. He knows every inch of every vineyard backwards. He is also my partner at COWCO. So we are joined at the hip. Two Paddocks is all about premium wine, and Dean himself is premium, no question.

I know this isn't very professional, but I think it's important to have people you actually *like* to work for and with you. That's usually my priority in hiring someone. People need to get along. And it's particularly important with a small company like ours. Their welfare, how they get on with each other, their safety, their sense of wellbeing, their knowing that they are valued and part of us…all these and more contribute to a good working environment. A happy place equals a happy wine. A healthy place equals healthy wines. That is why we go the extra mile to happy organics.

My Own Personal *Jaws*

IN 1987 I found myself on Hamilton Island in Queensland shooting *Dead Calm*.

It is a thriller directed by Phillip Noyce, and it co-starred Nicole Kidman and Billy Zane. While it got some mixed reviews, it seems to have stood up well, for all its flaws. We had to reshoot the ending because Warner Bros. were not entirely sure that Billy's character had, in fact, died. About seven or eight months after we finished, we were up on the reef again, with me finishing Billy off in the most gruesome manner. I see the *New York Times* rates it as one of the Thousand Best Films Ever Made. So that's something.

Working with Nicole was a considerable pleasure. You could tell she would be a great star; she had everything. Not least a fierce commitment to the job. Formidable, and a sweet, funny person to boot.

It was a very long shoot indeed—for all kinds of reasons, filming at sea can be agonisingly slow. Just the slightest change of breeze and everything looks different. Plus, our two hero vessels were sailboats, and that brings extra complexity. But I was grateful for the snail's pace. I met Noriko there, fell helplessly headlong in love and, after a long and arduous courtship, I finally got her to notice me. I needed all the time I could get.

George Miller was the producer, and having just done *The Witches of Eastwick*, he came up to Hamilton for a bit of R&R. While he was there, it became apparent we would need a second unit, otherwise the film would never get finished at all. There are effectively only three characters in the film, and my character spends quite a bit of it isolated from the other two. While Nicole's character is trying to survive on our yacht at the hands of a psycho played by Billy, her husband (me) is trying to survive on a sinking ship. George, it was decided, would direct me on the sinking ship.

I was delighted to have the legendary George in charge of me. I will never forget seeing the first *Mad Max* in Melbourne at a matinee in 1979. It was powerful and visceral and wildly entertaining, and unashamedly B movie and art house and sci-fi all at once. He's one of those directors, and there aren't many, that you would do anything for.

George decided that my character needed a little more of a challenge, apart from dodging dead bodies, half drowning and other attendant horrors. So they wrote in a whole shark story. As the ship takes on more and more water, a man-eating shark makes an entry and smells blood, my blood, in the water. I think we had three, possibly four, versions of the shark. The most primitive of these was a stuntman with a fin on his scuba tank. All that was required was a fin to circle the boat, but it turned out to be very hard to make this work. He was quite a big stunt guy, and somehow you could always sense his considerable non-shark-like bulk.

The most sophisticated version was a mechanical shark of sorts. He was affectionately known as Snappy Tom and, like Spielberg's mechanical shark, Tom was unreliable at best. The whole shark story was a lot of fun to film, and it came down to not just Man Running from Shark, but Man Versus Shark hand to fin. A fight in which I acquitted myself rather well. Well done, that man. At the same time, my character is becoming more and more deranged. You would, wouldn't you? At one point the poor bloke under severe pressure is singing a hymn from his childhood to keep his spirits up. 'Jesus Loves Me'. My idea, and I was rather proud of it.

But in the end the whole shark storyline was ditched. Heartbreaking. For the shark, at least. I'm not entirely sure why—perhaps it was just a bit much. I've asked George several times to add the shark scenes as an extra on a Blu-ray or some such. He claims they are all lost. I don't really believe him. Come on, George, you know where they are!

Thirty years later, I was working on *Sweet Country* in the desert near Alice Springs. We were shooting a scene in which the posse was around a campfire at night. Someone recites a poem. Someone else tells a story. We all get a turn. We can easily forget how people used to entertain each other before there was television and radio, when there was just a fire. My character, a farmer, is also something of a God-botherer. I suggested that I sing a hymn. I sang once again 'Jesus Loves Me'. This time our director, Warwick Thornton, God bless him, kept it in the film. It is a kind of funny, ridiculous moment and, dare I say it, a little touching too.

Anyway, we finished *Dead Calm*, and it worked pretty well, I'd have to say. At the very least it got me married. Steven Spielberg saw the film, he told me, and that as much as anything else was how I got cast in *Jurassic Park*. It's the switch on the train track once again. Very good luck for me.

As for my getting married, Noriko and I wed in 1989. We stayed married for almost thirty years. I think this speaks well of us both. She is a wonderful woman, and is the mother of my two fabulous daughters. She is very beautiful, is a brilliant cook and host, and I enjoyed all those good years with her. As in any marriage, we had the odd bad patch, but by and large we sailed along happily.

One of the things I found endearing about her was her English pronunciation. Like many native Japanese speakers, she tends to treat the letters 'l' and 'r' as interchangeable sounds. (Noriko speaks English well, but I never learnt Japanese, to my eternal shame.) When we first got together on *Dead Calm*, Australia was going through a 'general erection'. One of her best dishes is 'lack of ram'. She once left a note for me in which I was accused of being a 'stuben buster'. I'm sure I was just that.

Noriko is also one of the most brilliant hair and make-up artists in the world. Her work for Jane Campion, Liam Neeson and Nicole Kidman is testament to that. But enough already—let's allow her her privacy now.

One last story about this film. There is a macabre footnote to the public reception of *Dead Calm*. I was in Los Angeles when George and Phil tested the film with some American audiences.

My beautiful bride, Noriko.

There is a completely terrifying sequence near the beginning. It's the backstory to the main narrative, and explains why we, as a couple, are in trauma, and sailing peacefully in an attempt to heal. Nicole's character has a horrible car accident in which our child, a baby, is killed. In the crash the child goes straight through the windscreen of the car. So there I was, sitting in this audience, somewhere out in the Valley, watching the film. The hideous accident happens. At this, to my complete astonishment and horror, the audience laughed, clapped and cheered. I felt sick to my stomach, and had to leave the theatre.

*

I run into Nicole once in a while, and it's always a pleasure: she's funny, warm and affectionate. I also think she's one of the best actors around. See *Big Little Lies*, tell me I'm wrong. But *Dead Calm* put her on the map. And, for all I know, it put Billy Zane on *Titanic* as well.

I've only seen Billy Zane a few times since then. There was a party once at his place on Hollywood Boulevard. Kind of a strange party—I ended up doing a painting on the floor with Marilyn Manson. In hindsight that seems a little odd.

In 2000, however, Billy and I were invited for a week to the Moscow Film Festival. Here they were honouring Phillip Noyce, and the key film they were showing was *Dead Calm*. I didn't see a lot of Billy that week: he was seemingly super-glued to a six-foot, blonde Russian supermodel for the duration.

We did have one or two memorable nights out. Moscow was pretty wild then. We were staying at the venerable old Metropol hotel, just off Red Square, and to enter you always had to make your way through gangsters' bodyguards, who were to a man armed with machine guns. One night we ended up in a club at about 3 a.m. Very exclusive and, weirdly, not a lot of clientele. More women than men. One large booth had a bunch of about ten men and women—the women uniformly stunning and the men uniformly ugly. Our chaperone whispered urgently in my ear: 'Do not, whatever you do, even look in that direction. The man at the back of the booth is the Most Dangerous Man in Russia. Whatever you do, do not catch his eye.' I asked quietly what his name was. He went pale. 'Please! Please do *not* ask me that! I do not want to die.' Now that I think about it, perhaps it was Vladimir Putin himself?

We flew to an overnight cruise down the Volga. The boat was full of gamblers and filmmakers and clowns and all sorts. I woke up with the sun at about 5 a.m. with the worst vodka hangover of my life. As I sat on the foredeck, feeling desperately sorry for myself and sick as a dog, a mirage began to appear, glistening in the golden low sunlight. Strange huge golden onions. As we got closer it became clear that this was a massive church complex, and indeed it was one of the oldest and most revered monasteries in all of Russia. We stopped there and stumbled, marvelling, through the ancient buildings, and then, on the banks of the Volga, we were given the pleasure of a folkloric dancing and singing festival. It was charming and peculiar, and I wished I was a little less self-inflicted.

On the weekend, we were asked to a lunch party at the dacha of Nikita Mikhalkov himself. Mikhalkov was not only president of the festival, but he has an impressive body of work, including one of the greatest films ever made, *Burnt by the Sun*, in which he also stars. Quite a do, a beautiful place deep in a Chekhovian birch forest. Overlooking his political views for a minute (he is close to Putin), Mikhalkov is hospitable and charismatic. His brother was there, the great director Andrei Konchalovsky—I love *Runaway Train*.

Their father, the venerated poet, playwright and composer
Sergey Mikhalkov, was there. He is most famous for compos-
ing the stirring Russian national anthem, commissioned by Stalin
himself. He had a successful career as a Soviet, and as a post-
Soviet as well. That takes some doing.

And curiously, Prince Michael of Kent was there, with
Princess Michael. He looked spookily like the last tsar, the
one they shot in 1918. Indeed, he is closely related to all those
Romanovs. I have a feeling he might be a little close to one or
two oligarchs as well. Mikhalkov apparently is a royalist, so there
we go.

Moscow was wild and I enjoyed it. But a sad note on departure. I had a very nice translator for the duration, a pleasant
middle-aged woman who was also a distinguished professor at
Moscow State University. This was a holiday job for her. I was
grateful for her help. On departure I had about two hours to
kill at the absolutely hideous Moscow airport, having got there
early, as required. I asked her if I could buy her a drink upstairs
at the bar. She agreed. There wasn't much that I wanted to drink
there, but I suggested that we share a half-bottle of Bordeaux. It
was expensive, eighty dollars for the half, but it was just about
the only wine available. I paid, poured us both a drink, and she
sipped it thoughtfully.

I said, 'Why do you look so sad?'

She said, 'Do you want to know the truth?'

'Of course.'

'What you paid for that wine is more than I get paid in a
month.'

That made me sad as well.

A Setback

A while ago I had another PET scan. The news was not good. The chemo regime I've been under for the last eighteen weeks has been a failure.

This is something of a disappointment; back to square one. Four months of torture and I am as bald as a badger with nothing to show for it. Initially we were all very optimistic—the tumours were in retreat. However, they are on the march again, the bastards. I can feel them around my neck, something like a noose. Sorry to be a little macabre, but I think it's excusable. The subtitle for this book might be 'Notes from a Dying Man'.

But, back to positivity. I start a new regime on Tuesday. Chemo again, but new and I think somewhat experimental. Crossing all digits and we will see how we go. Every week for the next six months. Hey ho. With any luck my hair may return. More than anything I want my beard back. I don't like the look of my face one bit.

On the upside, I signed a contract with the drug company. It's an expensive treatment, very expensive, and my insurance won't pay. But, but, if I'm still alive in six months, it's free thereafter. *Free*, I tell you! Deal! Wait. I doubt these motherfuckers do *anything* for free. I think there might be a catch in there somewhere...

And just now I remembered, from more than sixty years ago, a board game that my American godmother, with the wonderful moniker Jean Paradise, sent me for Christmas when we children

were small. We loved board games at home. This one was called
Careers. We became fascinated with it. We liked Monopoly, but
this was better. Careers was played with dice. And it was about
more than accumulating property and money; it was about what
you did with your life. I remember some of the choices: Farming,
Big Business (Dad's favourite), Going to Sea, Exploring, Hollywood and, best of all, Astronaut. It didn't occur to any of us,
certainly not me, that any of these would be our future. Not
Hollywood, that's for sure.

There were penalties, as in most games, and the two worst
fates were the Park Bench or Hospital. We never had homeless
people in New Zealand in those days, so ending up on a park
bench never looked as bad to me as it might to someone in New
York City. Sitting in a park sounded, well, quite relaxing. And
until now, in my life, I've avoided the park bench okay, but lately
I seem to have copped a bit of the bloody hospital. In the game,
to get out of Hospital you had to forfeit half your money (American healthcare may not have changed all that much since then).
And to win you had to accumulate sixty points and achieve either
Fame, Fortune or Happiness, or some combination of the three.
Going to Sea got you lots of Happiness points, but not much
Money or Fame. A Scandal in Hollywood gave you more Fame
points, but reduced Happiness and Fortune.

So where am I up to? Have I won? I'm not sure. What points
have I accumulated? Happiness—quite a lot. Fortune—some
success. Fame—a little. Which of those is most important?
Happiness, of course.

I can tell you this with absolute assurance. I have met the
winners. I once spent time with a tribe on Vanuatu who are part
of the Prince Philip Movement, a sect that venerates the Duke of
Edinburgh. They are easily the happiest people I have ever come
across. And the reason, I believe, is this: they have faith and,

more importantly, they own absolutely nothing. They eschew everything from the west; even a T-shirt is too much. They live simple subsistence lives, wear only a grass skirt or a penis sheath, raise children, share their food…and that's it. They are unburdened and free. They laugh all day. Life is good.

Half their luck.

So where am I in the game? Have I got to sixty points? I don't know, but I am not finished yet. Onwards and upwards and we soldier on. Let's hope the spirit of my great-grandfather arrives, as he did in the relief of Kandahar. And may the dice be with me.

On Vanuatu with the happiest people I know.

Women Are Better

THIS might sound dumb. I don't care. I just think women are better. Better than me, at the very least.

Women are better at most things. Politics, that's one. Acting, that's another.

Better actors. It is sometimes proposed that we have one acting award. Men would never win a damn thing if they did that. We are outclassed all the time. Not that it's a competition or anything. And that's almost invariably the case with women. They work with you. That is gold.

As proof of all I say, here is a list of some of the great women I have been lucky enough to work opposite, alongside, under... whatever. In collaboration with.

This is *not* in any order whatsoever.

Anjelica Huston (*Family Pictures*)

Rachel McAdams (*The Vow*)

Laura Dern (three *Jurassic*s)

DeWanda Wise (*Jurassic World Dominion, Invasion*)

Rachael Blake (*Perfect Strangers*)

Kristin Scott Thomas (*The Horse Whisperer, Sweet Revenge*)

Anna Paquin (*The Piano, Flack*)

Sophie Okonedo (*Flack, Skin*)

Meryl Streep (*Evil Angels, Plenty*)

Victoria Hamilton (*To the Ends of the Earth*)

Lindsay Duncan (*Reilly, Ace of Spies*)

Rachel Griffiths (*Children of the Revolution, Ride Like a Girl*)

Susan Sarandon (*Irresistible, Blackbird*)

Kate Winslet (*Blackbird*)

Rachel House (*Hunt for the Wilderpeople, The Portable Door*)

Noomi Rapace (*Assassin Club*)

Lisa Harrow (*Omen III: The Final Conflict, From a Far Country*)

Mia Wasikowska (*Blackbird*)

Judy Davis (*My Brilliant Career, One Against the Wind, Children of the Revolution*)

Holly Hunter (*The Piano*)

Rose Byrne (*Peter Rabbit, Peter Rabbit 2*)

Teresa Palmer (*Ride Like a Girl*)

Bryce Dallas Howard (*Jurassic World Dominion*)

Helen McCrory (*Peaky Blinders*)

Romola Garai (*Angel, Mary Bryant*)

Rima Te Wiata (*Hunt for the Wilderpeople*)

Charlotte Rampling (*Angel*)

Cate Blanchett (*Little Fish*)

Mandy McElhinney (*House of Hancock*)

Carmen Ejogo (*Sally Hemings*)

Sigourney Weaver (*Snow White*)

Toni Collette (*Dirty Deeds*)

Greta Scacchi (*Country Life, Palm Beach*)

Odessa Young (*The Daughter*)

Rachel Ward (*The Umbrella Woman, Palm Beach*)

Lena Headey (*The Jungle Book, The Adventurer: The Curse of the Midas Box*)

Emily Blunt (*Irresistible*)

Joan Allen (*Yes*)

Heather Mitchell (*Rake*)

Keira Knightley (*Dr Zhivago*)

Wendy Hughes (*My Brilliant Career, Lucinda Brayford, Amerika, Two Twisted*)

Scarlett Johansson (*The Horse Whisperer*)

Olivia Hussey (*Ivanhoe*)

Marta Dusseldorp (*The Twelve*)

Isabella Rossellini (*Merlin*)

Kate Mulvany (*The Twelve*)

Kirsten Dunst (*Wimbledon*)

Stéphane Audran (*The Blood of Others*)

Annabelle Wallis (*Peaky Blinders*)

Miranda Richardson (*Merlin, Merlin 2, Rams, And Then There Were None*)

Sinéad Cusack (*My Mother Frank*)

Parminder Nagra (*Alcatraz*)

Helena Bonham Carter (*Merlin, Sweet Revenge*)

Isabelle Adjani (*Possession*)

Jodie Foster (*The Blood of Others*)

Jessica Lange (*The Vow*)

Maria Doyle Kennedy (*The Tudors*)

Kerry Fox (*Country Life*)

Imogen Poots (*A Long Way Down*)

Miranda Otto (*The Daughter, The Portable Door*)

Wendy Crewson (*The Vow, Bicentennial Man*)

I'm stopping there. It sounds like I'm bragging.

But, honestly, read that list. It's breathtaking. Half my luck, eh? What a privilege. Why actors of this extraordinary calibre were bothering with an ordinary chap like me, heaven only knows.

Only one of them made it clear I wasn't in her league. She may tell you if you ask.

I Turn into Fellini

WELL, not *that* Fellini, obviously, more Brian Fellini from Invercargill. I have been a Proper Director once, and once only. This was in conjunction with my old ally, the genius John Clarke.

The Fellini reference is a nod to John. John swore on his life that he'd met a chainsaw artist who used to do massive sculptures of koalas, kookaburras and so on, whose name was Trevor Monet. He was by his own account the great-nephew of Claude Monet. The urge to create art obviously ran strongly in his veins, and he expressed it in a very Australian manner. Lots of smoke, noise and weird wildlife. I'd like to believe that at least some of this is true.

John and I briefly had a small film company together, at least on paper. We looked for projects, and John found one. He decided to adapt two very Australian, very Melbourne, detective novels for the small screen. Crime fiction, written by Shane Maloney, featuring a hapless but uncommonly good amateur sleuth, Murray Whelan. I would direct one (*The Brush-Off*) and John the other (*Stiff*). In addition we would play small parts in each other's movies.

I had done this once before for John. He asked me to play a guest spot in his outrageously good series *The Games*. My character, Sam, is a possible 'transport consultant' for the upcoming Sydney Olympics. John had a healthy contempt for 'consultants', the sort of leeching bludgers who breed freely in a free-market free world. My main contribution was this: Sam, I suggested, was someone who spends more time having long lunches than doing any work. As a result, he is very gaseous, and much given to heartburn. It's a small thing, but I made the most of it. Burping and gassing all over the shop.

But back to *The Brush-Off*. I threw myself into this with uncommon abandon. I lived and breathed it for six months, or was it nine? It was captivating for me. I was there for the pre-production, and we were lucky to have Chris Kennedy designing both films. Casting was a wonderful thing—I called in a lot of favours, a lot of people who were friends or who I thought were great, and who were happy to come in for two or three days, more as a kindness than anything. I had a dream bunch of actors to work with.

First of all, we had David Wenham playing Murray. Wenham is about the best actor in Australia, and a very close friend. He's also very funny and gives a performance that works on many levels. We first see him, in my film, waking up with the worst hangover in the history of Melbourne in his shitty Melbourne flat. He stumbles in his jocks to his ghastly Melbourne bathroom.

David Wenham as Murray Whelan, with admirers.

We shot the wide in two takes. For the second take I gave him this direction—just as you pass camera, pause briefly and pretend to fart; I will put the fart noise in later in post. To my complete astonishment, as he passed the camera he paused and farted for real. Now, many actors can cry on cue. Real tears. That's amazing in itself. But very few indeed can fart to order. That is surely the mark of a great actor.

All the rest of the cast were outstanding as well. Dear old Bruce Spence, tall as a gum tree, playing an old queen arts administrator. Steve Bisley playing a crooked developer of some kind with all the right weight, very wry. I've loved him ever since that first *Mad Max*. He tears up the screen. Playing opposite him was my darling Heather Mitchell. If there were still damehoods for acting in Australia, she'd be first off the rank. Their characters are having a steaming affair in the film. In a horrific scene, when the hapless Whelan has to hide in a cupboard in the room where those two are having a very noisy bonk, I suggested for no good reason that they have a thing when they're having sex. They play doggies; very noisy, barking doggies. They loved the idea, and Steve plays it like a roaring alsatian, while Heather does a yapping chihuahua. It still makes me laugh to think about it. We play most of the scene on poor Murray in the cupboard, having to bear witness to this grotesquely loud canine activity.

Justine Clarke, one of my favourite actresses, was then, as now, most famous in Australia as a wholesome presenter on *Play School*. I had her playing against type as the sexiest thing on two legs. Funny, too. Subsequently, Justine has kindly sung at two of our big bash birthdays, and again she just fogs up your glasses. No one there will ever forget her steamy version of 'My Baby Just Cares for Me'. We had our friend Deborah Kennedy, who played John's wife in *Death in Brunswick*, playing closer to what we expect from her. There is no one in the world better at giving you the sort of look that makes you wither and die. Mick Molloy, that hilarious reprobate, we cast as a ne'er-do-well politician of a right-wing persuasion. We dressed him in a Wallabies track-suit, the sort of thing that John Howard would wear on his sad morning walks, accompanied by a security detail. Molloy was anything other than in great shape, and was just as risible as Howard as a wannabe Wallaby. And I had Tracy Mann playing Bisley's wife; I didn't know Tracy, but I've always thought she's about as good as it gets, so it was worth a shot. She said yes and she was terrific. And so it went. An old hero—Gerard Kennedy—makes an appearance. Robert Grubb, the funniest actor I know (we worked on *My Brilliant Career* and *Robbery Under Arms*), was wonderful as a cop. So many extraordinary actors.

The shoot itself was a dream, if an exhausting one. Ellery Ryan, whom we loved on *Death in Brunswick*, shot the film. Like all the best Australian crews, everyone went the extra mile. I was so completely absorbed in everything I was even dreaming the film at night.

I brought my little staffy, Fire, across from New Zealand to keep me company in Melbourne. Production found me a nice flat on about the tenth floor in a new building on St Kilda Road. One Saturday, I went out for dinner, leaving my dog behind. That night there were fireworks over the Yarra River. Any bangs or frights and Fire would invariably lose her mind. It's a dog thing. The flat had floor-to-ceiling windows and a perfect view of a huge firework display, explosions and all. When I came home, I found her in the spare room still terrified. I calmed her down, and she eventually settled at the bottom of my bed as always. It was only in the morning that I realised she had spectacularly shat all over the new white carpet in that spare bedroom. Poor little thing. I called in the carpet cleaners to no avail. I had to replace the entire carpet—cost two grand. So much for celebrations.

The sheer pleasure of working with other actors, actually directing them, I cannot fully express. Incidentally, it's amazing to me how infrequently one gets any direction at all from directors these days. I'm not sure why that is. Do they think that, once they've cast you, you just know what you're doing? I myself love getting input from a director—let's try this or that. It almost never comes. But every day on *The Brush-Off*, bouncing off my actors, exchanging ideas, coming up with stuff that made us laugh...what a gas.

And then, a few weeks in the cutting room, sitting over someone's shoulder. It was like the old days at the NFU; I loved every minute. Cezary Skubiszewski provided the music, endlessly inventive. The theme for Justine Clarke's character is almost as exciting as her appearance, and I still like a jive to it now and then.

The film was well received. The *Sydney Morning Herald* said it was the best telemovie of the year. We got four Australian Film Institute nominations: Best Telefeature, Best Screenplay, Best Actor, and even—wait for it—Best Director!

Would I do it again, on another film? No. It was just too damn exhausting. For all the thrills, I was depleted at the end. I vowed to stick with what I know—acting and making wine. That's more than enough. Leave directing to directors. Lucky bastards.

This Is Where I Am

THIS illness / recovery / rehabilitation...I know not what to call it. You take your pick, but please, no curses or spells...Be nice.

Whatever it is, it has had a transformative effect on my study, which has become a refuge, a snug, a place of comfort. I sit here now, awkwardly tapping away with just two fingers. I told you I was slow.

That was not always the case. I used to avoid my study altogether, or would drag my feet in here, and sit myself with reluctance to read something, a script, a proposal, an offer. The older I get, the less incentive I have to work. I remember reading an interview with an ageing Robert Mitchum in the *Guardian*, who was asked what he responded to in scripts. His answer: 'Great locations. And days off.' A tad cynical, I thought. But now I understand. Mind you, I am also hopelessly addicted to work, which in large part explains why there are a number of jobs on my CV that should be put out of their misery, shot with a silencer behind a woolshed somewhere. Fat chance. They sit brooding and unloved in the dark corners of the interweb. Forever.

The study, in addition, is a place I always felt vaguely guilty about. This, I am sure, has something to do with my upbringing. If my parents caught me curled up in a corner with a good book, I would be briskly shooed outside. A waste of a good day.

But now I love my study. I have been writing this book in here—is it a *book?*—and that has been a lifesaver these last six months. But, although I am alone in here, I am surrounded by people. Lots of people.

I started collecting vintage photography about thirty years ago. I've always been drawn to the infinite variety and complexity of the human face—portraits are a large part of my art collection. I decided I only wanted people in my study as I work. So the walls are covered with more than a hundred images of people, shoulder to shoulder. It's a hot mess of humanity.

Behind me are Diane Arbus's *Patriotic Young Man with a Flag, NYC, 1967*; Weegee's *Cop Killer*; Jürgen Schadenberg's *Miriam Makeba*; Ans Westra's *Carmen*, her elegant portrait of the drag queen; Jacques Henri Lartigue's *Gypsy Mistress*; Seydou Keïta's intriguing *Mali Police Inspector with Two Wives*; Max Dupain's *Nude*.

Before me, a wall of faces, including Rita Angus's portrait of a girl with different coloured eyes; Helena Bonham Carter's grandmother's watercolour of a tiny old lady in black entitled *But She Was Kind*; a carved wooden head with full moko tattoo from my dear friend Gordon Hatfield, carver and tattooist; a Soviet realist portrait of a tractor driver, circa 1936; Marti Friedlander's limpid and definitive portrait of Ralph Hotere; Louis Armstrong at home with his wife in Brooklyn.

But the golden thread through all of this is woven from images of my family, my loved ones. They spread from frames all over my desk and climb up the walls into the grand mix. In pride of place, my father inspecting the Guard alongside the Queen. There are my sons with my arms around them. All my grandchildren are there, my siblings. My darling Gaggie. So many loved ones. I am happy in their company.

I also own and love a painting by Nicholas Harding, a lush landscape. Nicholas and I had been going through cancer and chemo together, supporting each other as best we could. Then he began to fade fast, and in November 2022 he died. I felt like my pal had suddenly disappeared out the boxcar door. But it wasn't until I saw his last show, a few weeks after his death, and was surrounded by the ecstatic, vibrant bush paintings that he'd created with such courage and tenacity through those last enfeebling months, that I was gripped with true grief and reduced to helpless tears.

But I can't stay in my study all the time. Every day I am dragged away from the pictures and the portraits by the lorikeets, those raucous, riotously coloured mobsters that fly in from gangland elsewhere. I know full well I am subject to an abusive relationship here. I love them, and I think they love me. But the gang, sometimes fifteen strong, yell and bully me to feed them when they feel like it. I do what I'm told. Classic victim me. Listen. They are screeching at me now.

One of my avian friends.

Still More Stories from the Front

The Great Tree in the Desert

IN Australia, some of my best experiences have been working with First Nations actors, on Country.

Tommy Lewis was a wonderful friend and partner on *Robbery Under Arms*. We laughed all day, charging around on our horses. He told me lots of stories about life at home, way up at Katherine. I won't repeat them here but they were eye-opening for me. Wayne Blair was a tonic on *Rams* and lightened my load on some of those long, gruelling days.

I would always listen carefully to these guys, and would welcome even the slightest word of advice on what was not my turf. Spooky sometimes, though. One day I was walking up a track with Ernie Dingo, and he stopped dead.

'Uh oh. Bloody willy wagtail just walked in front of us. Gonna be a *bad* day, Sammy!'

Nothing bad happened that day and, you know, you're never *entirely* sure whether your leg is being pulled.

Hamilton Morris and I became very strong friends on *Sweet Country*. Deep mutual respect, and a warm-hearted, decent bloke. We took *Sweet Country* to the Venice Film Festival and it won the Silver Lion, I think it's sort of second prize. Very prestigious. Hamilton is the lead in the film but couldn't be found the week before we were due to go. He should have been there, but no show. I've never been told why. Great pity.

Hamilton and I were driving in a van once on the way to work through this spectacular, dry canyon country near Alice Springs. We passed a sign that simply said Big Tree. I was intrigued and got the driver to stop. We got out, and Hamilton and I wandered down the track, and found an immense gum tree in an old dry riverbed.

It was enormous, ancient and charismatic. I walked towards it and spent a few minutes in its company, embracing its huge trunk in the hippy manner. It was rather overwhelming.

I looked back at Hamilton, who was still at the edge of the clearing. It was time to go, and we walked together back to the van. I told him how powerful that tree had been for me. Hamilton shook his head and muttered, 'I wouldn't have touched that tree, mate.'

I looked back at him. I said, 'What do you mean, Hamilton?'

'Not my country, mate. I wouldn't touch it. Bad luck.'

I spluttered in indignation. 'Bad luck? Bloody hell, Hamilton. Why didn't you say something, why didn't you tell me not to touch it? You could have said something.'

He just grinned a bit and said nothing.

Whitefellas...

I wrote a note to a couple of First Nations actors last week. It's important to encourage the young from time to time. I will never forget the odd encouraging word I got as a young chap from some older actor I respected. (James Mason, for instance.) I don't know if these two respect me, but I wrote anyway. Keep an eye on them.

First of all, Mark Coles Smith. I've been watching Dylan River's excellent *Mystery Road: Origin*. I worked with Mark a few years ago, with Bryan Brown, on *Old School*. I thought he was really good; I hope I remembered to say something. But here he is, commanding as the lead in this series.

Then there is Rob Collins. What an actor. He has everything: looks, talent, charisma. I voted for him to be the new James Bond and he'd pull that off with aplomb.

Both these guys are true leading men. There are many good actors in the world. Leading men, actors who can carry a show, are rare.

Political Encounters

I first met Australian rugby great George Gregan at Sydney airport, waiting for my bags at the carousel. I was dozing on my feet, when I became aware someone was talking to me. He had a green blazer on, and I realised that I was surrounded by big men in green blazers. Hadn't a clue why, or who they were. The talking one was saying, 'G'day, Sam. I'm George. Big fan. Wanna come to the Test next week?'

I was baffled. I started to realise what the blazers were—these were the Wallabies, the Australian rugby team. I hadn't thought about rugby for years; I'd long ago lost interest. I liked this friendly bloke in the blazer, though, and I said, 'Yeah, sure, that'd be great. George, is it? Terrific.'

We've been friends ever since, and I am a rabid rugby supporter once more. Who do I support? Good question. The answer is: I am an All Blacks *supporter*, but I am a Wallabies *fan*. If pressed I might admit to being, on occasion, an Ireland *enthusiast*.

My friendship with George not only led me to enjoy rugby once again, it also meant, through Georgie's kindness, tickets to all sorts of good things. Before one of the games in Sydney at the Rugby World Cup in 2003, I was having a beer in the members bar with Bryan Brown and the journalist Mike Carlton. Bryan knows almost nothing about rugby union, and more than is healthy about rugby league. Sad. So Carlton and I were doing most of the chat.

Suddenly a familiar voice was right beside us. 'G'day, Mike. G'day, Bryan. G'day, Sam.'

We swung around and there was the prime minister, John Howard, glasses, weird grin and all. Not my favourite person in all the world, you'd have to say, not after *Tampa* and all the disgraceful children-overboard bullshit, not after the lies about Iraq. He struck up a conversation. To my complete dismay, bloody Bryan and Carlton faded away, leaving me alone with John Howard. Awkward.

Oh well, I thought, since we were stuck with each other, I might as well not waste the opportunity.

'John. Mate. Those kiddies, those little kiddies, John, that you've got locked up in those concentration camps. You've gotta do something about that. Get 'em outta there.'

'Oh yeah, Sam, well, you know it's not as easy as you think. They won't leave without their parents. You know...'

To my great satisfaction, he faded away as fast as my treacherous friends. See ya, John.

The Wallabies beat the All Blacks that year in the semi-final. Bryan and I were asked to say a few words before the game on the broadcaster Channel Seven, and afterwards at full time. By then we were both pretty drunk. I was maudlin, and Bryan was ebullient. I tried to say a few gracious words in defeat, but no one could hear me, as Bryan wouldn't stop bellowing, 'I come from a land down under,' over and over again. They never asked us back. Idiot.

The following weekend the Wallabies lost the final in the last minute after the famous Johnny Wilkinson drop goal. Bryan and I went back to the hotel where the Wobblies were staying for a drink. They had played the whole Cup brilliantly, much better than anyone expected, but now understandably they were gutted. I was appalled—no one from Rugby Australia was there, no one made a speech, no one gave a shit. The whole ballroom was quiet and sad. I turned to Bryan, who was drunk again, and said, 'Someone needs to say something. This is disgraceful. None of the big wigs are here, these boys are totally unacknowledged. It has to be you. Okay?' He was reluctant, but I was angry by now and I told him to bloody get up and say something.

He did. He stood swaying on a table and yelled, 'Hey! A bit of bloody shush, please! Shut up! Listen, just wanna say you blokes did great! Ya did! You're a great fuckin' team, and we fuckin' love ya!'

Perfect! The place erupted with cheers and hilarity, and the night ended really well. Good on ya, Bryan.

One other close encounter with an Australian politician, while I think of it. If I was in Australia on election day, I always enjoyed handing out how-to-vote cards for the Labor Party (an activity that is strictly forbidden in New Zealand). This was especially enjoyable in Double Bay, where I was living in the early 1990s. It's in the seat of Wentworth, until recently one of the safest Tory seats in Australia. Most of the voters I encountered at the polling booth hated the Labor Party. I'd laugh all day, trying to give them cards.

At the 1993 election the Liberal Party, led by opposition leader John Hewson, was expected to romp home. During the campaign I had spoken up for the arts on the telly, but the Liberal Party seemed to care little for Australian film or theatre or, for that matter, for any of the arts. I was therefore a marked man at the polling place. Towards the end of the day, to everyone's surprise, Hewson himself turned up. He'd dropped by to thank the volunteers, and was quickly surrounded by adoring Young Liberals, who were mostly wearing blazers and ties, and were by and large remarkably chinless.

In a moment of silence, I approached and held out a Labor card. 'Dr Hewson, I wonder if you might like something to help you decide how to vote?'

He looked up in surprise, grinned wryly and said, 'No thanks, mate.'

Suddenly, an angry woman with blonde, Princess Di hair was up close and in my face. It was Carolyn Hewson, the then wife of the leader of the opposition. 'We know who you are!' she snapped.

I chuckled, but it was a scary moment. The wife of tomorrow's prime minister apparently bore a grudge against me, and who knew what that meant?

Well, as it happened, against all predictions, Labor won. John Hewson's political career was effectively over. The next morning, I opened the doors of my house, and played 'Fanfare for the Common Man' as loud as I could over the rooftops of Double Bay. Oh, the relief. (It's only fair to add that, in the years following, John Hewson became something of an elder statesman, and is often critical of the Liberal Party of which he is no longer a member. I have come to admire him.)

Meryl Streep Has Pleasure in Inviting You

Rehearsing for *Evil Angels*, Meryl Streep and I got on really well. We were a team, and could make each other laugh. I'm not sure if this is still true, but Meryl's method around this time was this: if your character was against hers in the story, she would have as little to do with you as possible. In this film absolutely everyone is against Lindy Chamberlain (Meryl) and her husband Michael (me)—the press, the public, the jury, the police…everyone. So it was us against the world. Now, it was a big deal to have Meryl doing a movie in Australia, and all kinds of actors were happy to take the tiniest part, to spend a few days in the courtroom, for instance, just to watch Meryl work. Some of them were my friends, and I would need to explain why Meryl was a little stand-offish.

Anyway, we were friends now, and she was good enough to invite me to things. One night she was having the prime minister, Bob Hawke, to dinner. She asked Noriko and me to join them. I admired Hawke and was keen to meet him. He came on his own, on time, and left early. It was clear from the moment he entered the room that he didn't want to be there at all. I'd have to say, in all honesty, I have never sat at table with a ruder man. The distinguished Fred Schepisi was there, a great Australian and a great director, along with his charming wife, Mary. Hawke hardly acknowledged them. The same went for me and my wife. I could forgive that, but not his rudeness, his outright bad manners, to his hostess Meryl and her husband, Don. He couldn't be arsed even to make conversation. Why turn up at all, you boorish wanker, I thought.

By contrast, Meryl and Don asked us to join them and their kids at a Michael Jackson concert in Melbourne. Although I was never much of a Michael Jackson fan, Meryl had a private box in the stadium and it looked like something to do on a Sunday night in Melbourne. I had seen Michael years before that, when he was with the Jackson 5, in the Wellington Town Hall. This night, however, was full-on 'Thriller' and all the rest of the Michael Jackson stuff. Massive production, but not nearly as good, I thought.

'We're going back to see Michael after the show,' Meryl said, 'do you want to join us?'

Privately, I thought the show sucked, but I said, 'Thanks, Meryl, it was great, but we've got an early start in the morning and I think we'll go home to bed.'

The next day at work I asked Meryl what it was like meeting Michael Jackson. She was beaming. 'Oh, Michael is so great I cannot tell you.'

I asked what she meant.

'Oh, he is *so* charming. I mean, he wasn't interested in Don and me! Boring grown-ups! No. Can you believe it? He just wanted to play with the kids! They all sat on his knee. He loved the kids. The kids loved him. He was *wonderful*.'

I Prepare to Be Michael Chamberlain

Let me rewind the tape a fraction. You may not have seen *Evil Angels*, directed by Fred Schepisi and released in 1988, but you are probably familiar with one of the most extraordinary murder cases in Australia's history—the Lindy Chamberlain case. In short, the unfortunate Chamberlains lost their nine-week-old baby Azaria from their tent in the dark near Uluru in August 1980. Lindy saw a dingo leave the tent carrying something, but no one believed her, apart from her husband, Michael. She was convicted of the murder of her daughter and spent more than three years in prison. He was convicted of being an accessory after the fact. It was a grotesque miscarriage of justice; the unfortunate Chamberlains were crucified by the media, framed by incompetent police and loathed by the public at large.

In 1988 Lindy and Michael were exonerated and pardoned, and their convictions quashed, but it took until 2012 for a coroner to declare the child was taken by a dingo. This most horrible thing happened to a family who were so ordinary, so everyday, it should at the least give all of us pause. Anything, anything, could happen to you.

It's one thing to portray a fictional character. It is quite another to play someone who is very much alive. You have an extra burden of responsibility to bear, and at the same time you must tell the truth.

Michael Chamberlain was something of an enigma to me, and I was anxious to get to know him, even a little, before we started to shoot *Evil Angels*. Lindy was a considerably more dynamic character and was reasonably familiar to me, since I had seen her so much in the media. Michael seemed quiet, extraordinarily dignified under the circumstances, but elusive.

I needed to know him. They were kind enough to ask me to come and stay with them. They lived in a small community, largely consisting of Seventh Day Adventists—their church in which Michael was a pastor—somewhere north of Sydney. I jumped at the chance.

As I thought, Lindy was friendly and engaging. Michael kept his distance, suspicious probably. He had every reason to be, given the horrors they had both suffered (Lindy was not long out of jail). She could fill a room with her personality. Michael, on the other hand...you sometimes hardly noticed he was there.

I had three or four days with them and, happily, Michael began to thaw, and perhaps even to trust me. Two things struck me over that time. The first was their implicit and absolute faith. These were very religious people who knew, without a shadow of a doubt, that when they died they would be reunited with Azaria. No question. The separation from her was temporary. That faith,

Meryl Streep still cops flak for her accent in *Evil Angels*. It was, in fact, a completely accurate version of Lindy Chamberlain's hybrid New Zealand–Australian voice.

something I could never contemplate, gave them extraordinary strength through all those years of suffering.

The second was this—these were the most *honest* people I had ever met. They once took me to see a plot of land they had bought up in the hills on which they planned to build a house one day. This meant walking through an abandoned orange orchard there and back. It was spring and the orchard floor was covered with thousands of beautiful unwanted oranges. I said, Why don't we get some bags and take some home? They were both visibly shocked that I would even suggest such a thing. That would be theft. I loved that brief insight; it was key to everything.

I hope I served Michael well on the movie. Meryl was, of course, superb as Lindy, and was nominated for an Oscar. I tried diligently to convey his immense pain, his patient dignity. I admired him more than I can say, but I also bled for him, poor bastard. He was never as strong as her, and I think it broke him in the end.

We took the film to Cannes. I remember standing in front of a bank of hundreds of photographers, the two of us, and hearing the *clack clack clack* of a thousand shutters, and the shouts.

'Meryl! Meryl! Over here!'

'Sam! Sam! Get out of the way!'

I Cheat at Tennis

For some reason, Australia has a penchant for alpha males, moguls who make fortunes from mining or media. People like Rupert Murdoch or Kerry Packer or Clive Palmer. I played one—Lang Hancock, an immensely wealthy, larger-than-life bloke from Western Australia who was born in 1909 and died in 1992. He had the great good fortune, in the fifties, to discover the largest iron-ore deposit on the planet. His politics were extreme, both right-wing and racist. He became even more famous later in life for his marriage to Rose Porteous, a fabulously vivid woman who had been born in the Philippines and came to Australia in 1983, where she found a job working as a maid for Hancock. Rose was loathed by Hancock's daughter and successor Gina Rinehart, who is now often said to be one of the richest women in the world.

In 2015 the excellent Mark Joffe directed a mini-series called *House of Hancock* for Channel Nine, and I enjoyed playing Lang. Mandy McElhinney was superb as Gina. I don't think I did Hancock any disservice. I did, however, cheat on a few calls in a tennis scene—and thereby hangs my tale.

Years ago, I spent a weekend on the property of the impossibly rich Kerry Packer near Scone in New South Wales (Packer himself wasn't there). This was the headquarters of his polo empire. It was incredible—the ponies were better housed than most Australians, in a cathedral-like stable complex that sprayed a mist every few minutes over the nags, keeping them both cool and free of flies.

There were so many people working for Packer that he had houses all over the property, which even had its own pub where the staff would often gather of a Friday night. The boss liked to join the crowd over a beer and play billiards or snooker. Packer loved to win. The smart employee would discreetly allow that to happen. Stories circulated that Packer, whose temper was legendary, had been known, if beaten, to storm off into the night, having lost all of twenty bucks on the game. But the money wasn't the point. And his displeasure could be even worse if he sensed that you were *allowing* him to win. That was crossing a line.

Did Lang Hancock also want to win at all costs? What might happen when he was playing tennis with an underling? I had no evidence that Lang Hancock cheated at tennis, but on set, whenever I was receiving serve, I called the ball out.

Gina Rinehart was not a fan of the mini-series. After the first episode went to air she took Channel Nine to court and won the right to vet the second episode before it was screened. It went to air with 'agreed cuts', and with a disclaimer that it was a work of fiction, a 'drama' and not a 'documentary'. Channel Nine apologised and promised never to screen *House of Hancock* again.

One of Gina Rinehart's objections was to the scene on the tennis court. But the truth is that I am a rotten tennis player, and I simply...couldn't be arsed to chase the ball.

The Navigators, the Lepers

I spent almost a year making *The Pacific: In the Wake of Captain Cook*, fronting a six-hour documentary series. This was one of the best experiences of my life—we went from Alaska to Antarctica, from Tahiti to Tonga, from Aotearoa to Tanna, from Australia to Hawaii. I fell deeply in love with Polynesian people and their culture.

It is difficult not to have mixed feelings about Cook himself given the impact his three voyages had on the native peoples of the Pacific. His sailing into uncharted waters brought with it colonialism and all it entailed, not the least being diseases including syphilis and gonorrhea. These were swiftly followed by smallpox, Hansen's disease (leprosy) and others, none of which the islanders had any resistance to.

I formed an immense respect for Cook's courage and brilliance as an explorer and navigator, and as a leader of men. But that was matched by my awe for the Polynesian navigators who came before him. With an entirely different set of skills these men had enabled Polynesian people, using sea-going double-hulled canoes, not only to explore what amounts to one third of the globe, but to discover and settle the most remote points on the planet, from Hawaii to New Zealand, and I have no doubt South

America as well. This with no instruments or maps, but by observation of stars, birds, tides and currents.

The navigator would sit under the main mast, in silent reverie, for the entirety of these epic voyages, directing the course, which was plotted with extreme accuracy. Imagine if you can the difficulty, for instance, of finding Easter Island after you have set out from Hawaii, a distance of more than 7200 kilometres. If you miss it, the next stop is Antarctica. And death. And consider this—most islands in the Pacific, being no higher than a coconut tree, are easily missed.

In 1999, we were shooting *Molokai* in Kalaupapa. The movie was directed by Paul Cox and starred David Wenham. It was about Father Damien, a nineteenth-century missionary, now canonised, who devoted his life to caring for victims of Hansen's disease. I played Walter Gibson, prime minister of the kingdom of Hawaii. I wandered one day, in my Victorian garb, to the beach. In the distance, to my astonishment, was a double-hulled Hawaiian canoe under full sail, passing beneath the looming cliffs of Molokai. It was the *Hōkūleʻa*, which had been built in the 1970s to demonstrate and teach the extraordinary maritime skills of the Pacific islanders.

Almost twenty years later, in 2018, I found myself on the *Hōkūleʻa* under the command of the great Nainoa Thompson himself, the man who more than anyone else is responsible for the almost miraculous revival of Polynesian navigation. That was a privilege indeed. The *Hōkūleʻa* had undertaken many of these epic voyages, unguided by modern technology, as proof, if any were needed, of those ancient Polynesian skills.

But back then on the beach, in my stiff collar and top hat, I experienced a truly surreal moment. I felt that somehow I had slipped the bonds of time, and it was both exhilarating and unsettling at once.

And it was in Kalaupapa, shooting *Molokai,* that I met Nikau (not his real name). He was the youngest resident in the colony. He had been sent there at the age of five, taken from his family on suspicion of having Hansen's disease. Cruelly, he contracted the disease *after* he was dumped on Kalaupapa. He was, however, not an angry man, not at all. He was now in his fifties. He was gay, a handsome affable chap, slightly louche, a likeable man. He was a talented pianist, quite a feat given he only had half his fingers. He was a natural entertainer, and quite the criminal.

In the 1950s, a treatment was found for people with Hansen's disease. It wasn't a cure, but it meant they were not infectious, and eventually could leave quarantine as they saw fit. Most chose to stay, and Kalaupapa became a refuge for the unfortunate residents, since their deformities often made them feel stigmatised in the outside world.

Nikau, however, knew no shyness. He came and went as he

With the great Polynesian navigator Nainoa Thompson, in Honolulu.

pleased. He was widely travelled, and basically didn't give a fuck. The law meant nothing to him, wherever he was. I suspect if I'd been dealt the cards he'd been given in life I would have been lawless as well. He committed crimes with impunity in places as far away as Australia, mostly to do with drugs and prostitution.

His modus operandi was apparently as follows. On being locked up, he would request an interview with the prison governor. Here he would make it known that he was a gay leper. Invariably, within a day or two, a side door would be opened and Nikau would quietly become a free man once more.

On my last night on Molokai, Nikau was the life of the party. I was staying with Wenham, and got up at first light with the worst hangover in the history of parties. I staggered down to the lonely beach and went to sit on a large white sandy log under a coconut palm. I bounced off the log, which roared in fury. It was the biggest, angriest white seal imaginable, but luckily too fat and tired to chase me.

Last heard of, Nikau was doing time on the Main Island for attempting to import a small amount of methamphetamine back to Kalaupapa some ten years after we were with him in 1999. I guess no one is falling for his bad-boy ruse any more. I do hope he's still alive, and happy.

He has had to navigate a more difficult ocean than I can imagine.

A Knighthood

On 20 June 2022, I became Sir Sam.

Or, as Bryan Brown insists, Sir Nigel. I knew he'd be annoying about this. My only consolation is that the news is probably more annoying to him than Sir Nigel is to me.

In 2006 I was honoured to receive a DCNZM (Distinguished Companion of the Order of New Zealand). At the time this was the equivalent of a knighthood, titles having been abolished by the Labour government in 2000. The family all went to Government House in Wellington, and the governor-general decorated me with a big star on my chest and a cross around my neck. The great All Black Brian Lochore was just before me. I didn't look very convincing, but he certainly did.

Then, a couple of years later, National was back, and restored knighthoods. All those who had received the equivalent in the intervening years were invited to take the title if they wanted to. I declined. This for a number of reasons, not least because of the stick I knew I would get from friends and colleagues, like Bloody Bryan Brown. There was also a certain amount of vaguely lefty republican sympathy under all that. But, regardless, I just didn't feel quite senior or deserving enough. Back in 1991 when I was made OBE, I had a quiet chuckle at this. The OBE recipient right after me on the (alphabetical) list was honoured for 'Services to the Raspberry Industry'. A raspberry, a Bronx cheer, a loud one, right behind me.

In 2022 I thought about all that again. Two things prompted this. First of all, my friend, nemesis and neighbour, Grahame Sydney, got knighted. The idea of bloody Sydney sounding more grand than me was both hilarious and unbearable. Next the distinguished author and also a friend, Vincent O'Sullivan, decided to convert his DCNZM to a KNZM.

Why was I being so precious about this? The last time I saw Sir Eion Edgar he pressed me again. Don't be a bloody fool, go on, take it. Eion died about three weeks later, after extraordinary service to the community and to the country. I couldn't measure any contribution I'd made to anything at all against his. But he was insistent.

I'm senior enough now. Seventy-five is knocking on a bit, truth to tell. Also, I may not be all that long for this world. In addition, if you're in the arts, and in particular an actor, to be knighted is a rare thing. There is a sense, therefore, in which a title for an actor shows that we take this profession seriously. Acting is valued by the community, by the country. So I sort of think this is on behalf of all my acting colleagues from Aotearoa.

My grandson Caleb, wearing my knighthood regalia. Suits him more than me.

There is only one other acting knight or dame in New Zealand—Dame Kate Harcourt. She has reached the marvellous age of ninety-five.

But perhaps I'm rationalising. Perhaps I just want to be full of myself for a day or two. Too big for my boots. So far up myself I can't see daylight. Or maybe the train of thought was thus: Oh, fuck it, I've got cancer. Why not?

The Latest from the Nurses' Station

HERE'S the thing about nurses. They are the ones who look after you. I love them unconditionally.

Last time I was dealing with cancer, I was in St Vincent's Hospital for about eight days. I underwent an operation, largely performed by a robot. I never saw the robot, but I'm reliably told that it looked very much like those octopus things that build cars nowadays. Eight arms. I didn't get to see it because the anaesthetist, a smiley Aussie bloke, had knocked me out before they wheeled me into the operating theatre. The last I saw, he was holding two large bottles of something.

'I hope you're giving me the good stuff?' I said.

He said, 'Sam, mate, you see this here? This is the stuff Michael Jackson loved. And this other one—that was Prince's gear.'

I laughed briefly, and then stopped. 'Wait a minute. Didn't they both…?'

Next thing, some hours later, I woke up back in my room. I hadn't died.

The post-op was pretty painful, so I was on quite a lot of morphine. Morphine is all very well and good. But it had one serious side effect. I built up a lot of gas, as somehow it stops your bowel from letting things go. My stomach began to swell to alarming zeppelin promotions and was very uncomfortable indeed. I would have paid anything for a long, loud fart. Still, the pain relief was almost worth it.

My main nurse was an angel from Nepal, called Winnie. She was my friend: caring and kind. And funny too.

One day, though, I said, 'Winnie, I haven't had my shot today.'

'Mr Sam. On a pain scale of one to ten, where are you?'

I lied and exaggerated. 'Oh, eight…eight and a half, Winnie.'

She saw right through me. 'No, Mr Sam. That's enough now, finished on the morphine.'

I turned into the saddest, most pathetic Kings Cross junkie

Morphine man.

imaginable. I begged, I pleaded. 'Winnie, you are my friend! Please, please, Winnie. Please don't be so mean, Winnie. I'm in pain. Pleeeaaase!'

She held the line. And that was it. She was, of course, right.

The fart was disappointing. It just sort of subsided over a few days—no noise, no fun.

For this last lot of treatment I've been going to hospital and overnighting. This may change if we go into a different regimen again, and it could be a five-week stay, if you survive it. T-cell lymphoma is a bastard, and this one is aggressive. I've had to ask my doctor to rephrase something twice. She is inclined to say, '*If* we get you into remission…'

'Look,' I say, 'it's just a little word, but could you change it to *when* we get you into remission?'

She smiles sweetly, but does not correct this critical phrase. Some things about cancer make you hypersensitive. And I'm all for a little optimism right now.

I am beginning to look like a guinea pig, I think. My beard

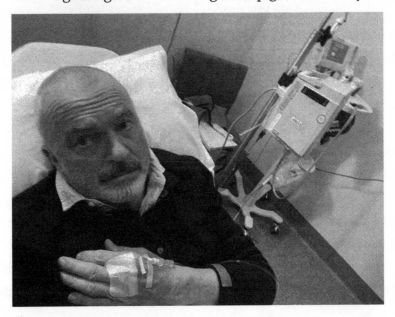

Chemo is not a lot of fun, to be honest.

has made a reappearance. Or perhaps I am a lab rat. I am the *only* person in all New South Wales on this new stuff. We will see if it is the game changer some think. Watch the death notices in the meantime.

I'd prefer to live. It's more interesting, I think, than whatever happens next. I don't believe in an afterlife, certainly not one with angels and harps. I do believe, I know, that you become quite literally part of the universe again. Every atom of my body, every part of my essence, is as old as the universe itself. It is imperishable, and although I won't be reassembled in a white gown on a cloud, I will be around, disassembled, until the end of time.

I have no fear of death, none whatsoever. That's not courage; that's just realism. I don't particularly want to die on my own, that's all. I am a single man and there is no one here to hold my hand, no partner to see me out. So if it comes to that, I think I'll die over there with the nurses. They've seen it all before and there will be a minimum of tears and fuss, if any. I will have got all my beloved family well clear by then.

The nurses at St Vincent's at the moment are almost universally Irish. I completely delight in their accents. Apart from Susie, the head honcho, who has a name I can spell, all the others have names that are ridiculously difficult. Only the Irish would think to spell Neve as Niamh. Or Sersha as Saoirse.

The name of my pal on *Peter Rabbit*, Domhnall Gleeson, is pronounced 'doenull'. Everyone gets it wrong; it must drive him mad. He was presumably named by his brilliant father Brendan, whose own parents must have made the sensible decision not to spell the infant Breandann. I am not immune to this. My third name is spelled Diarmaid, pronounced 'Dermot'.

No wonder the Irish never had any imperial ambitions, unlike the English. No one else in the world could have read the orders.

I'm Not Ready to Leave You Yet

SOME people cling on, even after death. You just can't shake them.

My uncle Tony Elworthy was one of those. Tony was a chipper, smiling bloke, but quite what he was doing married to my Aunt True one will never know. She had had one great love in her life, and it was not Uncle Tony, but a man who was killed in the war. For the rest of her days, she kept this man's photo beside her bed, the marital bed. An everyday cruelty, I would've thought; but for all that they had four children, and my cousins are really good value.

Like me, Uncle Tony had a brilliant older brother—Baron Sam Elworthy of Timaru—and suffered in his shadow all his life…That would be my guess. (I would like to have been there on the day my brother was first asked, 'Are you Sam Neill's brother?' Up until this time I had had thirty years of people asking me if I was Michael Neill's brother. A petty thought, I grant you. I say it in the most affectionate way. I do love my brother.)

Charles ('Sam') Elworthy had a distinguished war career in bombers, and later became not only the Marshal of the RAF, but Chief of the Defence Staff in the UK. He was also Governor of Windsor Castle, Knight of the Garter, made a Lord and so on. It's a very long list of accomplishments.

Uncle Tony was much more of a muddle. He was a very good pilot himself, but was turned down for the RAF, to his bitter disappointment. Later he became obsessed with gliding, and set several records for distance, time and all the things that matter to gliders. But his actual working career was not all that red-hot. I remember him importing German bubble cars made by such famous names as Messerschmitt or Heinkel, for which there was no appetite at all in a postwar New Zealand. Epic fail. He had a farm too, but hated farming. He was good at fixing things and making stuff, but on two occasions managed to lose fingers in a bandsaw. He was one of those people who could've done any number of things, but he was brought up in a conventional way at a conventional school, so his undeniable talent as a cinematographer, for instance, would never be realised. For all that he was always cheerful and I liked being around him.

Uncle Tony wanted his ashes scattered across Aoraki Mount Cook, and the Mackenzie Country he so loved. My cousin Mark, who flies small planes, took the urn up into the skies as per his wishes, accompanied by a friend. They circled for a time to get more height; up where Uncle Tony would've been at his most

Uncle Tony and Dad.

peaceful, gliding above the clouds. When Mark judged that it was the right time to set him free, he told his friend to let him go. The window was opened, the urn was shaken out and all the ashes blew, instead of out into the clear blue sky of the Southern Alps, straight back into the cockpit. The two of them were covered in ashes; they were choking on Uncle Tony.

There was nothing for it but to fly back, covered in ash, all the way to Timaru. When they landed they brushed themselves down, vacuumed the old man out of the plane and put him back as best they could into the urn. Eventually he was scattered over some very ordinary lawn. Dear old boy—talk about coming back to earth.

Another post-mortem clinger was Sebastian Black, my brother's closest friend. Sebastian also taught English at Auckland University. He was an eccentric character, with a beard that would have put Santa to shame. Wildly opinionated, and on a good day fizzing company. He was very English under all that hirsute stuff. He was, by all accounts, a riveting lecturer. He and his partner, Judith Binney, the distinguished historian, lived right next door to Michael. I went to a memorial for him at a little restaurant in Parnell, and at least twenty people got up and spoke, not only fondly, but also in glowing terms about what an extraordinarily good influence he had had on their lives.

All this was true, but it wasn't the full story. I got up and said, entirely fairly, that on the contrary Sebastian had been a very *bad* influence on me. I used to stay with them when they lived in a sort of semi-communal way in a big old house on St Stephens Avenue. I would hitch up to Auckland to stay with my brother, and it was always an eye-opener. I'd get up early in the morning, for instance, and make myself a cup of tea; more than once, a completely naked girl would wander languorously out of Sebastian's room and make a cup of tea beside me. I wouldn't know where to look. He also had a reasonable supply of marijuana in the days when it was an unknown area for me. I'm pretty sure the first (and last) time I did acid was something to do with Sebastian. This was bohemian living, Sebastian was at the centre of it, and I found it intoxicating. It was also an intensely left-wing political place, and the intellectual discussion was way over my head.

Sebastian's boho air was always rather undermined by his intrinsic and obvious Britishness. He was probably the last pipe smoker in New Zealand. Not just a pipe, but a Sherlock Holmes bendy job. He wore posh pink trousers, and floral shirts from Liberty. And there was that rumbling, stentorian voice that spoke of Rugby School and Oxford. I even saw him in a striped cricket blazer once.

Sebastian had served in the French Foreign Legion. He'd apparently been jilted by someone at university, and on a romantic impulse joined up, and found himself serving in Algeria during the War of Independence. Terrible decision. He was badly wounded and wore a few battle scars from that time. This was an unjust war, and he hated it. In hindsight anyway; he served his full five years. After recovering from his wounds, he was made quartermaster-general, which meant supplying provisions to the troops. The officers demanded *bifteck*, beef steak, but Sebastian discovered if you served them far cheaper black-market mule (smuggled by the enemy from Morocco), they couldn't tell the difference. He pocketed the change, and when he returned to England it was enough to put him through university again.

Judy had died a few years earlier, and Sebastian's wish was that his ashes, mixed with hers, should be scattered in the surf at his favourite beach north of Auckland, released into the deep blue Pacific. Not an unreasonable request. When the day came, a few friends and loved ones assembled, words were said, and it was the right mixture of sadness and gratitude one can find at such times. They waded out into the surf for the great liberation of Sebastian and Judy, to pour their ashes into the waves.

Unfortunately, none of them had calculated how far out in the surf to empty the urn. Things were a little premature and, as is the way with surf, whatever's in it generally comes back at you. *Woosh*, the urn was emptied. I have had various accounts of what happened next. My favourite is this. Almost immediately at least two people were covered in wet Sebastian ashes. Head to toe. Not a good look. Sebastian had no intention of going to sea; he was going to cling to people as long as he could. I'm sure it was Sebastian—Judy would exit gracefully as always. Now, it's one thing to vacuum an uncle out of an aeroplane, quite another to get all those sodden ashes off one's person. A shower was found at the beach, and that was pretty effective. But it did mean that a lot of Sebastian went down the drain.

Two more ashes stories quickly while I remember. A family in Wales, friends of Mum's, received a most welcome gift every Christmas from relatives in the US. This in the severely food-rationed war years. It contained all the ingredients for a most delicious Christmas cake—flour, sugar, fruit, cinnamon probably, nuts, cherries, spices—everything you could not get at the shop, and a real treat.

One year it came with a small packet of white powder, obviously something wonderful and American, and that went into the cake along with the rest.

A letter arrived, delayed, a few weeks later. Great Aunt Hermione had asked to have some of her ashes scattered in Wales, and would they be so kind? See in the parcel a small packet of powder. It was too late. They had consumed the remains of Great Aunt Hermione.

Lastly, another family story. Mum's cousin Edith Somerville was in her day a rather famous writer from County Cork. She and her writing partner, Violet Ross, wrote as a team: Somerville and Ross. They wrote a number of novels, mostly about the sort of people they knew and indeed were. They rode to hounds and fished—country gentlewomen. They were most famous for a series called *The Irish R.M.*, which was adapted into a very successful television series some years ago, starring Peter Bowles.

They were clearly devoted to each other, and lived together for years at Edith's large Georgian family house in Castletownshend, Drishane House, until Violet died. Edith continued to write under Somerville and Ross still, saying she was in contact with Violet via a medium. One of us once asked Mum if they were lesbians. Mum looked askance, and replied, 'Darling, they wouldn't know *how!*'

After Violet died, Edith's express wish was that she be buried alongside Violet in her grave behind the gothic St Barrahane's Church of Ireland. The church sits on a rocky promontory above the village, which tumbles down the hill to a beautiful small harbour.

Finding space for Edith in the grave proved problematic—it was pretty much solid rock, and they were at a loss as to what to do. The answer was a very Irish solution. Someone thought perhaps some small explosive might be a shortcut and, this being Ireland, someone knew someone who knew someone who was with the local IRA boys. They were happy to help, and indeed had the explosives to hand.

But wouldn't you know it, the IRA boys slightly overdid things. They blew Violet's grave to bits. There was an enormous explosion and the village was covered in debris and such remains as there were of Violet as well.

Yes, some people are hard to shake, even after death.

A Fateful Phone Call

I am waiting for the phone to ring. It's a call that could be fatal or fateful. Stand by—I will let you know.

I spent a lot of yesterday in hospital. This was my fourth PET scan. You glow in the dark, which is good, because inside the tunnel you need a glimmer—it is pitch-black in there. I am not claustrophobic, luckily—you are in there for a good hour. I zen out and quite enjoy the peace.

The first PET scan confirmed I had stage III cancer, with tumours galore. And that I needed chemotherapy.

The second confirmed the chemo was working, and the tumours were in retreat.

The third confirmed that the chemo was *not* working, and the tumours were on the march again. And that we would abandon the first chemo in favour of a new drug.

The fourth will tell us if the new chemo is working, and we are on course. Or that I am a doomed man.

I have turned the phone off silent mode. Stand by. My haematologist, Dr Lavee, said she would call me this morning, having seen the scans. I half dread and half look forward to what happens next...

Okay, she has texted. It is time to talk. I am trying to breathe calmly. I wonder what news. You will be the first to know. Stand by...

Oh my God. I'm just trying to absorb this now—it seems so unlikely. The news is good, better than good. The new drugs are working. They are working to the extent that I am in something called full metabolic remission. The tumours have gone.

Remission! Now! I still have to persist with this stuff, it seems, but right now there is *no cancer* in my body.

What the hell? A few hours ago I was a dying man. Dying with dignity. Now I'm a living man, with every intent of going on living and living and living. Dignity abandoned!

Now, *that's* a phone call.

Chapter the Last:
Where Are They, Daddy?

IN 1995 I made a film called *Restoration*, with Robert Downey Jr., Meg Ryan, Hugh Grant, David Thewlis and Ian McKellen. It's based on one of my favourite novels, by Rose Tremain. I play King Charles II, and I think I was rather good in it. I'm too nervous to go back and check, so I'll leave you to do that.

This Charles is powerful, randy, capricious, dangerous, seductive and oh so smooth. A dream part, like a pavlova cake, and I consumed it with gusto. Michael Hoffman directed this film—it's stunning to look at, in part due to Eugenio Zanetti's design, but also the most extraordinary wardrobe, including mine, by James Acheson. I looked a million pounds, if not guineas. Waistcoats galore, enormous hats sporting ostrich feathers, blooming breeches, thigh-high boots, moustaches, spaniels, you name it. I looked so fabulous I hardly needed to act, but I acted my pants off anyway. The pants, come to think of it, the underpants, were the real thing. James is such a stickler for detail that even what you wore around your privates was exactly what the king would've worn in 1660. No Jockey support for me, oh dear me, no.

We shot much of it at Shepperton Studios, and I made sure that the family came out on the biggest day of all—the wedding of Robert Merivel. This gilded event took place around an ornamental lake inside a sound stage. There were swans, ladies in waiting, an enormous banquet...everything was excessively gorgeous. Beautiful Polly Walker, playing my mistress, is being married off to the hapless Merivel, while the king, her lord and master, looks on. You cannot imagine how resplendent I was.

I was sitting in my trailer when the word came that my family had arrived. I ensured that I was fully kitted out to make the maximum impression. I particularly wanted to wow Elena, who was about four or five then.

There came a knock on the trailer door. I flung it open; my hat could hardly fit through the door let alone the rest of my sumptuous costume, but I leapt anyway in all my glory to the ground before them. I was sure they would faint and swoon at first sight, and indeed there were gasps of admiration from most. Apart from the little one. She looked baffled. Nothing made

As Charles II. Hello, ladies!

sense, it seemed. Now I myself felt disappointed.

'Daddy?' she said in a quiet voice.

I leant down to her, almost tumbling under all the weight of jewellery draped around me. 'What, darling?'

'Daddy, where are they?'

'What, Bubs? Where are what?'

'Daddy, where are the…where are the dinosaurs?'

Sigh.

Photo credits

IMAGES INTEGRATED IN TEXT

Sam Neill and family: 3, 5, 6, 7, 9, 25, 41, 49, 51, 64, 75, 78, 81, 88, 91, 105, 110, 115, 145, 152, 158, 168, 172, 190, 192, 265, 273, 284, 304, 333, 347, 353, 364, 378, 381, 384, 385, 388

Peaky Blinders: Landmark Media/Alamy Stock Photo: 16

The Windmill Theatre: Matthew Lloyd, http://www.arthurlloyd.co.uk: 38

Roger Donaldson: 121

Sleeping Dogs: NZ On Screen: 123

My Brilliant Career: New South Wales Film Productions/Ronald Grant Archive/Alamy Stock Photo: 133

Death in Brunswick: United Archives GmbH/Alamy Stock Photo: 146

The Piano: RGR Collection/Alamy Stock Photo: 230

From a Far Country: ITV/Shutterstock: 246

Marti Friedlander: *Ralph Hotere, Dunedin,* black and white photographic print, 203 x 254 mm, E. H. McCormick Research Library, Auckland Art Gallery Toi o Tāmaki, on loan from the Gerrard and Marti Friedlander Charitable Trust, 2002: 257

Black Phoenix, 1984–88, Port Chalmers, by Ralph Hotere. Burnt wood and metal. Purchased 1988 with New Zealand Lottery Board funds. © Reproduced by permission of the Hotere Foundation Trust. Te Papa (1988-0030-1/AA to BZ): 261

Dean Spanley: Moviestore Collection Ltd/Alamy Stock Photo: 296

The Dish: TCD/Prod. DB/Alamy Stock Photo: 317

Reilly, Ace of Spies: ITV/Cinematic Collection/Alamy Stock Photo: 324

Portrait of Ed Limato: courtesy of Firooz Zahedi: 327

The Jungle Book: © Disney 1994: 333

The Brush-Off: courtesy of Lisa Tomasetti: 358

Evil Angels: TCD/Prod. DB/Alamy Stock Photo: 373

Restoration: PictureLux/The Hollywood Archive/Alamy Stock Photo: 396

IMAGES IN PLATE SECTIONS

Sam Neill and family: various

My Brilliant Career: courtesy of Margaret Fink/The National Film and Sound Archive

Possession: Gaumont/Oliane Productions/Marianne Productions

The Piano: Moviestore Collection Ltd/Alamy Stock Photo

My Brilliant Career: New South Wales Film Productions/Ronald Grant Archive/Alamy Stock Photo

Sweet Country: courtesy of David Jowsey

Athfield House: courtesy of Euan Sarginson

Naish House: courtesy of Lauren Major

Sam Neill at The Last Chance vineyard: Ross Land/Getty Images